THE GROWTH OF CONSTITUTIONAL
POWER IN THE UNITED STATES

BY CARL BRENT SWISHER

THE GROWTH OF
CONSTITUTIONAL POWER
IN
THE UNITED STATES

UNIVERSITY OF CHICAGO PRESS
CHICAGO · ILLINOIS

CHARLES R. WALGREEN FOUNDATION LECTURES

University of Chicago Press · Chicago 37

Agent: Cambridge University Press · London

FOREWORD

✵

THE study of the Supreme Court of the United States
constitutes a subject of perennial interest both to the
student of jurisprudence and to the layman. No institution in the world occupies such a unique position. It is not
alone a court of law, but a supreme tribunal of arbitration
rendering final decision upon complex problems of economics,
sociology, and political science. It has often been contended
that training in law is not so essential for a justice of the Supreme Court of the United States as training in the social
sciences. One may very well understand the reason for this
position if one notes the hundreds of cases handled by the
Supreme Court which involve an understanding of factual
material and the application of social principles.

Professor Swisher, in this present volume, gives us a careful
analysis of the Court within our rapidly changing social structure. In addition to presenting a substantial amount of background material, he considers the problems of the Court today
and in the years to come. Under the sponsorship of the Charles
R. Walgreen Foundation these lectures were given on the
campus of the University during the Spring Quarter, 1945.
The co-operation of the author and the University of Chicago
Press now enables the Foundation to publish this series of
lectures as the sixteenth volume of its "Studies of American
Institutions."

JEROME G. KERWIN
Executive Secretary, Charles R. Walgreen Foundation
for the Study of American Institutions

PREFACE

❋

THE present generation of political scientists has concerned itself largely with specialized work in administration, legislation, politics, theory, law, and other subordinate subjects rather than with study of the constitutional system as a whole. This preoccupation with specialities is only natural. We assume that the substructure of our governmental institutions is well established. We deem it more important to create or examine new devices and ideas than to cover old ground for the purpose of showing the relation between basic values and mechanisms, on the one hand, and the substance and the froth of change, on the other. Yet the proper education of American youth and correction of the perspective of people who function as experts and operate in terms of masses of detail require periodic return to the process of generalization about the constitutional system. Therefore, without pretense of covering the entire subject, this volume seeks to relate our evolving institutions one to another and to a unified whole, with some reference back to fundamentals as envisaged when our Constitution was adopted.

As always, the author is indebted to many people. The book is the product of an invitation to deliver a series of lectures at the University of Chicago which was extended by Professor Leonard D. White on authorization from Professor William T. Hutchinson, Executive Secretary of the Charles R. Walgreen Foundation for the Study of American Institutions. Professor White provided facilities in the Department of Political Science for preparation of the lectures and gave wise counsel concerning them. Since the lectures took shape from a background of teaching and writing at the Johns Hopkins University, indebtedness must be expressed to those graduate students who have aided in clarifying the conception of American constitutional development which provides the theme of this analysis. Miss Elsie B. Snow aided in the preparation of the Index.

CARL BRENT SWISHER

JOHNS HOPKINS UNIVERSITY
October 1945

TABLE OF CONTENTS

*

I

DEMOCRATIC CONCEPTIONS OF THE CONSTITUTION

✻

DURING the past third of a century our constitutional system has undergone the ravages of two major wars and a major depression. It has suffered or profited, as the case may be, by the collapse of innumerable governmental traditions and has become the source or the channel for a flow of governmental power so great as to stagger the imagination. It has felt the impact of great changes in other lands as, during the same period, other governments more or less firmly fixed in the ways of democracy which the first World War was fought to make safe have surrendered to mystical ideologies and highly unmystical dictatorships, while a decadent monarchy of a great country has given way to something which calls itself communism and which, in its release of power, has presented a startled world with a magnificent demonstration of productive energy and military might. Truly, the old order changeth!

The constitutional disturbance created in the United States by the first World War caused profound uneasiness. A blithe disregard of civil liberties expressed itself in red-baiting activities after the war had come to an end and brought a vicious Ku Klux Klan back into existence. Businessmen feared encroachments on their rights by continuation of wartime regulation of enterprise in time of peace. Above all, thoughtful persons were convinced that the constitutional system with its safeguards as to liberty and property could not stand the strain of still another major war. We know the sequel. At the end of that other major war—a war incomparably more tremendous and costly than its predecessor—the time is ripe for an examination of the ship of state to discover the condition in which it is weathering the storms.

Such an examination of our constitutional system requires careful scrutiny of the changes which war and depression and, behind these two, the development of mass-production industrialism have brought about. It requires study of the application of simple machinery to the performance of tasks which are ever increasingly complex. It requires understanding of the shift in ideological background from that of Edmund Burke and Adam Smith and Alexander Hamilton and Thomas Jefferson to that of Herbert Hoover and Wendell Willkie, Henry Wallace and Franklin D. Roosevelt. Most of our attention throughout this volume will be given to events of relatively recent years and to the current status of our constitutional system. Yet of constitutional systems, as of human beings, it is true that knowledge of the life-history of the patient is essential to adequate diagnosis. For that reason we shall make some use of early history when conditions and climates of opinion differed greatly from those of the present day.

Furthermore, because terminology and conceptions in statecraft often lack definiteness of content and contour, it will be necessary to discuss terminology and to make clear the varying senses in which it is used. Words, indeed, and the intellectual and emotional content which people give to them, must often be treated not merely as keys to understanding but as the very stuff of government. Since "ideas are weapons," the words which symbolize them are instruments of tremendous power. Our Constitution may be said to consist both of a verbal framework and of a kind of panoramic entity which its words symbolize in the minds of the American people. So rich and varied is that symbolism that no dictionary, however full, can give more than a suggestion of its content. To discover what the Constitution meant at the time of its adoption, we must add to textual study an examination of what the men of that time thought a constitution was and, more particularly, what they thought our Constitution was. The same is true if we would discover its meaning today or at any intervening period. Without necessary change in the words themselves, the color of the Constitution may follow public sentiment through all the variety of the spectrum. Indeed, we can paraphrase the comment of Charles E. Hughes that "the Constitution is what the judges say it is" to add with equal truth the generalization that, in the long run, "the Constitution is what the people think it is." This is no less true because the multiple, complex, and conflicting conceptions of the people at times signify that the Constitution is a most bewildering creation. The purpose of the analysis which follows is in part to discover something of the original meaning of the Constitution and of the meanings which have been attached to it from time to time down through the years, in order that we may be able more adequately to appraise the living Constitution of today.

A conception which is basic and commonplace in connection with any constitution is that it provides for government. It prescribes or describes the exercise of governmental power. In the light of this conception every state has a constitution. It may have a good constitution or a very bad one, but it has a constitution whether written or unwritten or, as in the instance of our own Constitution, a combination of the two. Without a constitution there is no government and no state. Although the term might reasonably be applied to the whole area of the flow of governmental power, its use is usually limited to activity near the source, to rules of operation which seem to be fundamental, as distinguished from those extensions of public law which lie at the periphery of the administrative process. For example, we describe as "constitutional" those rules and principles which outline the establishment of Congress or the presidency, or the judiciary, whereas we do not ordinarily apply the term to the rules issued by a department head for the organization or reorganization of a governmental bureau.

Within the dimensions of this basic conception of a constitution as a center and source of power, the concern of the critic is principally as to whether the constitution provides enough power or adequately efficient methods for its exercise to achieve the ends of the society it is intended to serve. Thus the principal defect of our first federal constitution, the Articles of Confederation, was that it gave too little power to achieve the ends of the newly established Union. For example, it did not give the power of taxation or power to control interstate or foreign commerce, and it failed to provide a feasible mechanism for self-amendment so as to generate or release additional power which might be needed. In terms of another illustration, a source of anxiety at the time of the Civil War was the question whether the Constitution authorized the waging of war against states in rebellion. Again, amid the depression of 1929 many people questioned whether the Constitution gave adequate power to deal with the crisis. In terms of this conception, furthermore, the great problems in connection with the powers actually given are those involved in making the most effective use of those powers. In considerable part the problems of government are problems of effective administration.

To people everywhere, however, and perhaps particularly to the people of the United States, a constitution has meaning other than that of the vital conception of giving power. Those meanings are restrictive and in certain areas absolutely negative. They color and often confuse our thinking on constitutional matters. Emphasis upon them at times so restrains the exercise of power as almost to defeat the basic purpose of the

Constitution. These qualifying conceptions may be listed as follows:

1. Any constitution worthy of the name must forbid government to do certain things.

2. It must require that certain things be done only in prescribed ways.

3. It must require that government operate strictly according to rule.

4. It must—or at least our Constitution must—embody the spirit of "rightness."

5. It must be federal.

6. It must divide the powers of government among three co-ordinate branches.

7. It must base government upon the consent of the governed.

Because of the influence of these conceptions in molding the course of American constitutional development, they must be examined more at length, as to both origins and more recent applications. First of all, the conception of a constitution as an instrument which inevitably forbids the doing of certain things seems to root back into beliefs in the existence of natural rights—rights which are so fundamental that a healthy society cannot function without their preservation. Such beliefs are formulated in many different kinds of statements and are variously related to concepts of natural law, natural justice, and divine law and formulations under still other terms. Suffice it to say that they run back through most of recorded history. The development of the American conviction that certain areas of control were altogether forbidden to government came through our British heritage from at least as far back as Magna Carta. The conviction grew rapidly amid the experience of the American colonies. It was boldly formulated in the Declaration of Independence and in most of the state constitutions which were adopted around the time of the writing of the Declaration. Among the important areas of immunity from control, freedom of religion came into realization with freedom for those of the dominant Christian faith of a particular colony; it spread to freedom for all Christians—with the delayed and reluctant inclusion of Catholics—and then to freedom for persons of all faiths or no faiths at all. Freedom of speech was regarded first of all as a most important immunity for legislators—that is, for the formulators of governmental policy. Protection spread to the people generally as the people themselves came to be regarded as the legitimate governors of themselves and of the community. Freedom of the press developed with similar gradualness as the people became increasingly aware of the importance of public discussion of public issues. So great at times has been the emphasis on the purely negative characteristics of a constitution, on prohibitions of the exercise of power rather than on the giving of power, as to create the false impression that the primary function of a constitution is negative rather than positive. Important as are the negative functions, their existence would have no point were there no positive functions on which to exercise restraint.

Closely related to the conviction that a constitution must altogether forbid the doing of certain things was the conviction that certain wrong methods of performing necessary community functions must be forbidden and "right" methods must be enforced. Crimes could not be punished by bills of attainder or ex post facto laws. Searches and seizures should be made only with warrants issued upon probable cause. Indictments had to be by grand jury. A man was entitled to trial by a jury of his peers. The conception of a jury as consisting of exactly twelve men and of a verdict of guilty as requiring a unanimous vote became clearly fixed. Trial had to be in terms of the various if not very definite component factors of due process. Double jeopardy and compulsory self-incrimination were to be outlawed. The place of trial had to be relatively close to the place where the alleged crime had been committed. "Excessive" bail could not be required. "Cruel and unusual" punishment could not be authorized. A prisoner could not be denied the privilege of the writ of habeas corpus whereby the cause of his detention could be inquired into by the judiciary. Government could not keep the people in subjection by denying them the privilege of keeping and bearing arms, and it could not quarter soldiers in the homes of the people without their consent.

These two conceptions, that is, conceptions of both substantive and procedural areas into which government could not enter, were fairly clear in the minds of the American colonists before the separation from the mother-country. Either Parliament or the king—depending on the strategy of the particular argument—was denounced for violation of various of the areas, and the conduct denounced was likely to be characterized as "unconstitutional." In other words, the colonists read into the British constitution their own conceptions of areas of freedom which government could not violate. The conceptions were native to England, but the colonists refined and clarified them and codified them in bills of rights which were included in most of the early state constitutions. Although several years passed before the inclusion of bills of rights in state constitutions became virtually unanimous, sentiment in their favor was so strong, and they had come to be regarded as such an essential part of a constitution, that to many people the adoption of the federal Constitution drafted in Philadelphia in 1787 was unthinkable without the inclusion of a bill of rights to keep government out of areas in which it did not belong.

The belief in the immunity of certain areas from governmental intervention was a part of the philosophy of natural rights. It was generally accepted and was usually expressed as an integral part of that philosophy, oftentimes along with statement of a social contract theory of the origin of government. In the Virginia Declaration of Rights, for example, which antedated the Declaration of Independence by approximately a month, the doctrine was broadly stated in the following language:

That all men are by nature equally free and independent, and have certain inherent rights, of which, when they enter into a state of society, they cannot, by any compact, deprive or divest their posterity; namely, the enjoyment of life and liberty, with the means of acquiring and possessing property, and pursuing and obtaining happiness and safety.

The similarity of this statement to that of the Declaration of Independence will be noted. Pennsylvania used similar language in a Declaration of Rights drafted shortly after the Declaration of Independence was proclaimed. It included the following section:

That all men are born equally free and independent, and have certain natural, inherent and unalienable rights, amongst which are, the enjoying and defending life and liberty, acquiring, possessing and protecting property, and pursuing and obtaining happiness and safety.

Other state constitutions contained similar general statements or specific statements clearly intended to implement the same general beliefs. The beliefs were not the exclusive property of the men who did the drafting. They represented the dominant political philosophy of the time. The purpose of the statements was to incorporate that philosophy into the law of the land.

The federal Constitution which was drafted in Philadelphia in 1787 was submitted for ratification without a bill of rights. It contained, however, a preamble expressing the purpose to "secure the blessings of liberty to ourselves and our posterity." While it is true that the preamble does not have the force of law and is often characterized as a mere gesture on the part of the framers, gestures are not made without a purpose. This one was made in recognition of the prevailing belief that the function of government was to preserve liberty and not to destroy it. Furthermore, a number of provisions which states included in their bills of rights were incorporated into the body of the federal Constitution. Among them were prohibitions of bills of attainder and ex post facto laws, provision for jury trial, and a restricted definition of treason. The framers doubtless thought that they were further protecting the essentials of liberty by setting restrictions upon state power such as that which forbade the states to impair the obligation of contracts. Alexander Hamilton, in No. LXXXIII of *The Federalist,* contended that the language of the preamble was "a better recognition of popular rights, than volumes of those aphorisms which make the principal figure in several of our state bills of rights, and which would sound much better in a treatise of ethics than in a constitution of government." He contended further that the whole Constitution might be interpreted as a bill of rights.

It will be recalled that the protests of Hamilton and other defenders of the Constitution were ineffective in quelling the uneasiness of many people who felt that the Constitution should contain a bill of rights which was identifiable as such. This uneasiness led to an understanding that amendments to the Constitution would be submitted as soon as the Constitution became operative. Such was the origin of the first ten amendments which, although they contained no broad, philosophic statements about the sphere of government, did seek to delimit the sphere of operations of the federal government in specific instances. Although in later years the philosophy of natural rights has been submerged in language much less philosophic in character, the assumption that the sphere of government is limited is largely unshaken. The controversies which rage over the subject involve not so much the question whether limits to governmental action exist as questions as to what the limits shall be.

The conception of a constitution as providing for government strictly according to rule, with equal treatment of all men in like positions, has been firmly fixed in the minds of the American people. Like the conception of limited government, it grew out of a philosophy of natural rights and of human equality. It aided in the intrenchment of protective procedures, such as jury trial, which shelter the accused from unjust discrimination, and it had an impact generally upon the development of machinery for lawmaking and law enforcement. It provides much of the definable content of the word "constitutionalism," which is used in contrast with descriptive terms signifying mere rule of force. Take, for example, the following quotation from *Constitutionalism, Ancient and Modern,* by Charles McIlwain:

Perhaps never in its long history has the principle of constitutionalism been so questioned as it is questioned today, never has the attack upon it been so determined or so threatening as it is just now. The world is trembling in the balance between the orderly procedure of law and the processes of force which seem so much more quick and effective. We must make our choice between these two, and it must be made in the very near future. If we are to make that choice intelligently it would seem reasonable, whether in the end we decide for law or for force, that we should retrace the history of our constitutionalism—the history of force is plain enough—should try to estimate its past achievement, and should consider the nature and effect of the forces which have been arrayed against it.[1]

There is an element of deception, it is true, in contrasting "orderly procedure of law" with "processes of force" and labeling the former as "constitutionalism." A constitution must provide for the use of force in the exercise of the positive functions of government, and a regime of force must operate with a certain amount of order or it will degenerate into chaos. It is

[1] Charles Howard McIlwain, *Constitutionalism, Ancient and Modern* (1940), p. 3. For an illuminating discussion of definitions of constitutions see Edward M. Sait, *Political Institutions* (1938), chap. XV. See also Howard Lee McBain, *The Living Constitution* (1927), chap. i.

a human failing that we tend to apply the term "constitutionalism" to those constitutional systems of which we approve and to characterize the others as demonstrations of the rule of force. Even so, there is value in the relative conception of orderliness and impersonality in the application of law. It can be a potent weapon for the defense of individual or minority rights against tyranny in office.

In the United States the conception found expression in the provision of the Massachusetts constitution of 1780 which dealt with the separation of powers and ended with the words, "to the end it may be a government of laws, and not of men." In writing the opinion in *Marbury* v. *Madison*, which was decided in 1803, Chief Justice Marshall remarked that "the government of the United States has been emphatically termed a government of laws, and not of men,"[2] and argued that, in order to deserve such a high appellation, it must furnish a remedy for the violation of a vested legal right. Another chief justice, William Howard Taft, declared in 1921:

Our whole system of law is predicated on the general fundamental principle of equality of application of the law. "All men are equal before the law"; "This is a government of laws, and not of men"; "No man is above the law"—are all maxims showing the spirit in which legislatures, executives, and courts are expected to make, execute, and apply laws.[3]

Justice Sutherland, speaking for the Supreme Court in 1936, condemned an action of the Securities and Exchange Commission by saying that it violated

the cardinal precept upon which the constitutional safeguards of personal liberty ultimately rest—that this shall be a government of laws—because to the precise extent that the mere will of an official or an official body is permitted to take the place of allowable official discretion or to supplant the standing law as a rule of human conduct, the government ceases to be one of laws and becomes an autocracy.[4]

[2] *Marbury* v. *Madison*, 1 Cranch 137, 163 (1803).
[3] *Truax* v. *Corrigan*, 257 U.S. 312, 332 (1921).
[4] *Jones* v. *Securities and Exchange Commission*, 298 U.S. 1, 23–24 (1936).

The contrast of government of laws with government of men has been much criticized. It is contended that laws are without vitality apart from the men who interpret them and carry them into execution and that all government is essentially government of men. Woodrow Wilson declared that "constitutional government is *par excellence* a government of law,"[5] but used the expression in terms of use of law by the judiciary to restrain administration. At the present time, as will be shown more at length hereafter in this volume, it is the advocates of a free hand for administration who scoff most loudly at "a government of laws and not of men," while lip service continues to be paid to it by those who oppose the extension of governmental power and the further development of administrative agencies. But, apart from the merits of this particular controversy, the essential theme that government must give like treatment to all men in like positions and that the probable treatment should be discoverable in advance by reference to the rules has always been and still is deeply rooted in popular sentiment.

The conception of the Constitution of the United States as an embodiment of fundamental rightness is also well intrenched. Identification of constitutionality with rightness has been at once the bane of judicial existence and the principal guide to judicial interpretation of the Constitution. We are pretty firmly convinced that what is essentially right can be rationalized in terms of the Constitution by any judge who is up to the performance of his task and, conversely, that anything that is wrong is in some way in violation of the Constitution.

It is almost as difficult to state the reasons for the growth of the conception as it is to present clearly the attitude itself.

[5] Woodrow Wilson, *Constitutional Government in the United States* (1908), p. 17. For further discussion of the concept see Edward S. Corwin, *Twilight of the Supreme Court* (1935), chap. iii.

Part of the explanation and part of the difficulty lie in the tendency to identify all law, law of any kind, with rightness. Experience over long periods has shown that the ease or difficulty of law enforcement varies with the extent to which the law in question has the approval of the community—the extent to which it is regarded as right. The popular approval given first to the common law of England and then to the Constitution of the United States was in no small part the product of the skill of judges in interpreting the law in terms of the conceptions of rightness which were prevalent among the people. The whole tradition of our legal system involves a careful mixing of morality, precedent, and logic. The language of the common law is thickly infused with arguments and premises selected from principles of morality or natural law or natural justice. Since the common law represented the mold of our legal thinking, it is not surprising that we dealt with the Constitution and constitutional interpretation after the same fashion. As already indicated, furthermore, there was in our British heritage a tendency to identify constitutions as a whole with bills of rights. An instrument which was calculated to protect rights must itself almost inevitably be righteous.

But the process of sanctification of our Constitution grew out of still other factors than our traditional attitude toward law and constitutions. As part of the strategy of securing adoption, the friends of the Constitution magnified the defects of the Articles of Confederation and the excellence of the proposed substitute. It began to be suggested that the hand of God had guided the hands of the draftsmen. Even shrewd old Benjamin Franklin, whose career had not been particularly one of religious leadership, suggested a comparison between the ancient Jews who had rejected Jesus as the Messiah and the Anti-Federalists who opposed adoption of the Constitution.[6] So effective were the efforts to sanctify the Constitution

[6] John Bigelow (ed.), *The Complete Works of Benjamin Franklin,* IX (1888), 434–39.

that by the time of its adoption it had taken on something of the character of a holy document.[7] Federal judges during the years immediately thereafter spread the gospel of the greatness and rightness of the Constitution as they went from place to place to administer federal justice. Counsel before the courts and politicians interested in legislation and administration found it expedient to refrain from attacks upon the Constitution itself; instead, they sought to control its interpretation. It was no uncommon event, for example, when a one-time opponent of the adoption of the Constitution indignantly excoriated Federalists for action alleged to be unconstitutional.

Since hostile criticism of the Constitution almost ceased with its adoption and, in the language of Woodrow Wilson, "gave place to an undiscriminating and blind worship of its principles,"[8] it became the task of judicial interpreters to find in the principles of the Constitution the basic moral principles of the period. Illustrations may be found particularly in Supreme Court decisions handed down during the regime of Chief Justice Marshall. In *Marbury* v. *Madison* the Chief Justice shuddered at the obloquy which would be cast upon the jurisprudence of the country if it failed to provide a remedy for the violation of a vested legal right.[9] In *Fletcher* v. *Peck,* facing an attack upon vested rights by a state legislature, he generalized as follows: "It may well be doubted whether the nature of society and of government does not prescribe some limits to the legislative power; and, if any be prescribed, where are they to be found, if the property of an individual, fairly and honestly acquired, may be seized without compensation?"[10] In a concurring opinion in the same case, Justice

[7] See Frank I. Schechter, "The Early History of the Tradition of the Constitution," *American Political Science Review,* IX (November, 1915), 707–34.

[8] Woodrow Wilson, *Congressional Government* (1885), p. 4.

[9] *Marbury* v. *Madison,* 1 Cranch 137, 163 (1803).

[10] *Fletcher* v. *Peck,* 6 Cranch 87, 135 (1810).

Johnson wrote as follows: "I do not hesitate to declare that a state does not possess the power of revoking its own grants. But I do it on a general principle, on the reason and nature of things: a principle which will impose laws even on the Deity."[11]

In the Dartmouth College case the same conception of natural rights or natural law is revealed. Marshall admitted that Parliament would have had power to annul a contract. "Yet," he declared, "the contract would at that time have been deemed sacred by all."[12] In the same case, in discussing whether or not the charter of Dartmouth College was nullified at the time of the Revolution, Justice Story found a negative answer in a principle of the common law and added that "this maxim is equally consonant with the common sense of mankind, and the maxims of eternal justice."[13]

In the development of law, however, as in other fields, "new occasions teach new duties," and "time makes ancient good uncouth."[14] Even moral principles have to be interpreted not merely in terms of conceptions of bygone eras but also in harmony with those that are current. In the bankruptcy case of *Ogden* v. *Saunders*, Marshall found himself in a minority of the justices with disagreement over what constituted the obligation of a contract which a state was forbidden to impair. The case involved application of a state bankruptcy law. The majority of the Court, evidently in sympathy with the social sentiments which had led states to relieve debtors from impossible burdens through bankruptcy legislation, held that the obligation of a contract consisted of the legal provisions on the subject which were in force in the state at the time when the contract was made. Since bankruptcy legislation was

[11] *Ibid.*, p. 143.
[12] *Dartmouth College* v. *Woodward*, 4 Wheaton 518, 643 (1819).
[13] *Ibid.*, p. 707.
[14] James Russell Lowell, *The Present Crisis*.

among those provisions, enforcement of the bankruptcy legislation did not violate the obligation of the contract. The majority evidently understood Marshall as holding that the obligation of a contract was the moral commitment made by the parties to the contract and not just an obligation created by law. In the face of criticism Marshall admitted that it was the legal and not the moral obligation of the contract which the Constitution preserved,[15] but his argument leaves the reader with the suspicion that "legal" to him meant some principle of natural justice rather than merely the statute of a state. However that may be, the purpose in presenting these materials is to suggest that moral arguments give sanctity to law in general and to interpretations of the Constitution as long as, but only as long as, the moral arguments can be kept in harmony with the current moral conceptions of the community.

While in later periods the molding of constitutional interpretation through the injection of moral principles has been more carefully concealed behind technical legal terminology,[16] the practice has continued, particularly in connection with the application of the due process clauses. Two illustrations will suffice. Said Chief Justice Taft in 1921:

> The legislative power of a state can only be exerted in subordination to the fundamental principles of right and justice which the guaranty of due process in the 14th Amendment is intended to preserve.[17]

Said Justice Roberts in 1943:

> The due process clause of the Fourteenth Amendment requires that action by a state through any of its agencies must be consistent with the fundamental principles of liberty and justice which lie at the base of our civil and political institutions, which not infrequently are designated as "the law of the land."[18]

---

[15] *Ogden* v. *Saunders*, 12 Wheaton 213, 338–39 (1824).

[16] See Charles G. Haines, *Revival of Natural Law Concepts* (1930).

[17] *Truax* v. *Corrigan*, 257 U.S. 312, 329 (1921).

[18] *Buchalter* v. *New York*, 319 U.S. 427, 429 (1943).

In summary on this topic it should be repeated that the Constitution has been accepted as a righteous instrument and that it has been kept righteous by the infusion of new conceptions of rightness as they developed in the national community. If even fairly specific language in the Constitution happens to conflict with the dominant sentiments of the community, enforcement is likely to be lax or nonexistent—as witness our experience with provisions of those amendments calculated to protect the rights of Negroes and our temporary experience with the ill-fated Eighteenth Amendment. If the dominant sentiment of the community as to "what ought to be" deviates away from previously accepted interpretations of the Constitution, the judiciary will refrain from falling into line only at its peril. He who witnesses changes in our conceptions of rightness but nevertheless expects constitutional interpretations to remain unchanged has much yet to learn about the character of our institutions.

Like the conceptions previously discussed, the conception of federalism as an essential characteristic of our constitutional system and as a check upon the exercise of arbitrary power is deeply rooted in the history of the Colonial period. Government on American soil has been federal ever since England established or won control over the American colonies. The colonies always had a measure of local jurisdiction over local problems and a measure of responsibility to the government in London in matters which were not essentially local. Federalism was as much a part of our governmental folkways as was administration of justice in terms of common-law principles and practices. There is little evidence that the American revolutionaries, or the more levelheaded among them, at any rate, ever seriously contemplated giving up the essentials of federalism. When they declared themselves free and independent states, they had in mind freedom from the mother-country. But to some extent from the very beginning they expected the breaking of transoceanic ties to be compensated for by union among themselves. If perchance they talked about the reservation of full sovereignty in each state, they accompanied such talk by actions which belied their words. Government under the Articles of Confederation, and even that which preceded the formal adoption of the Articles, provided for more of central control over American affairs than had been exercised from London, but it followed a long familiar pattern. The Constitution as adopted in 1789 provided for a further increase of central power but again without fundamental modification of the pattern. Professor McLaughlin has summarized the point as follows:

The principle of federalism was recognized, formulated and legalized by the Constitution; the new government was given its distinct sphere of action and was made the recipient of a body of powers, carefully named and carefully deposited in their proper places; but in the selection and deposition little needed to be done but to follow the practices of the old British colonial system.[19]

Although later years brought much talk of secession from the Union and the actual attempt at secession which brought on the Civil War, the talk and that attempt did not imply an abandonment of federalism in the sense of atomistic dissolution. All that was seriously contemplated was separation into smaller federal unions, with the lodgment of varying amounts of power in central governments. On the other hand, in spite of the recommendations of such diverse commentators as Alexander Hamilton and Harold Laski, there has been at no time a strong popular sentiment on behalf of complete centralization of government in the United States. The alleged drift in that direction, which takes its impetus not from arguments but from the force of imponderable events, causes uneasiness on the part of men whose beliefs on the subject root back into

[19] Andrew C. McLaughlin, "The Background of American Federalism," *American Political Science Review*, XII (May, 1918), 240.

centuries of American experience with federalism. The alleged drift and the reasons therefor and the popular appraisal of it will receive further attention elsewhere. For the moment it is sufficient to say that current problems of federalism call for most serious attention on the part of thoughtful people.

The conception of the separation of powers as an essential characteristic of our Constitution and as a check upon the exercise of arbitrary power also roots back into our Colonial history.[20] It has been said that the persuasive writings of John Locke and Montesquieu had much to do with our adoption of the device. Textbooks have even offered explanation as simply as in the following language: Montesquieu went to England to discover what could be learned about British institutions that might have value in reform of the French government. He mistook the rise of the cabinet system for the development of the separation of powers and went home and wrote a book about it. Americans read his *Spirit of the Laws* and proceeded to write his misconception of the British constitution into our own fundamental law.

What actually happened was not so simple as that—or, if it was equally simple, it was very different. Americans undoubtedly knew the writings of Locke and Montesquieu and other political theorists of our late Colonial period. They were steeped in theories of natural rights and social contract and in discussions of devices for giving power without paving the way for tyrants. But, beyond all that, they had long known the operation of the separation of powers in their own governmental experience. This was particularly true in colonies in which governors, on the one hand, were appointed by the king and colonial legislatures, on the other, were chosen locally. Crystallized sentiment in favor of the separation of powers

[20] See Benjamin F. Wright, "The Origin of Separation of Powers in America," *Economica*, XIII (May, 1933), 169–85; Malcolm P. Sharp, "The Classical American Doctrine of the Separation of Powers," *University of Chicago Law Review*, II (April, 1935), 385–436.

was reflected in most of the early state constitutions either in general statements on its behalf or in the undiscussed adoption of the principle. For example, the Virginia constitution which was adopted June 29, 1776, contained the following provision:

The legislative, executive, and judiciary departments, shall be separate and distinct, so that neither exercise the powers properly belonging to the other: nor shall any person exercise the powers of more than one of them, at the same time. . . . .

The Maryland constitution contained the following provision:

That the legislative, executive and judicial powers of government, ought to be forever separate and distinct from each other.

The fullest statement was the much-quoted section of the Massachusetts constitution of 1780, which read as follows:

In the government of this commonwealth, the legislative department shall never exercise the executive and judicial powers, or either of them; the executive shall never exercise the legislative and judicial powers, or either of them; the judicial shall never exercise the legislative and executive powers, or either of them; to the end it may be a government of laws, and not of men.

In the drafting of permanent constitutions other states which did not incorporate statements such as those quoted set up governments in terms of the principle of the separation of powers.

Apart from emergency instruments such as the first constitution of South Carolina, the only important constitutional document which did not provide for the separation of powers was the Articles of Confederation. The Articles, although they provided for "perpetual union" of the states, were concerned as much with legitimatizing what had been done and was being done by the Continental Congress as with planning peacetime government for the long future. The Continental Congress had evolved as an agency of protest against British abuses and, largely without design on anybody's part, had gradually slipped into the position of a governing agency. In the light of all the circumstances, including its preoccupation with winning the war, it is hardly surprising that, when it undertook the task of establishing a clearly legitimate government, it created that government in its own image.

Even though the government represented by the Continental Congress and authorized by the Articles of Confederation represented something of a novelty on American soil, it ought not to be said that the form of the government was responsible for its unpopularity during the years which followed the war. The fact of its unpopularity, however, coupled with the fact of the comparative popularity of the state governments, is important in explaining why the members of the Philadelphia convention, almost as a matter of course, patterned the new government after the governments of the states rather than after its direct predecessor.

So it was that the federal government fell into line with the traditional experience of the American people in the matter of the separation of powers. The principle survives and apparently still has a healthy public sentiment behind it. The ends which it serves and the problems which it creates will be discussed later.

The conception of our Constitution as basing government on the consent of the governed is at once important and difficult to explain. It does not necessarily mean democracy in the sense of rule by all the people in their capacity as voters. It will be recalled that, in presenting the Virginia Plan to the Constitutional Convention, John Randolph deplored the existence of too much democracy in the states and lauded those checks by which democracy was restrained. The Constitution exempted federal judges from operation of the elective process and provided that election of the President and United States senators should be indirect. Executive and administrative officers other than the President and Vice-President were to be appointed rather than elected. As to those officials who were elected, furthermore, the determination of the franchise was left to the states, which customarily limited the right to vote in terms of age, sex, race, status (as slave or bond servant), property, and religion.

The conception of "consent of the governed," therefore, was not identical with a conception of each individual as a direct participant in the governmental process. If we search for meaning in the Declaration of Independence, we find the doctrine stated in the following language:

We hold these truths to be self-evident, that all men are created equal, that they are endowed by their Creator with certain unalienable rights, that among these are life, liberty and the pursuit of happiness.— That to secure these rights, governments are instituted among men, deriving their just powers from the consent of the governed.

In the light of this language the conception has all the vagueness of the diverse statements of the theory of the social contract. As used in the Declaration it was an instrument to justify revolution against a government which had perpetrated a long list of abuses. In the light of the language of the entire document, "consent of the governed" seems to imply a compound of the right of a certain amount of local self-government, on the one hand, and, on the other hand, the right to "righteous" government by the ruler. It included the content of prevalent theories of natural rights and also the beliefs which had evolved down through the years since Magna Carta as to the right of at least some of the people to have something to say about how they were to be governed. It could support the slogan of "No taxation without representation," even though actually the men who voiced it were probably much more concerned about escaping taxation than with winning the right of representation. Implying, as it could be said to do, government from within the group of the governed rather than from without, it could be used in breaking American ties with a nation across the sea which to the American people was growing steadily more alien.

The history of the conception since the Revolution and since the adoption of the Constitution has been similarly vague and similarly important. Even though it was not inseparably linked with a commitment to universal suffrage, or perhaps even to suffrage at all in the modern sense of the term, it has supported the steady expansion of the right to vote. On the other hand, it has been used to justify criticism of or resistance to government on the part of sections, classes, or interests which believed that as sections, classes, or interests they had rights which were subject only to government to which they themselves gave consent, as distinguished from the consent given by the larger group in which the group in question constituted a minority. When the federal government prescribes certain treatment of the colored race, the white people of the "solid South" wax indignant over the fact that their consent has not been given as to the governmental mandate. Wet areas once emphatically denied that they had given their consent to the establishment of national prohibition, and they asserted their freedom accordingly. Other groups make similar use of the conception. In general, however, there is recognition that consent goes with those measures which promote the larger welfare of the nation, the special interests of minority groups to the contrary notwithstanding. Once again, government must be "right" in order to be "constitutional."

So much, then, for an introductory discussion of American attitudes toward constitutions in general and our Constitution in particular. In summary, these attitudes reflect not merely an understanding of the Constitution as a source and channel of governmental power but also important conceptions which influenced the shaping of the original Constitution and its interpretation thereafter. The doing of certain things by government is and must be forbidden. Certain things must be done only in prescribed ways. Government must operate strictly according to rule. The essence of government must be "rightness." Federalism and the separation of powers are indispensable devices in the government of the United States. Government must rest on the consent of the governed. These conceptions, quite as much as the exact language of the Constitution or the logic of arguments based upon it, help to mold constitutional government in the United States and guide our thinking about constitutional matters as we adapt government to the needs of a new era. The most obvious fact in this brief account is the imprisonment of the power-giving agency within a stockade of restrictions, the giving of power with one hand and the blocking of power with the other hand, or, seemingly, with many hands. The current and fundamental question about the process is whether restraint in terms of the restrictions herein discussed is vital to the democratic process or whether it goes so far as to prevent achievement by government of the ends which society is seeking more and more to achieve through political organization.

II

SHIFTING BOUNDARIES OF FEDERALISM

✻

THE American people today, as throughout most of the history of the United States, hear dire predictions of the imminent collapse of our federal system. The federal balance, the lamentation runs, is being destroyed; state lines are disappearing; the states are being transformed into mere tools of the federal government. If the appraisal continues to what is usually regarded as its logical conclusion, it culminates in the forecast that most of our liberties are about to be lost and that dictatorship is about to be intrenched in Washington—or in the solemn and portentous assertion that these disasters have already occurred. Although such predictions concerning our federal system are novel only in incidental characteristics, their utterance in the current era of political ferment justifies an examination of existing relations between the federal and state governments. As has already been said, resort to a federal system in the United States was originally conditioned in part by the federal character of our Colonial heritage. However, other considerations than those merely of precedent entered into its adoption, and other considerations must justify its maintenance if it is to be maintained. At the outset of our inquiry, therefore, it is well to seek, in terms of public welfare, justification of the federal relationships for which the Constitution provides.

Federalism rests on the principle that political problems are likely to be solved most effectively if the task of solving them is allocated to the people who, at once, are most affected by the problems and know them most intimately. In the minds of many people, furthermore, it is assumed that the very act of solving one's own problems is conducive to the development of the highest qualities of citizenship in the community. In terms of territory and population, the area of responsibility for the solution of problems is commensurate with the area of affectation. Such areas vary tremendously from problem to problem. If it were feasible administratively and otherwise, we should have ideally an ever changing pattern of federated areas engaged in solving an ever changing panorama of problems. While maintenance of such a fluctuating pattern is not feasible, we do approach it, in fact, in the variety of jurisdictional areas to which the performance of varied political tasks is allocated. In addition to the deeply grooved outlines of the federal and state governments, for example, we have within the federal government administrative areas such as Federal Reserve districts and the Tennessee Valley Authority; while states make use of counties, municipalities, and special districts for education, irrigation, drainage, and various other purposes. States also find it desirable at times to enter into combinations with other states for particular governmental purposes, as in the instance of the Colorado River Compact and the New York Port Authority.

For the most part, however, the governmental units involved in the solution of our major problems are the states and the federal government. And, as Woodrow Wilson has said, "The question of the relation of the states to the federal government is the cardinal question of our constitutional system. It cannot be settled by the opinion of any one generation, because it is a question of growth, and every successive stage of our political and economic development gives it a new aspect, makes it a new question."[1]

Only in a very general way does the Constitution fix the

---

[1] Woodrow Wilson, *Constitutional Government in the United States* (1908), p. 173.

boundaries between the federal and state governments. Although it delimits the powers of the states by certain negative signposts, the prohibitions, such as that no state shall impair the obligation of contracts, or take life, liberty, or property without due process of law, are subject to wide ranges of interpretation. Although the Constitution gives to the federal government only the powers delegated to it or reasonably to be implied from its provisions and reserves all other powers to the states or to the people, many grants of federal power are in terms so general as to provide no clear peripheral lines. What are the limits of the federal power to regulate interstate commerce, for example, or the powers incidentally to regulate local affairs through the war powers, the taxing power, etc.? Nobody know except the Supreme Court; and that tribunal professes definite knowledge only as it decides the specific questions brought before it in particular cases. A general philosophy of interpretation is expressed by Justice Murphy in the following language:

We derive much of our strength as a nation from our dual system of federal government. To promote the harmonious working of that system the general clauses of the Constitution which broadly delineate the boundaries of state and national power should be construed by appraising the respective state and national interests involved and striking a balance which gives appropriate recognition to the legitimate concerns of each government. Since those boundaries are not absolutes, the question necessarily is one of reasonableness and degree.[2]

Although Justice Murphy's statement was incorporated in a dissenting opinion, the principle was probably acceptable to all his colleagues. For that reason it is worth emphasizing the fact that "appropriate recognition," "legitimate concerns of each government," "reasonableness," and "degree" are extremely general terms into which almost any content might be

[2] Dissenting, *Pacific Coast Dairy* v. *Department of Agriculture*, 318 U.S. 285, 304 (1943).

fitted. While in cases in which the facts resemble the facts of other cases previously decided the justices find it necessary to give close attention to precedents, their statements of principle as to boundary lines between state and federal jurisdictions, like the language of the Constitution itself, leave broad discretion in their hands. In the light of this fact, the drawing of such lines might be expected to involve chronic warfare among the interests affected by the decisions. So it does, and so it has always done. Particular battles have come to an end and particular stretches of the boundaries have been established, but the warfare has continued. In our analysis of the character of federal relationships it is well to examine some of the constitutional controversies which were settled during our early history, some which have persisted throughout the life of the Constitution, and some which are in important respects peculiar to the present day.

The scope of the authority of the federal judiciary with respect to the states was long a subject of bitter controversy. In an early battle over the subject the judiciary met a rebuff at the hands of the people. When, in 1793, citizens of South Carolina brought in the Supreme Court of the United States a suit against the state of Georgia, the latter state refused to take official cognizance of this alleged offense to its dignity except to file a protest against the jurisdiction of the Court.[3] When the Court decided for the creditors, the resentment of a number of states at the affront to state dignity involved in permitting suits against states by mere citizens was sufficient to bring about adoption of the Eleventh Amendment, which withdrew from the federal courts jurisdiction in suits against states brought by citizens of other states or foreign countries.

Thereafter, however, the judiciary, apart from relatively minor instances, succeeded in overcoming state resistance. For example, in 1815 the court of appeals of Virginia reached the

[3] *Chisholm* v. *Georgia*, 2 Dallas 419 (1793).

solemn conclusion that the Supreme Court of the United States had no power to reverse a decision of the highest court of a state even though the case involved a question of conflict between a state statute and a federal treaty. But, through an opinion by Justice Story which Charles Warren has called "an opinion which has ever since been the keystone of the whole arch of federal judicial power,"[4] the Supreme Court rejected the argument of the Virginia court.[5] Justice Story pointed out that the jurisdiction of the Supreme Court did not depend upon the court from which the case in question came. Rather, the Constitution conferred upon that tribunal jurisdiction in cases involving the federal Constitution, laws, and treaties. If the exercise of this jurisdiction in cases coming up from state courts seemed to impair the sovereignty of the states, it was, he declared, only one of many instances in which the people had limited state sovereignty by the adoption of the Constitution. To take another example, when in 1830 the state of Missouri protested indignantly at being haled before the Supreme Court in a case involving bills of credit issued in violation of the Constitution, Chief Justice Marshall replied piously that "this department can listen only to the mandates of law, and can tread only that path which is marked out by duty."[6] The Missouri protest was without avail.

States had similar experiences with the federal judiciary in other kinds of cases. They challenged restrictions based on the contract clause, the commerce clause, the slavery clauses, and other provisions of the Constitution. For the most part the judiciary stood firm in the assertion of its authority to define the constitutional limits of state powers. Apart from the effect of the Civil War itself in defining such restrictions, by the time

[4] Charles Warren, *The Supreme Court in United States History* (1926 ed.), I, 449.

[5] *Martin* v. *Hunter's Lessee*, 1 Wheaton 304 (1816).

[6] *Craig* v. *Missouri*, 4 Peters 410, 438 (1830).

the war was fought the federal judiciary had put itself into a firm position with reference to its authority over the states.

The tensions of state-federal relations revealed themselves along still other lines. The Virginia and Kentucky Resolutions at the end of the eighteenth century marked the agonies of adjustment to the federal enforcement of policy in conflict with local sentiment and stimulated development of theories of nullification. The Burr Conspiracy a few years afterward called attention to the fact that the Union might not continue with its then distended dimensions. The disaffection of Federalists during the War of 1812 as revealed by the Hartford Convention and by other activities and utterances showed how frail was Union sentiment when it clashed with dominant economic interests. The southern nullification movement in connection with tariff legislation emphasized the same point. The drift of the South toward secession because of slavery and other sectional interests kept the Union in a precarious position until the outcome on the battlefield settled the fact that the Union was indissoluble.

The Civil War brought about a series of adjustments in state-federal relations. The Thirteenth, Fourteenth, and Fifteenth amendments curtailed or eliminated powers of the states with respect to slavery, citizenship, suffrage, legal procedure, and other matters. The federal government set up what came to be called "carpetbag governments" in a number of southern states and supported them with federal troops, abandoning them only after experience proved that local governments without the support of politically effective members of local populations would never be able to stand on their own feet. Furthermore, the federal government began expansion of legislation based on the commerce clause, its power over elections, the recently adopted constitutional amendments, and other powers, expansion of which until the war had been held back by southern sensitivity about federal encroachment.

If, in spite of the statements of doctrine by the Supreme Court, doubt remained as to the power of the federal government to exercise its authority in intimate competition with the local administration of local affairs, that doubt was now obliterated.

In the meantime, the passing years were slowly and inconspicuously bringing about another kind of change in the federal system. The original states and the other states established during the early years had been centers of intense local patriotism. To many people it was more important to be a citizen of South Carolina or Virginia or Pennsylvania than to be a citizen of the United States. The newly established federal government was almost an alien institution to which secondary loyalties attached with extreme slowness. That government became better and better known to succeeding generations, however, and, to the people settling new states, it came gradually to assume a position of primacy. Citizens of the new state of Iowa, for example, who had probably been born within the confines of other states, might be expected to have a deeper loyalty to the Union, which they had always known, than to the newly established government of the state of their adoption. Such matters of sentiment have great influence on the operations of government. Citizens of Georgia may have felt a genuine patriotic resentment at what they regarded as encroachment of the federal government upon the proper sphere of state authority. If citizens of Oregon, on the other hand, had anything of the same kind of feeling, it burned feebly by comparison with that of the older states, which took such pride in their local sovereignty.

All this is not to say that problems of federalism were on their way to solution through submergence of the states by the federal system or that men stopped debating legal questions in terms of state-federal relations. Federal sentiment remained and still remains too deeply intrenched in the minds of native Americans for such easy eradication. The difference is that, whereas a citizen of Alabama might once have trembled with rage at some federal flouting of the sovereignty of the "Cotton State," the average citizen of the relatively young state of Arizona—like many of the now highly mobile citizens of even the oldest states—does not in the same sincere fashion draw his sword in defense of the virtue of outraged Arizona. To him the federal government may seem less alien than the government of the state. He will feel a thrill at the sight of the American flag, whereas he may not know whether his state has a flag.

Disciplined and honest thinking about federalism is one of our greatest needs. Throughout our history a great deal of the controversy over the proper dividing-lines between the spheres of state and federal action has raged in terms of insincere and confusing arguments. Whereas the arguments have been based nominally upon constitutional interpretations, the concern of the contenders has usually not been with the question whether the power in controversy should be exercised by the federal government or by a state government but whether it should be exercised at all. Many of the great constitutional decisions of our early years—decisions which we traditionally praise for their farsighted nationalism—were not decisions paving the way for contemplated exercise of national power. For many reasons—including southern distrust of a federal government ultimately to be dominated by the North—the broad exercise of power by the federal government was not seriously contemplated. The immediate effect of judicial assertion of the existence of broad federal power in certain areas was not to bring about the exercise of that power by the federal government but to prevent the states from exercising it. So-called "nationalist" decisions were not so much truly nationalist, therefore, as they were prohibitions in support of laissez faire. When, on the other hand, the federal government did eventually begin the sweeping exercise of its powers, the self-appointed mouthpieces of nationalistic enthusiasm became quickly very much concerned about federal encroachments upon the powers of the states.

It behooves us, therefore, to take thought before drenching our handkerchiefs when the National Association of Manufacturers and the American Bar Association bewail the prostrate position of the states before the federal colossus. These mourners are not shedding tears over the lamentable condition of New Hampshire and North Carolina and Montana and Texas but over the enterprise caught in the grip of the federal regulatory hand. Whether that enterprise merits our sympathy is at the moment not the question. The point is that the argument is hopelessly confused by the strategy of its use. Spokesmen for the enterprise seeking to avoid regulation seek shelter from the would-be regulator by crouching within the confines of that government which at the moment is not trying to regulate at all or by lodgment in a mythical no-man's land between the spheres of the two governments. If we are to think clearly about federalism, we must disentangle the issues of state-federal relations from those of freedom of enterprise versus control. True, the subjects are related. The questions of degree of control, centralization or decentralization of control, and efficiency of control take us back to the principles upon which federalism rests. But if arguments based upon federalism are to illuminate the subject rather than becloud it, they must not conceal the fact that oftentimes the real question at issue is the question whether control is to be exercised at all rather than whether the agency of control should be a state or the federal government. In the light of this fact we may find that the basic question is one of public policy, a political question, and not at all a question of law.

The fact that decisions bearing upon federalism are confused by the obfuscation of contending parties should not be taken to indicate that no legitimate disagreements over jurisdictional lines remain to be resolved. Questions as to the right-

ful spheres of the respective governments are constantly arising. They appear usually in connection with the projection of
newly exercised power from one government or another. They
arise in cases involving state and federal taxes of various kinds,
state and federal statutes bearing upon interstate and intrastate commerce, the exercise of state police power, the making
of federal grants to the states, control of primary elections, and
various other subjects. In spite of a background of a century
and a half of experience, the Supreme Court finds the establishment of boundary lines an exceedingly difficult task and
at times it finds it necessary to abandon old determinations and
establish new lines which are more acceptable in the light of
current thinking. To illustrate this point we shall examine a
number of changes in position which have been made since
the beginning of the New Deal administration in 1933.

In 1941 the Supreme Court formally abandoned an interpretation of the Tenth Amendment which for many years had
been used to check the extension of federal power over matters
which had once been considered primarily local. The Tenth
Amendment provides that "the powers not delegated to the
United States by the Constitution, nor prohibited by it to the
states, are reserved to the states respectively, or to the people."
The amendment was read in early decisions as if it meant
that the exercise of a power granted to the federal government
must stop at the point at which it began encroachment upon
matters which had traditionally been regarded as under local
jurisdiction. Here, as already indicated, the interpretation became an instrument not so much of local patriots as of interests
opposing regulation as such. Experience with child labor illustrates the point. Employers were for many years able to defeat
legislation against child labor in many states on the ground
that such legislation in one state would put its industries at a
competitive disadvantage with other states in which child
labor was not prohibited. Yet, when Congress enacted a stat-

ute prohibiting shipment in interstate commerce of goods produced by child labor, the Supreme Court, which embodied a philosophy hardly less opposed to governmental restriction of enterprise than that of the interests affected, was persuaded to hold that the statute unconstitutionally invaded the province of the states. Said Justice Day: "The grant of authority over a purely federal matter was not intended to destroy the local power always existing and carefully reserved to the states in the 10th Amendment to the Constitution."[7] When Congress attempted to achieve the same end through use of the taxing power, the Supreme Court blocked it in the same fashion.[8]

The interpretation stood as a bar to federal legislation not only on child labor but on hours of labor, wages, and many other subjects. Although the opinion of the Court is so confused as almost to defy analysis, the same conception of peripheral impotence of the federal government apparently guided the decision of the Supreme Court in *United States* v. *Butler*,[9] in 1936, in which use of the processing-tax device for the regulation of agricultural production was held unconstitutional. By this time, however, hostility to regulation from any source was becoming more clearly recognized as the motivation to use of the restricted interpretation. With the beginning of personnel changes on the Supreme Court in 1937, administration leaders began to plan legislation in terms of which they could ask the Court to overrule the child-labor case which was based on the commerce clause and abandon a logically untenable position. The Fair Labor Standards Act of 1938 provided the desired opportunity by establishing federal control of hours, wages, and child labor in connection with goods produced for shipment in interstate commerce. In *United States* v. *Darby*, decided in 1941, the Supreme Court over-

[7] *Hammer* v. *Dagenhart*, 247 U.S. 251, 274 (1918).

[8] *Bailey* v. *Drexel Furniture Co.*, 259 U.S. 20 (1922).

[9] *United States* v. *Butler*, 297 U.S. 1 (1936).

ruled the child-labor case and corrected the earlier misinterpretation of the Tenth Amendment in the following language:

> The amendment states but a truism that all is retained which has not been surrendered. There is nothing in the history of its adoption to suggest that it was more than declaratory of the relationship between the national and state governments as it had been established by the Constitution before the amendment or that its purpose was other than to allay fears that the new national government might seek to exercise powers not granted, and that the states might not be able to exercise fully their reserved powers.[10]

The decision makes it clear that the traditional sphere of state activity is immune from federal invasion only to the extent that the right of the invader is limited to the exercise of some power directly given or implied in the Constitution. If this conclusion provokes the horrified comment that under the color of exercise of the commerce power or the taxing power the constitutional balance between the states and the federal government may be destroyed, the answer, or one answer, at any rate, is that the Constitution does not provide for any such balance. It gives certain powers to the federal government, denies certain powers to the federal government and to the state governments, and leaves the remaining powers to the states and to the people. These remaining powers consist only of the powers not granted to the federal government and not forbidden to the states. An exercise of the federal commerce power or of any other federal power is not limited by the fact that the states have residual powers outside the scope of the powers granted. Our logical difficulty here is that we tend to confuse a reasonable interpretation of the words of the Constitution by importing a conception of something which the words perhaps ought to have included but which they do not actually say. We are convinced—or many of us are convinced, at any rate—that good government in the United States de-

[10] *United States* v. *Darby*, 312 U.S. 100, 124 (1941).

mands the preservation of the states as strong governmental agencies. We fear that the logical extension of the powers granted to the federal government will hamstring the states in the performance of local functions. We therefore indulge in untenable reasoning to show that something which is at least not more definite than "the spirit of the Constitution" limits the exercise of legitimate federal powers. Currency is given to such untenable lines of argument by the arguments of counsel—and by the judges who accept them—wherein the motivation is not necessarily the preservation of a balanced federal system but is rather the protection of enterprise from undesired federal control. We leave ourselves confused by the hopeless intermingling of questions of public policy—some of them avowed and some concealed—with questions of public law as answered by the language of the Constitution.

The field of taxation provides illustrations of a number of shifts in federal boundary lines which have been made since 1933. Since taxation provides the lifeblood of any government, courts recognize the fact that the power to tax must be preserved. On the other hand, since it is an efficient and potentially dangerous weapon in the hands of those who wield it, its use must be carefully hedged with safeguards. Without such safeguards, it "involves the power to destroy." In a federal system it might involve the power to destroy not only private enterprise subjected to inequitable levies but also agencies of the federal partner. As to taxation of private enterprise, the Constitution provides that direct taxes must be apportioned among the states according to population and that indirect taxes must be uniform. Both state and federal taxes must conform to due process of law and state tax measures must not deny equal protection of the laws. Yet these restrictions are subject to wide ranges of interpretation. In the matter of the encroachment of one government upon another by means of the taxing power, interpretation is largely a matter of reliance upon broad principles of the Constitution. The door to disagreement among those who have different conceptions of public policy is left wide open.

The history of controversies over taxation of the instrumentalities of one government by the other government dates back to *McCulloch* v. *Maryland*,[11] in which Chief Justice Marshall, uttering the famous dictum that "the power to tax involves the power to destroy," held invalid a Maryland statute taxing the notes of a branch of the federally chartered Bank of the United States. From this holding the Supreme Court developed in subsequent cases the principle of reciprocal immunity of federal and state instrumentalities from federal and state taxation.[12] The principle was easy to administer except for the difficulty of identifying marginal instrumentalities of government, and for many years it seemed to operate in the public interest. As the scope of governmental activity expanded, however, the area of exemption from taxation increased to formidable proportions. Exemption of the salaries of millions of employees of one government or the other became a serious matter in face of the need for increased revenue to pay increased costs of government. Retreat of huge sums of money into tax-exempt securities, securities of which neither the principal nor the income could be taxed, began to be regarded as a menace to the public welfare.

In the face of the changing situation people began more seriously to question the validity of tax exemptions based on the absolutist principle that the power to tax involves the power to destroy. In a dissenting opinion written in 1928, Justice Holmes challenged the principle which Marshall had enunciated:

In those days it was not recognized as it is today that most of the distinctions of the law are distinctions of degree. If the states had any

[11] 4 Wheaton 316 (1819).
[12] See *Dobbins* v. *Commissioners of Erie County*, 16 Peters 435 (1842), and *Collector* v. *Day*, 11 Wallace 113 (1871).

power it was assumed that they had all power, and that the necessary alternative was to deny it altogether. But this Court which so often has defeated the attempt to tax in certain ways can defeat an attempt to discriminate or otherwise go too far without wholly abolishing the power to tax. The power to tax is not the power to destroy while this Court sits.[13]

The changing attitude gradually worked its way into majority opinions. The Supreme Court began to trim down the concept of government instrumentalities which were exempt from taxation. Then, in 1939, it virtually wiped out the concept as far as the exemption of government salaries from nondiscriminatory taxation was concerned.[14] As a result the salaries of the millions of men and women employed by state and federal governments are now subject to both state and federal taxation. While no decision has yet cleared the way for reciprocal taxation of income from government securities, the principle is not greatly different, and a decision to that end would not occasion great surprise. To people more concerned about the health of governmental establishments than about exemptions from equitable responsibilities for support of their governments the new trend in decisions seems eminently desirable.

Since the beginning of the depression thoughtful people have been deeply concerned about preserving unhampered the taxing power of the states. The sweeping extension of federal power has been due to many causes, but one of them has been the ease with which the federal government could tax and borrow, in contrast with the economic and legal difficulties under which the states operate. States which relied heavily upon general property taxes as sources of revenue found property-holders unable to pay even the normal levies, and widespread sale of property for delinquent taxes was both politically and economically disastrous. Many states turned to

[13] *Panhandle Oil Co.* v. *Mississippi* ex rel. *Knox*, 277 U.S. 218, 223 (1928).

[14] *Graves* v. *New York* ex rel. *O'Keefe*, 306 U.S. 466 (1939).

other forms of revenue. Sales taxes proved profitable sources, but they also created serious problems. They could be collected on local sales, but they could not constitutionally be collected on sales made in interstate commerce. Quick to sense their own immediate interest, customers began wherever possible to buy in interstate commerce rather than locally. To counteract this disruption of local business, some sales-tax states then enacted so-called "use taxes" to be levied on the local use of goods which had been bought in interstate commerce and on which no sales tax had been paid. To the surprise of many people who thought the use-tax device would be held unconstitutional as an interference with interstate commerce, the Supreme Court found it constitutional.[15]

The giving of constitutional sanction to the employment of use taxes to match sales taxes which could not constitutionally be collected made it possible for the states to raise revenue which would not otherwise have been available and, therefore, to perform functions which otherwise would have gone unperformed or been performed by the federal government. The Supreme Court also aided the states by enlarging their powers as against earlier interpretations with respect to what is loosely called "double taxation." The Court had previously taken the position that intangible property could be taxed only in the state of the domicile of the owner. In 1939, however, it held that this restriction did not extend to states in which protection was given to the intangible property even though the owner's place of domicile was in another state.[16] How deliberately the Court was remolding constitutional law to enable the states to compete with the federal government in the expan-

[15] *Henneford* v. *Silas Mason Co.*, 300 U.S. 577 (1937). See Robert C. Brown, "The Future of Use Taxes," *Law and Contemporary Problems*, VIII (summer, 1941), 495–505. For the altitude of the Court toward sales taxes affecting interstate commerce see *McGoldrick* v. *Berwind-White Coal Mining Co.*, 309 U.S. 33 (1940), and *McLeod* v. *Dilworth Co.*, 322 U.S. 327 (1944).

[16] *Curry* v. *McCanless*, 307 U.S. 357 (1944).

sion of power we are not informed. But it requires no stretching of the imagination to picture the result achieved as within the contemplation of the men who made it possible.

Collection of use taxes approaches and at times belongs within a category of activities which result in what are known as interstate trade barriers. By means of measures allegedly enacted for legitimate tax purposes or purposes of legitimate licensing or inspection, states have sought to keep as much as possible of their internal business in the hands of their own people by excluding commodities and services from without the state. Where discrimination against interstate commerce is clearly the dominant purpose of the state statute, the Supreme Court disposes of it as an unconstitutional invasion of the federal field. Such a case recently came up from Florida. The legislature required inspection of all cement used in the state which was brought in from outside the state but not of that which was produced locally. The inspection fee proved to be sixty times the actual cost of inspection. The state legislature unwisely disclosed its purpose by saying in the statute that importation of cement "amounts to unfair competition being forced on this great industry in Florida." The Supreme Court had no difficulty in finding the act unconstitutional.[17]

Oftentimes, however, neither the over-all purposes nor the over-all effects of a particular statute are sufficiently clear to guide the judiciary in weighing constitutionality. It proves impossible for a judge to weigh the statute in terms of related measures and their administration or even to weigh the particular controversy before it in the light of other incidents of the administration of the same act. Justice Black has taken the position that, since the Supreme Court cannot deal systematically with such problems, it ought to exercise self-restraint in curbing state activities, leaving it to Congress to survey and, if necessary, to legislate upon the relations of state tax and

[17] *Hale* v. *Bimco Trading Co.*, 306 U.S. 375 (1939).

police measures to interstate commerce and property in other states. His argument runs as follows:

Judicial control of national commerce—unlike legislative regulations—must from inherent limitations of the judicial process treat the subject by the hit and miss method of deciding single local controversies upon evidence and information limited by the narrow rules of litigation. Spasmodic and unrelated instances of litigation cannot afford an adequate basis for the creation of integrated national rules which alone can afford that full protection for interstate commerce intended by the Constitution. We would, therefore, leave the questions raised . . . . for consideration of Congress in a nation-wide survey of the constantly increasing barriers to trade among the states. Unconfined by "the narrow scope of judicial proceedings" Congress alone can, in the exercise of its plenary control over interstate commerce, ... on the basis of full exploration of the many aspects of a complicated problem devise a national policy fair alike to the states and our Union. Diverse and interacting state laws may well have created avoidable hardships. . . . . But the remedy, if any is called for, we think is within the ample reach of Congress.[18]

Although Congress has not undertaken any such survey of state-federal relations as that suggested by Justice Black, the Supreme Court has leaned somewhat toward the policy advocated by him in its leniency toward state laws which encroach upon interstate commerce. Such a policy has its dangers, however, as Justice Jackson has pointed out:

The extent to which state legislation may be allowed to affect the conduct of interstate business in the absence of congressional action on the subject has long been a vexatious problem. Recently the tendency has been to abandon the earlier limitations and to sustain more freely such state laws on the ground that Congress has power to supersede them with regulations of its own. It is a tempting escape from a difficult question to pass to Congress the responsibility for continued existence of local restraints and obstructions to national commerce. But these restraints are individually too petty, too diversified, and too local to get the attention of a Congress hard pressed with more urgent matters. The practical result is that in default of action by us they will go on suf-

---

[18] *McCarroll* v. *Dixie Greyhound Lines, Inc.*, 309 U.S. 176, 189 (1940).

focating and retarding and Balkanizing American commerce, trade and industry.

I differ basically with my brethren as to whether the inertia of government shall be on the side of restraint of commerce or on the side of freedom of commerce. The sluggishness of government, the multitude of matters that clamor for attention, and the relative ease with which men are persuaded to postpone troublesome decisions, all make inertia one of the most decisive powers in determining the course of our affairs and frequently gives to the established order of things a longevity and vitality much beyond its merits. Because this is so, I am reluctant to see any new local systems for restraining our national commerce get the prestige and power of established institutions.[19]

The materials quoted from Justices Black and Jackson illustrate the diversity of opinion now prevailing on the Supreme Court as to state laws infringing upon interstate commerce and related matters. In spite of the differences, however, the tendency since 1937 or earlier has been to uphold state statutes unless their unconstitutionality seems obvious. Most of those held invalid have been in the field of civil liberties, which will be discussed in another chapter.[20]

But if the tendency since 1937 has been to uphold state legislation of which the constitutionality has been challenged, the attitude toward federal legislation alleged to encroach upon local jurisdiction has reflected more than a tendency. In this period the enactment of new statutes and the application of old ones to extend the exercise of federal power have proceeded almost entirely without judicial restraint—or, at any rate, without restraint from the Supreme Court. In a sense, what has happened is that the Supreme Court has gotten out of the way of Congress and largely out of the way of the states and has limited its activity to rationalizing approval of the measures which the respective legislatures choose to enact.

[19] *Duckworth* v. *Arkansas*, 314 U.S. 390, 400–401 (1941).

[20] For an important decision of this kind involving both civil liberties and interstate commerce see *Edwards* v. *California*, 314 U.S. 160 (1941).

The reasons for judicial abdication are not such as to indicate that judicial checks are permanently a thing of the past, but for the time being, at least, responsibility for the shaping of our federal system is being exercised largely by the states and by what are commonly called the political branches of the federal government. Amid these changes it has become clearer that the justification of federalism lies not so much in the compulsions of the written Constitution concerning the sovereign integrity of the states as in the need of the people for the preservation of local government. The Supreme Court, which in earlier years often employed constitutional interpretation of the federal principle to protect enterprise from control quite as much as to protect federalism, now more carefully decides cases in such a way as to leave a maximum of power in the hands both of the federal government and of the states.

How, then, is American federalism taking shape? The following are offered as tentative generalizations. First, the normal development of industrialization in the United States, the depression, and the current war have given rise to the exercise of power by our so-called federal government which was undreamed of even a decade and a half ago. The federal character of our constitutional system has caused a certain amount of friction and has required a great deal of deviousness in the justification of this exercise of power but has not seriously impeded it. Second, as a direct result of federal grants-in-aid and as an indirect result of the lack of a comparable amount of initiative on the part of the states, the federal government has become in many matters the architect of the policy administered by the states. Third, in spite of these facts, however, the states remain custodians of power not merely commensurate with that exercised in earlier years but substantially greater.

Of the growth of federal power nothing more needs to be said at the moment. As for federal influence over state policy, the subject is intricate and difficult. The states are generally unable to resist the seductive appeal of federal grants. Particularly in the poorer states and to some extent among the people of all the states, there is a feeling that largess from the federal treasury may cost them little or nothing, whereas state expenditures bring about the inevitable morning-after headaches of painful taxation. The federal government can always borrow money. Belief in the necessity of balancing the federal budget at some time is much less firm than it once was. If it is not necessary to balance that budget, we can borrow indefinitely and the expenditures will cost us nothing. Even if we may have to balance the budget sometime, we do not have to do it now. Since we have other things to worry about now, why worry about that until the time comes? Go ahead borrowing and spending and leave the worrying to Washington or to posterity. Many of the states have constitutional restrictions against extensive borrowing. While it might be possible to amend these restrictions out of the constitutions, it probably would not be worth while to do so, since the credit of a state going in for excessive borrowing without a compensatory revenue program would quickly disintegrate and since it is possible to get money from the federal government without all that trouble.

There are less disreputable approaches to the problem. If expenditures are to be reimbursed, the federal government, which has jurisdiction over the larger area, can reach taxable wealth or activity wherever it can be found and can therefore tax more equitably than can the states. In view of the interconnectedness of welfare in all the states, the national community must solve welfare problems if, for example, they exist in states financially unable to solve them—or lacking in the public spirit necessary for their solution. As a nation we cannot afford to have festering sores of poverty in our cities or desert wastes of ignorance throughout vast areas. Health and education for all are vital not merely to the localities but to the United States as a whole. Problems which cannot be solved locally must be solved by the union of localities—by the nation.

Furthermore, as the costs of government increase and the burdens of legitimate taxation grow heavier, increased attention must be given to the equitable allotment of those burdens. The duplication of heavy federal and state tax burdens at the same point may be disastrous, even though each, standing alone, is not unreasonable. The need for integration of federal and state tax programs, if it goes unmet, may give rise to a demand that all taxes be collected by the federal government for allotment to the federal and state governments, respectively. Such a device would take much of the remaining substance out of local independence and local responsibility.

We can say, then, that certain dominant tendencies in American economic development and certain tired spots in the moral spine of the American people endanger the vitality of local government in the United States. Were the states now nonexistent—could we conceive of such a possibility—it is most unlikely that we should re-create them. The tendency toward centralization, uncurbed by the resisting power of intrenched institutions, would probably be irresistible. But we still have the states, and, if they are weak in will and lacking in imagination, they have not shriveled in dimensions of power. They have more employees, spend more money, and perform more functions than ever before. Whatever may be the situation in the distant future, they still have substantial tax resources in spite of the competition of the federal government. Furthermore, even though some federal molding of state policy inevitably accompanies state acceptance of federal grants, such control has not yet been harmonized with our traditional thought about state-federal relations. In short, if the states are worth saving, there is still time to save them.

The question, therefore, becomes one of public policy rather than merely a matter of accepting the inevitable.

Are the states worth saving? Alexander Hamilton, who at the beginning of our life as a nation did much to pave the way for the growth of American capitalism, thought even at that time that the states were not worth preserving in the form of independent sovereignties. Harold Laski, as of 1939, thought the states a luxury of an expanding capitalist system—a luxury which we could no longer afford now that capitalism had reached the stage of contraction and decline. They seemed to him to have become instruments of capital for obstruction and evasion of legitimate control of our economy by the central government, with no functions of their own which that government could not better perform.[21]

We can say of Hamilton that, with all his greatness, he was not one of the Founding Fathers to whom we owe obligations for the safeguards of our governmental system. Although we credit him with the vision necessary to achievement, we do not credit him with the wisdom and caution necessary to avert disaster. As for Laski, much that he says about use of the states as instruments to avert legitimate control is too obviously true. Yet it is also true that for every safeguard we must pay a price in inefficiency and abuse. The characteristics of human nature which led Hamilton's contemporaries to write prohibitions and checks into the Constitution are just as much the characteristics of men today. Tyrants are not merely relics of antiquity. They are not merely German, Italian, Spanish, and—if it can be said without creating a diplomatic incident—Russian. They are of the ranks of men wherever power is given without restraint and without limit. A major purpose of our federal system is to divide power so as to diminish the intoxication

[21] Harold J. Laski, "The Obsolescence of Federalism," *New Republic*, XCVIII (May 3, 1939), 367–69. Reprinted in A. N. Christensen and E. M. Kirkpatrick, *The People, Politics, and the Politician* (1941), pp. 111–17.

which goes with it, so as to reduce the prospect of tyranny when power is given, as inevitably it must be. With the tremendous increase in power now flowing through government and certain to continue to flow, the need for checks and for division becomes greater than ever before.

But the need for the states is not merely negative. Local government has its own peculiar values. It is the ideal forum for the practice of democracy. Democracy justifies itself not so much by efficiency of administration as by development of character in a participating citizenship. Something vital to the good life of a community is lost when the people abandon control to rulers at a distance, however wise and beneficent the rulers may be. A fatherly voice in the White House may be a menace as well as a comfort if it lulls the people into forgetting that the salvation of mankind is a matter not merely of faith but also of conscious striving on the part of all. Only at distant intervals do a citizen's obligations to the nation reveal themselves so clearly as to call for hard thought and concrete personal effort. His local obligations are more obvious. If he grows as a participating citizen, the growth is likely to be in connection with his local responsibilities. The states and their subordinate organizations are needed because of the school for living which they are.

If it is true that the states are needed, why the tendency to regard them as outmoded institutions? It is due, first of all, to the growth of mass-production industrialism in the United States, which has called for the uniform exercise of great regulatory power—power which can be exercised only by the federal government. Matters once subject only to local jurisdiction have oftentimes been caught indiscriminately in the tide of national activity and swept along with it. In the second place, the logic of centralization, the hypnotic quality of immense power, and the anesthetic quality of uniformity have temporarily dulled our interest in the less big, the less powerful, and the ununiform. It has seemed altogether proper to invite federal aid to feed the hungry, clear slums, promote education, build highways, and perform innumerable other functions rather than expect the local community to rise to the occasion when by taking proper thought and making the effort it could meet those of its own needs which are not occasioned by conditions outside its jurisdiction. We have tended to forget that the people of the United States are none other than the people of Illinois and Maryland and forty-six other states and certain territories and possessions. We have tended to forget that, while for waging war and certain other national purposes we must be banded tightly together as a nation, it is only when we are loosed individually or working in smaller groups that most of us can grow as responsible citizens and perform those varied functions which give color and flavor to the life of a community.

Our position, therefore, is that the preservation of the states and the revitalization of their activities along with the growth of the power of the federal government—in a word, the maintenance of a federal system—is essential to the highest welfare of the people of the United States. Federalism must change with our growing industrialism, but it is not necessarily doomed by it. Furthermore, its fate does not rest primarily with the Supreme Court, or Congress, or the President, but with the people themselves. They have strong state institutions which have not more than begun to disintegrate. These institutions, as servants of the people and not as tools of the lawless for the prevention of control, can promote that local welfare which makes up the higher welfare of the people of the United States.

III

THE PENDULUM OF CHECKS AND BALANCES

✳

THE separation of powers, like federalism, provides a check upon unlimited accumulation of power in the hands of an individual, an oligarchy, or an agency. Although enunciation of the principle goes back at least as far as Aristotle and although credit for its popularization on American soil belongs in part to the Britisher, Locke, and the Frenchman, Montesquieu, it was practically indigenous in the American colonies. The colonists embodied it in the state constitutions as both a familiar and a necessary institution. They accepted it as necessary because they knew the capacity of men to lose perspective and self-restraint when they became possessors of unchecked power. They knew also the value of checks upon individuals and agencies, not necessarily to prevent action altogether but to restrain the passions of the moment until sober reflection could verify the wisdom of proposed measures.

Like federalism, the separation of powers has been a source of friction throughout our history. As in connection with federalism, jurisdictional lines have shifted with changing conditions inside and outside the government. Like federalism, the separation of powers is today under attack as an instrument so outmoded and inefficient that the United States can no longer afford to maintain it. Much of the criticism comes from sponsors of administrative agencies which merge in themselves legislative, executive, and judicial powers and which resist interference from the judiciary proper and at times from Congress and the President as well. Part of the subject will be left for discussion elsewhere in connection with the growth of administrative agencies and administrative law. The purpose at this point will be to analyze past struggles among the three traditional branches of government and the various shifts of power from one branch to one or both of the others. The current discussion, therefore, will deal with the exercise of the power of judicial review, the exercise of presidential power over legislation and judicial action, and congressional efforts to dominate administrative policy and the functions of the judiciary.

Resort to the separation of powers does not imply that the three branches of government are to be enemies or that the function of each branch is to restrain the other two to a point of complete inaction. Separation and checks are negative. A government cannot govern by negation alone. The Constitution provided for the meshing of the wheels of government in such a way that the governmental machine could function as an integrated mechanism. The mere identification of separate and co-ordinate branches, however, constitutes an invitation to rivalry and jealousy. The high degree of self-consciousness of each of the three branches during the first decade under the Constitution got in the way of the smooth co-operation which may have been contemplated by the framers. At any rate, even though the branches were manned by many of the framers themselves and by others who thought in harmony with them, relationships from the start were exceedingly formal. Although he worked in collaboration with members of Congress in many matters, the ponderous rectitude of the first President made impossible easy relationships and thoughtful interchange with him. The procedure whereby he delivered his messages to Congress was exceedingly formal. After he had delivered his address orally to a joint assemblage of the two houses, each house prepared a formal address in reply and went en masse to his quarters, where a spokesman read it to him, whereupon the President in turn delivered a rejoinder in the verbose language of diplomacy.[1] It would have been hard to devise a method of interchange which would more completely insulate the legislative and executive departments one from the other. Thanks to the good sense of Thomas Jefferson, the whole procedure was abandoned when he chose to ignore it to the extent of sending written messages to Congress and to maintain most of his contacts with that body through personal relationships with individual members.

Other events of the first decade illustrate the self-consciousness and concern for the preservation of departmental dignity which tended to rigidify the separated branches of the government. John Adams suffered a ridiculous amount of mental anguish in deciding how he should comport himself at once in the two capacities of vice-president of the United States and president of the Senate. The Senate, which the Constitution made a consulting body with the President for the making of treaties, declined to sit with him and to discuss a proposed treaty until it had had an opportunity to meet in his absence and work into its new position. When the House of Representatives asked the President for information about the making of the Jay Treaty, the President replied in peremptory language that the making of treaties was a function of the President and Senate in which the House of Representatives did not participate and into which it had no right to inquire. As for the Supreme Court, the President consulted with Chief Justice Jay on many legal matters, but when the President, through his Secretary of State, requested an advisory opinion from the Supreme Court as a body, the Court replied courteously but firmly that it could give opinions only in the due course of judicial proceedings. Both Washington and Adams recognized the importance of the immediate initiation of right

[1] See Carl B. Swisher, *American Constitutional Development* (1943), pp. 48–49.

practices and of making them traditional in the government. Their administration fulfilled the purpose of the Constitution in establishing the three branches as separate units, but they did their work so well as to discourage that flexible co-operation which ought to have become a part of the tradition of the government.

Jefferson improved somewhat relations between Congress and the President. He largely abandoned the formal methods of communication and operated through personal contacts with officers and influential members of the two houses. If for various reasons the legislative and executive departments were sometimes sharply at odds, they fought nevertheless at closer range. Jefferson at times, and apparently reluctantly, assumed a dominance which it would have been hard to justify in terms of his democratic philosophy. He was not always averse to presenting the legislators with a *fait accompli*, as in the instance of the Louisiana Purchase, so that they found it necessary to back him up. Although in neither scope nor method did his conduct resemble that of the administration which came into power in 1933, he seems occasionally even to have drafted or participated in the drafting of bills which were planned for introduction in Congress by his friends.

Jefferson's methods in bringing about greater co-operation between the legislative and executive branches of the government were essentially personal methods, the success of which turned predominantly upon the character of his own personality and the personalities of the men with whom he worked. This being true, his methods could not be institutionalized in such a way as to provide a pattern for subsequent administrations. His immediate successor, at any rate, James Madison, while lacking in the somewhat forbidding characteristics of the first two presidents, was unable effectively to get together with his Congress even under circumstances wherein the acceptance of executive leadership over Congress might have been deemed necessary for the winning of a war. James Monroe demonstrated little more capacity for leadership of the co-ordinate branch than did his predecessor.

If Jefferson's administration did little to institutionalize better relations between the executive and legislative branches of the government, it witnessed and was in part responsible for a wider separation of the judiciary from the other two branches of the government. A wider separation developed from the fact that the judiciary remained for a considerable time in the custody of Federalists, while the other two branches fell into the hands of Jeffersonian Republicans. Because of this division, partisanship joined institutional rivalry to prevent smooth functioning of the government. Since the merits of the controversy need not greatly concern us, a brief summary of the departmental-partisan conflicts will suffice. The most influential members of the federal judiciary were ardent partisans not merely of the federal government but of the Federalist leadership as well. In their rabid enforcement of the Alien and Sedition Acts they antagonized the Jeffersonian Republicans, who were bitterly opposed to those measures. Shortly before retiring from office, the "lame-duck" Congress of the Adams administration furthered the intrenchment of the Federalist party in the judiciary by authorizing the appointment of some sixteen circuit judges to perform functions hitherto performed by justices of the Supreme Court. The resignation of Chief Justice Ellsworth made it possible for President Adams to appoint John Marshall in his place, thus frustrating the hopes of Jefferson to capture the leadership of that tribunal. The resentful Jeffersonians got rid of the sixteen new Federalist judges by repealing the act creating their offices and sought to purge other offending judges through impeachment proceedings. By this device they succeeded in replacing one intermittently insane district judge, but they failed in a major effort to get rid of a member of the Supreme

Court—Justice Samuel Chase of Maryland. These proceedings naturally added to the bitterness between the two parties and among the branches of the government.

One phase of the partisan conflict led to the decision in *Marbury* v. *Madison*,[2] in which the Supreme Court, through Chief Justice Marshall, for the first time clearly rationalized the doctrine that the federal judiciary had the power to declare acts of Congress invalid because of conflict with the Constitution. In providing for the government of the newly created District of Columbia, Congress had authorized the appointment of such a number of discreet persons to be justices of the peace as the President should think expedient. President Adams immediately nominated the unconscionable number of forty-two persons, and the nominations were immediately confirmed by the still Federalist Senate. Some of the commissions remained undelivered when the Adams administration expired, and the officers of the Jefferson administration refused to deliver them. *Marbury* v. *Madison* involved a suit by one of the appointees to compel delivery of his commission.

The opinion of the Court, as well as the actual decision rendered, was a masterpiece of political strategy. With all the solemnity that could be packed into judicial utterance, Marshall showed that Marbury was entitled to the commission which had been denied to him and declared that, unless we cast upon the jurisprudence of our country the obloquy that the government of the United States failed to deserve the appellation of a government of laws and not of men, it was necessary to assume that the laws of the country provided Marbury with a remedy for his loss. Most conveniently, however, when it appeared that the Chief Justice would have to issue a writ of mandamus to Jefferson's Secretary of State and to witness the probable refusal to obey the writ, Marshall escaped from

[2] 1 Cranch 137 (1803).

this predicament by finding that the act of Congress which gave the Supreme Court jurisdiction in this case was unconstitutional.

It was the early part of this long and unanimous opinion that further antagonized the Jefferson administration toward the judiciary and widened the breach between that branch of the government and the other two branches, even though it was the latter part of the opinion which made the decision one of permanent importance in our constitutional history. Therein Marshall phrased superbly the obligations of a court to adhere to the language of the Constitution when there was conflict between the law of the Constitution, on the one hand, and the law which, on the other hand, found expression in a federal statute. We are not to assume, of course, that, if the Supreme Court had not on this occasion asserted its power of judicial review over acts of Congress, the power would not thereafter have been asserted. The Supreme Court and other courts had already exercised the power of review, even though the former had not previously found any statute in conflict with the Constitution. Marshall's justification of the power came, however, at a strategic moment in the Supreme Court's struggle for prestige, and it was voiced in such a way that the enemies of the existing judiciary found it hard to make an effective attack upon this particular portion of the decision. The right of the Court to exercise this power was not thereafter seriously challenged, even though more than half a century passed before another federal statute was declared unconstitutional.

In his handling of the trial of Aaron Burr and in many of the opinions in which he established for all time—or for all the time that has thus far passed—his voice as the leading voice in the molding of our constitutional law, Marshall further intrenched the judiciary as an agency independent of, and oftentimes antagonistic to, the executive and legislative branches of the government. The long interval of partisan strife during this formative period of our governmental institutions undoubtedly had a permanent influence in insulating the judiciary against co-operative interchange with Congress and the President.

Following the administration of Thomas Jefferson the presidency was occupied for a number of terms by men who, however profound their statesmanship, were not richly endowed with capacity for executive leadership. The dominating personality of Andrew Jackson re-energized the office and made it the successful competitor of leadership in Congress by such men as Daniel Webster, Henry Clay, and John C. Calhoun. He won important victories over Congress not so much by persuasion or ability to co-operate as by shrewd maneuvering and by the capacity to coerce Congress by appeals over its head to the people. However, although Jackson succeeded in getting some new legislation which he desired as well as in preventing enactment of measures to which he was opposed, the legislators as well as the President drew blood in the course of the strife. For the first time in the history of the Constitution the Senate exercised its responsibility in connection with the appointing power to prevent the appointment of a cabinet officer whom the President had nominated. Establishment of the precedent of rejecting a cabinet officer was important, even though appointment of the same man, Roger B. Taney, to the higher office of Chief Justice was later successfully completed. For the period of his own administration Jackson warded off congressional control of cabinet officers through statutes prescribing specific duties for those officers. Under existing statutes the Secretary of the Treasury was directed to deposit government funds in the Bank of the United States. When Jackson ordered the secretary to use selected state banks as depositories instead of the Bank of the United States, he refused to obey, whereupon the President peremptorily removed him from office. Perhaps unfortunately, however, the precedent did not prevent the development of entangling lines of responsibility in later years through legislation governing the conduct of officers who were at the same time responsible to the President for the execution of his policies.

Jackson's attitude toward the judiciary was as unyielding as his attitude toward Congress. He may not actually have said, in connection with a decision of which he disapproved, "John Marshall has made his decision, now let him enforce it," but the words are too characteristic to seem untrue even if they were never actually uttered. He was in a favorable position, furthermore, in that Chief Justice Marshall, even though as unbending as in earlier years and still idolized by many people, was no longer the dominating figure he had been when in his prime. Marshall and a number of other justices died while Jackson was President, leaving to him and his successor the opportunity almost completely to reconstitute the Supreme Court. Taney, the new Chief Justice, was the man who had helped Jackson phrase doctrines limiting the sweep of some of Marshall's opinions. He took the then seemingly heretical position, for example, that when the President acted in his legislative capacity, that is, when he was deciding whether to approve or disapprove a bill passed by Congress, he was not bound by decisions of the Supreme Court in deciding whether the proposed measure was constitutional. This deviation from the widespread assumption of complete infallibility of the Supreme Court in the field of constitutional interpretation was no doubt a relatively minor matter, but it was significant of the attitude which for many years thereafter restrained the Supreme Court as the articulate voice of the body politic.

From the Jackson period until the Civil War the imminence of sectional strife molded the course of constitutional development. Congress, like the people, was divided, and, because a large section of the people was opposed to the exercise of broad national powers, it refrained from the exercise of such powers. The divided people chose weak presidents, perhaps in part because they would not be ready to make use of strong leadership until the factional conflict had been resolved in one way or another. The Supreme Court divided its votes in case after case involving issues of slavery and issues of other kinds on which turned questions as to the exercise of state or federal power. It almost wrecked itself when in the Dred Scott case it failed skilfully to dodge the question that was dividing the nation and attempted by judicial decision to heal the breach between the North and the South.

When the South attempted to secede, on the other hand, leaving the federal government to administration by one of the hitherto contending factions, strong leadership was immediately in demand, and as a result both the President and Congress sprang into action. It may be that the election of Abraham Lincoln to the presidency on the Republican ticket was an accidental result of the disintegration of the opposing parties. At any rate, he showed a capacity for leadership which the presidency had not witnessed since the days of Andrew Jackson. Although military hostilities broke out in April, 1861, Lincoln chose not to burden himself with congressional interference and refrained from calling Congress into special session until the following July. In the meantime he called the state militia into federal service, issued a call for volunteers, blockaded the ports of the southern states, and took various other steps which he deemed necessary to the waging of a successful war. When Congress arrived on the scene, it could hardly do otherwise than give its support to the measures which the President had already initiated.

Congress refused to remain long in the position of a rubber stamp. It created a joint committee on the conduct of the war which inquired into all the details of the subject, sponsored bills for enactment, and gave advice to the President, the cabinet, and the army. Legislators differed greatly in their ideas as to how the government ought to operate for the purpose of winning the war. Some of them evidently cared very little about the constitutionality of procedure as long as the war was waged successfully. Others believed that the President, as commander-in-chief of the Army and Navy, had virtually full powers for war purposes. Still others, however, believed that in his capacity of commander-in-chief the President was in a position completely subordinate to the control of Congress. The war continued to a close without formal answer to the question. Once Congress was permitted to assemble, it became and remained an active participant in the management of the war. The amount of conflict which took place was minimized to some extent by the genuine humility of the man who happened to be President—a man who could act firmly on the basis of his own judgment and yet admit the possible rightness of the critics who firmly believed him to be in the wrong. A traditional defect in the operation of the principle of the separation of powers has been the product not of the principle itself but of the lack of humility and of consideration for the judgment of others—qualities exceptional men like Lincoln have possessed to a high degree.

The Supreme Court remained for the most part in the background while questions which were fundamentally constitutional were answered on the battlefield. When the war began, the Court stood discredited by the Dred Scott decision. Chief Justice Taney made matters worse by his circuit-court decision in the Merryman case,[3] in which he held that only Congress could authorize suspension of the privilege of the writ of habeas corpus and that the President had exceeded his powers in taking action without authorization from Congress. When he sent a copy of his opinion to Lincoln as a reminder that one who was sworn to take care that the laws be faithfully exe-

[3] *Ex parte Merryman*, Federal Cases No. 9487 (1861).

cuted should not himself violate them, Lincoln replied indirectly in a message to Congress that he did not believe that he had violated any law. In any event, the entire body of federal law was being resisted and failing of execution in nearly one-third of the states. "Must they be allowed to finally fail of execution," he asked, "even had it been perfectly clear that by the use of the means necessary to their execution some single law, made in such extreme tenderness of the citizen's liberty that practically it relieves more of the guilty than of the innocent, should to a very limited extent be violated?"[4]

Only by the narrow margin of five to four did the Supreme Court uphold the presidential blockade of southern ports prior to the time when Congress sanctioned exercise of that power.[5] Although Chief Justice Taney and probably other members of the Court deemed the Conscription Act and the Proclamation of Emancipation and other acts of the Lincoln administration to be unconstitutional, the war came to an end without Supreme Court decisions on these questions. After the war the Court, with a majority of Lincoln appointees, denounced military trials for civilians in areas outside the theater of war where the civil courts were open[6] and annulled restrictions on the right to practice law in federal courts on the basis of previous participation in the rebellion.[7] The so-called Legal Tender Acts were stricken down[8] and then restored to validity again.[9]

Even so, however, the Supreme Court remained on the fringes of the controversy over reconstruction which raged

[4] James D. Richardson (ed.), A Compilation of the Messages and Papers of the Presidents, VI, 25.

[5] Prize Cases, 2 Black 635 (1863).

[6] Ex parte Milligan, 4 Wallace 2 (1866).

[7] Ex parte Garland, 4 Wallace 333 (1867).

[8] Hepburn v. Griswold, 8 Wallace 603 (1870).

[9] Knox v. Lee and Parker v. Davis, 12 Wallace 457 (1871).

between Congress and the President. The so-called "radical" leaders of Congress differed from the President as to the severity with which the defeated South was to be treated. They resented, furthermore, the relatively vigorous exercise of presidential power in competition with the power of Congress. With the assassination of Lincoln and the succession of Andrew Johnson, who was obviously a much less able figure, congressional leaders expected once more to have their way in control of the government. Johnson surprised them by fighting for the moderate treatment of the South for which Lincoln had stood and for the powers of his office. When he vetoed reconstruction measures, Congress retaliated by passing them over his veto. It prevented his making appointments to the Supreme Court by providing that no vacancies should be filled until the membership, which had increased to a total of ten, had been reduced to seven. It sought to prevent his removing from office members of the cabinet and other Lincoln appointees by conditioning removals of officers appointed with the consent of the Senate upon the giving of the consent of the Senate to the removal. When Johnson dismissed the Secretary of War in violation of this restriction, the House of Representatives impeached Johnson, and the Senate lacked only one vote of a conviction as a result of which he would have been removed from office. In a word, the presidential office, which during the Civil War had attained prestige and power hitherto unknown, had now swung to the opposite extreme, sinking to a new low in public esteem or, at any rate, in the esteem of the legislative branch of the government.

When Congress enacted drastic reconstruction measures over the veto of the President, critics of the legislation looked to the Supreme Court to strike it down. It was clear, however, that an attempt to defeat the pet measures of Congress would invite an attack which the Court, with its prestige not yet fully restored, would be unable to ward off. In two of the cases which were brought before it the Court was fortunately able to find that it had no jurisdiction.[10] It took jurisdiction in another case, however, and heard arguments and was about to give a decision when Congress averted conflict by passing an act to withdraw jurisdiction of the Court in the class of cases involved. Over the protest of two of its members the Court accepted this invitation to avoid trouble.[11]

From the Civil War until the beginning of the twentieth century the balance of power in the federal government was lodged in Congress. The Supreme Court, it is true, trimmed down some of the legislation calculated to preserve order in the South and protect the rights of the Negro, and it set aside other measures to the extent that between 1865 and 1900 it handed down some twenty-four decisions in which acts of Congress or parts of acts were held invalid. The Court had no sustained and positive leadership through that period, however, such as that which John Marshall had provided over a period of similar length, and the trend of its decisions, if there can be said to have been a trend, was largely negative in the sense of the use of due process clauses and other clauses of the Constitution to maintain the freedom of enterprise.

The presidency during the same period was in the hands of men who, whatever their merits in other respects, lacked strength as executives. If this generalization be questioned as applied to Cleveland and McKinley, the answer is that, in general, Cleveland as a matter of principle restricted the exercise of his powers to the execution of policy expressed in acts of Congress. As for McKinley, not even the occasion of a foreign war brought the presidency to the fore as the dominant institution of government.

In his study of *Congressional Government*, which was pub-

[10] *Mississippi* v. *Johnson*, 4 Wallace 475 (1867), and *Georgia* v. *Stanton*, 6 Wallace 50 (1867, 1868).

[11] *Ex parte McCardle*, 7 Wallace 514 (1869).

lished in 1885, Woodrow Wilson declared that "the actual form of our present government is simply a scheme of congressional supremacy"[12] and that "the predominant and controlling force, the center and source of all motive and of all regulative power, is Congress."[13] The judgment of this thoughtful political analyst is to be given substantial weight, even though tradition has it he wrote his book at the Johns Hopkins University without taking the forty-mile trip from Baltimore to Washington to observe Congress in action. Wilson's attitude was not the product of narrow hostility toward Congress. It was the product of his belief that the interactions of the separated powers operated in such a way as to give power without responsibility and to permit action without integration of policy.

As at present constituted, the federal government lacks strength because its powers are divided, lacks promptness because its authorities are multiplied, lacks wieldiness because its processes are round about, lacks efficiency because its responsibility is indistinct and its action without competent direction. It is a government in which every officer may talk about every other officer's duty without having to render strict account for not doing his own, and in which the masters are held in check and offered contradiction by the servants.[14]

Wilson's criticism suggested the desirability of substituting for our system of divided and subdivided power one similar to the parliamentary system of Great Britain wherein legislative and executive powers are integrated in a responsible cabinet.

The experience of Theodore Roosevelt in the presidency suggested that congressional domination of the government might have come about largely by default and that an executive with a strong personality and with a program of his own still had opportunity for leadership. Roosevelt lacked the

[12] Woodrow Wilson, *Congressional Government* (1885), p. 6.

[13] *Ibid.*, p. 11.

[14] *Ibid.*, p. 388.

humility and the human sympathy of Lincoln and the finesse of Jefferson for dealing with legislators, but he had a capacity similar to that of Jackson for capturing the imaginations of the people and winning their support. It is true that the people as well as Congress probably wearied of so much strenuousness in the White House and felt relief when Roosevelt departed to hunt lions in Africa. Nevertheless, they—and Woodrow Wilson, too—learned from Roosevelt something of the potential dynamics of the presidential office. If Congress actually enacted more of the measures advocated by Taft than of those advocated by Roosevelt, it seems clear that the influence of the earlier chieftain had at least an indirect effect on the achievements of his successor.

The presidency of Woodrow Wilson tends to be remembered largely in connection with his leadership in wartime. It should not be forgotten, however, that his earlier peacetime leadership was hardly less dynamic and was probably more skilful than that exercised by Theodore Roosevelt. He successfully sponsored the Federal Reserve Act, the Federal Trade Commission Act, and the Clayton Act, and he would doubtless have extended the list of important statutes but for the outbreak of war in Europe. He tried to establish close relations with Congress by resuming the practice—which had been abandoned since the presidency of Jefferson—of oral delivery of messages to Congress. When efforts at personal contact failed to win success in leadership, however, he was not averse to lashing out wrathfully at offending legislators, as in his denunciation of the "little group of willful men" who defeated congressional support for his plan to arm merchant ships.

Unlike Lincoln in his handling of the Civil War, Wilson as a war President attempted to secure in advance congressional sanctions of the steps which he proposed to take. When congressional support came too slowly, however, he sometimes acted without it or in advance of it, and in his management of Congress he led with the stern hand of an experienced schoolmaster. He anounced in no uncertain terms that he would have no interference by a modern successor to the joint committee on the conduct of the war with which Lincoln had had to cope. He publicly denounced senators who had the temerity publicly to criticize his administration of the war. In short, while seeking legislative support for his acts as President, he came close to taking the position that Congress was under compulsion to ratify the policies which he saw fit to adopt. In his postwar struggle for the creation of a League of Nations and for American participation in it he came close to public gloating over the fact that the Senate would find it impossible to reject the League of Nations without rejecting altogether the treaty of peace—and that, he seems to have assumed unquestioningly, the Senate would never dare to do. When the Senate refused to follow him, he went over the head of that body to the people, but the people, who had previously denied his request for the return of a Democratic Congress, again failed to give their support.

The reaction against Wilson's leadership was in part a component of the whole blind reaction of the American people against the inevitable coercion of wartime control. It was a part of the "return to normalcy." It was characterized by a backswing of power from the President to Congress, wherein was the battleground of most important political struggles on the national level during the next decade. During that decade the presidency, under the leadership of Harding and Coolidge, as successors to Wilson, who lived out the last two years of his administration in defeat, offered little positive leadership and sought principally to restrain such attempts at leadership as were made by a badly divided Congress. The Supreme Court aligned itself in part with the forces of negation in restraining the exercise of regulatory power by federal and state governments.

As President, Herbert Hoover made the unpardonable mistake of letting the national economy slip into the worst depression in our history during the course of his administration. He tried to atone for it by stolid assurances to a frightened people that the national economy was fundamentally sound and that prosperity was just around the corner, but the stock market seemed ungratefully to punctuate each of these utterances by slumping to a new low. When Hoover saw that it was necessary to offer more than verbal assurances—and he did offer a great deal more—he found himself handicapped by the loss of popular support, which is the reward of all but the most skilful of political leaders when disaster occurs under their administration. At the end of his first two years in office the people handicapped him by electing a Democratic House of Representatives. Although the Democrats were probably not much more obviously lacking in confidence in the President than the Republicans, they had a peculiar stake in withholding their support in that the failure of Hoover's administration would facilitate the return to power of the Democratic party. Hoover found himself blocked at almost every turn, and— whether or not the sequence be one of cause and effect—the depression grew worse and worse. At the end of his first and only term the people took revenge on Hoover for his misfortune and theirs by voting him out of office via the process of electing Franklin D. Roosevelt.

When Roosevelt took the oath of office in March, 1933, the frightened and bewildered people and a mildly exuberant but equally bewildered Democratic Congress were eager to accept his confident leadership. One representative spoke the sentiments of many when he voiced the slogan "In Roosevelt I Trust!" and boasted of the fact that he was voting blindly for a bill sent from the White House for enactment. Congress was so eager to enact some of the measures prepared under the direction of the President that standing committees fought for the prestige involved in sponsoring them. So complete was White House domination of Democratic thought and action in Congress that Republicans tellingly chided their Democratic colleagues by asking them periodically, "What do you think you think today?" The practice of executive preparation of legislative measures, which in previous administrations had been indulged in only surreptitiously, was carried on at such length at session after session of the Roosevelt administration that it came to be accepted as good form.

Although Roosevelt encountered minor difficulties with Congress immediately after the close of the "honeymoon period," with the result that he became the most prolific of all presidential authors of veto messages, his first serious troubles were with the judiciary, and it was in connection with his bill to reform the judiciary that he met his first sharp rebuff from Congress. From 1900 through 1934 the Supreme Court had handed down some forty decisions in which acts of Congress were declared invalid. The decisions had been pretty well averaged out over the years and at no time had been grouped in such a way as seriously to interfere with an integrated program of administration. During 1935 and 1936, on the other hand, a total of eleven cases were decided in such a way as to block or forecast the blocking of most of the New Deal program. Early in 1937, shortly after his election for a second term, Roosevelt retaliated by sending to Congress for enactment a bill to provide broadly for reform of the judiciary and to provide specifically for authorization to appoint new members of the Supreme Court to sit alongside justices over seventy-and-a-half years of age who chose not to retire. The bill brought a terrific furor on the part of enemies of the New Deal and shocked many friends of the administration who continued to view the Supreme Court as a hallowed institution.

The Supreme Court judiciously shifted its position with regard to controversial measures while the bill was before Congress—or, rather, one justice shifted his position and another announced his intention of early retirement—with the result that enactment of the bill no longer seemed necessary. With a sweeping gesture of righteous indignation, the Senate then killed the bill. On the surface the President appeared to have met a resounding defeat. It was a defeat about which he had no reason to feel badly, however, in the light of the fact that since 1936 the Supreme Court, with the exception of one minor provision, has found no act of Congress to be in conflict with the Constitution.

One of the most irritating decisions of the Supreme Court had been that in which the Court held that the President had no power to remove a member of the Federal Trade Commission in violation of the statute governing the subject.[15] Although in 1926 the Court had settled a question about which lawyers had speculated since the Johnson administration by holding that Congress could not restrict the power of the President to remove executive officers even though appointed by and with the advice and consent of the Senate,[16] the Court now held that this exemption did not extend to members of the independent regulatory commissions, which were quasi-legislative rather than executive in character. The decision meant that such commissions, which were growing rapidly in number, would remain in important respects free from presidential control. When the President's Committee on Administrative Management reported a plan for reorganization of the executive branch of the government, it advised in a general way that these commissions be broken up into their component parts and that their nonjudicial functions be allocated to organizations in the executive branch of the government. The

[15] *Humphrey's Executor* v. *United States*, 295 U.S. 602 (1935).
[16] *Myers* v. *United States*, 272 U.S. 52 (1926).

commissions, and the Interstate Commerce Commission in particular, proved to have almost as many friends as the Supreme Court. The position which the President's Committee took on this incidental point and on certain other individual points had the effect for a considerable time of blocking all provisions of much-needed legislation on the subject of executive reorganization. Roosevelt's first reorganization bill went down to defeat amid a popular clamor against dictatorship in the presidency. One of the odd bits of diplomacy in the matter was the publication of a letter to an unnamed friend in which Roosevelt solemnly denied that he was seeking to make himself a dictator.[17]

As might be expected, the outbreak of the second World War brought further extension of presidential power. Custom had already sanctioned drastic enhancement of presidential power in time of war. The process of enhancement picked up in 1941 where it had left off in 1918. Illustration of the initial attitude of President Roosevelt toward Congress in time of war can be found in the message of September 7, 1942, in which he urged the enactment of legislation for the control of farm prices. He asked Congress to act before the first of October ensuing, declaring that "in the event that the Congress should fail to act, and act adequately, I shall accept the responsibility, and I will act." He asserted that the President had power under the Constitution and existing statutes to take measures necessary to avert a disaster in the form of sky-rocketing prices, which would interfere with the winning of the war. He had determined to consult Congress in the matter because such consultation was consistent with his sense of responsibility as President and with his deep and unalterable devotion to the processes of democracy. He could not tell, however, he said, what powers might have to be exercised in order to win the war. "When the war is won, the powers under

[17] *New York Times*, April 1, 1938.

which I act automatically revert to the people—to whom they belong."[18] Although Congress resented being dealt with in this peremptory fashion, it completed enactment of the desired legislation soon after the established deadline had been passed.

Further growth of interdepartmental friction was revealed when in February, 1944, Roosevelt expressed even greater intolerance for the judgment of Congress on matters of policy in a message vetoing a tax bill. In one respect, he declared, it was "not a tax bill but a tax relief bill providing relief not for the needy but for the greedy."

The bill is replete with provisions which not only afford indefensible special privileges to favored groups but sets dangerous precedents for the future. This tendency toward the embodiment of special privileges in our legislation is in itself sufficiently dangerous to counter-balance a loss of a very inadequate sum in additional revenues.

Taking a partisan share in the recrimination being indulged in by the tax experts of the Treasury Department and of Congress, respectively, he declared that the complicated character of income-tax forms was not the fault of the Treasury Department but was "squarely the fault of the Congress of the United States in using language in drafting the law which not even a dictionary or a thesaurus can make clear."[19]

The language of the veto message so enraged Senator Alben Barkley, Senate floor leader, that he delivered a speech denouncing the veto message and resigned as floor leader—to be enthusiastically re-elected by his colleagues. Part of the message, he declared, was a "calculated and deliberate assault upon the legislative integrity of every member of Congress." He declared that if Congress had any self-respect left, it would override the veto and enact the bill into law.[20] Congress speed-

[18] *Congressional Record*, LXXXVIII, 7044.

[19] *Congressional Record*, XC, 1959.

[20] *Ibid.*, pp. 1964–66.

ily followed his advice, and President Roosevelt took the reaction so seriously that he immediately disclaimed any intention of attacking the integrity of members of Congress.[21]

Although the influence of Congress upon the conduct of the war and upon administration of the government generally in time of war beyond making necessary appropriations and enacting the statutes requested was not conspicuous, it did continue to perform an indirect but important function through investigations by its standing committees and special investigating committees. Although administrators showed resentment at inquisitorial interference, the so-called Truman Committee and certain others did important work in discovering and giving publicity to facts about the conduct of the war. The power seems to have been abused at times, as in the instance of the so-called Cox Committee, which, until a change was made in the chairmanship, acted as if its deliberate purpose was to besmirch a particular federal agency against which its chairman had a grudge; but this and other instances of abuse were not sufficient to condemn the judicious exercise of the investigatory power. A Senate subcommittee ran headlong into a presidential obstruction when it attempted to compel testimony from one of the President's confidential assistants, but the threatened clash, which grew out of a controversy following almost immediately upon the bitter exchange over the tax bill just mentioned, was averted when Roosevelt shrewdly avoided it by instructing his assistant to give the desired information in the case at hand. Other outbursts of ill will beween the two allegedly co-ordinate branches of the government took place on occasions when Congress refused to make appropriations for particular agencies until particular officers had been removed and, when appropriations for particular agencies were made, with the reservation that no

[21] *Ibid.*, pp. 2050–51.

money appropriated was to be spent on the salary of particular individuals.[22] The probable ill effect of interdepartmental friction upon postwar international relations became so apparent that the State Department began systematic consultation with members of the Senate on the conduct of foreign affairs, and President Roosevelt, after his return from the conference at Yalta, made an effort to establish more friendly relations with Congress. President Truman, building on the prestige which he already had in Congress, sought at the beginning of his administration to cement better relations between the legislative and executive branches and to avert the conditions of intra-governmental warfare which had prevailed immediately after the close of the Civil War and the first World War.

Thus far in this discussion we have pursued a running account of important checks which each of the three branches of the federal government has exercised upon the other. In the light of the facts presented let us restate the principle governing the adoption of the separation of powers and appraise the effectiveness of the device in terms of the ends to be achieved. One of the purposes, of course, was to provide a scheme of classification and organization of the men who were to operate the government, roughly according to the functions which were to be performed. It is not generally questioned that in a rough way the functions of government fall logically into categories of legislative, executive, and judicial characteristics. Since in every government there must be some differentiation of functions, classification of personnel along these lines will, in general, be accepted as reasonable.

The careful separation of powers as provided for in the Constitution, however, apart from specific overlappings, has the additional important purpose of using two of the three

[22] For discussion see Robert E. Cushman, "Civil Liberty after the War," *American Political Science Review*, XXXVIII (February 1944), 1–20.

branches of the government as restraining agencies to prevent the exercise of tyrannical power by the third. The record shows the constant operation of the system to attain this end. Persuasive evidence that the system has worked is found in the record of accusations by each branch or by the sponsors of each that one or both the others are seeking to exercise tyrannical power and must be restrained. Jackson, Lincoln, Wilson, and Franklin Roosevelt have been denounced as would-be dictators or as dictators *in esse*. Jackson is said to have characterized the United States Senate as "damned scoundrels."[23] He and Johnson and Wilson and Franklin Roosevelt evidently believed that the country had to be saved from domination by the aggregation of irresponsible men which constituted Congress. Government by judiciary and domination by "the nine old men" have been denounced with similar fervor. Representatives of each of the three branches have not merely viewed with alarm but have bent their efforts to the prevention of the menace of tyrannical rule by the others.

We can take at its face value Franklin Roosevelt's statement that he had no desire to be a dictator, and the same statement can probably be made about all his predecessors. In spite of the conduct of the radical Congress of the Johnson administration and of Congress in other periods, it is probably equally true that the legislative body never had any considered plan for taking the government entirely into its own hands. In spite of the strategic care with which John Marshall imprinted principles of government upon the minds of the people and in spite of the wily and hardheaded obstructionism with which the Supreme Court in other periods substituted its will for that of Congress and the President, it cannot be assumed that the Court ever consciously planned completely to subordinate those agencies. All this, however, is to say little more than that

[23] Charles Warren, *The Supreme Court in United States History* (1926), I, 802.

the conscious desire to rule illegally has not been a highly influential factor in American constitutional experience. It leaves out of consideration the fact that men and agencies lose perspective in the tendency to identify the welfare of the country with their own conceptions of government and with the maintenance of themselves in the unrestrained exercise of power. The angry protest of each branch at what it tends to regard as the unjustifiable interference of other branches oftentimes provides the best possible evidence that checks upon the swollen ego of the protestant are very much in order.

It is true that the branches of government cannot be classified, respectively, as saints and sinners, with the former appellation attached to the interfering agencies and the latter to the agency attempting some positive action. The interference may be far more shortsighted and unpatriotic than the action that is restrained. The fact remains, however, that on no important occasion of intergovernmental conflict thus far in our history would the complete elimination or subordination of the restraining branch or branches of government have left us with an entirely satisfactory solution even of the problems immediately at hand. As for the effect of such elimination upon the solution of other problems as they arose, it would have deprived us of the instruments needed to correct the distorted perspective of aggressive individuals and agencies.

It is true that the exercise of checks often prevents the immediate realization of ends which by farsighted people have been discerned as desirable long before the masses of the people come to realize their importance. Developments may be restrained until large numbers of people are educated by verbal teaching or by circumstance to understand that the proposal in question is desirable. All this, however, is just to say that the processes of democracy are slow and that we pay the price of slowness for the fulfilment of our belief in democratic government. As far as the past is concerned, it is relevant to state that as a nation we seem thus far not to have done badly by comparison with other nations, in spite of the snail's pace at which government at times seems required to move. Gradually, if belatedly, we make intergovernmental adaptations as the functions of government expand and change. Under the drive of necessity the character of much congressional legislation is gradually changing and the processes of legislation are undergoing scrutiny for the purpose of making much-needed reforms. The executive branch of the government undergoes periodic reorganization, and administrative machinery and techniques are worked out for the performance of functions which are peculiar to the economic order in which we live. The judiciary likewise undergoes periodic modernization. As to the suggestion that the entire structure of our government ought to be reorganized, however, and the device of the separation of powers eliminated, the case is at least not yet proved. To that group of Americans who, while professing a belief in democracy, urge the adoption of the British parliamentary system as a substitute for our own, it may be suggested, among other things, that our form of government has maintained a vitality of contact with the electorate which has not characterized the British government during the war crisis. If that fact be attributed not to the forms of government but to the difference in tradition and to the fact that Great Britain has been in the actual theater of war, the fact remains that, whatever the stresses and strains within the interstices of our governmental system, the results achieved entitle it to distinction not inferior to that of any other government in the world.

IV

CONSTITUTIONAL SOURCES OF EXPANDING POWER

✶

ONE of the most remarkable facts about the American constitutional system is that, as far as the giving of power is concerned, the constitution drafted for the union of the original thirteen states in the relatively primitive era of the 1780's continues in the 1940's to serve as the constitution of the most highly industrialized and powerful of the great nations of the world. Unless we are to impute supernatural wisdom to the framers, we must assume that succeeding generations have found meaning in terms of grants of power which the framers themselves never suspected in the work of their hands. In the language of Justice Holmes, "when we are dealing with words that also are a constituent act, like the Constitution of the United States, we must realize that they have called into life a being the development of which could not have been foreseen completely by the most gifted of its begetters. It was enough for them to realize or to hope that they had created an organism; it has taken a century and has cost their successors much sweat and blood to prove that they created a nation."[1] In a sense it is true of the power-giving phrases of the Constitution, as Charles A. Beard recently said of the Preamble, that "it is a case of men's building better than they knew."[2]

The flow of power exercised by the federal government has

[1] *Missouri* v. *Holland*, 252 U.S. 416, 433 (1920).

[2] Charles A. Beard, *The Republic* (1943), p. 3.

its source in many constitutional phrases and combinations of phrases. All of them are important. The importance of each of them fluctuates somewhat with time and circumstance. Some of them much more than others have been the sources from which or the channels through which sweep the tremendous outpourings of governmental power which is released under the guidance of the government in Washington. It is to the most outstanding of these sources or channels that our discussion in this chapter is to be limited. It will not be possible, indeed, to give more than passing mention to such important sources as the appointing power, the power to build post offices and post roads, and the power to enact uniform laws on the subject of bankruptcy, important as these powers have been at times and still are. Rather it will be necessary for us to limit our discussion principally to the commerce power, the power to tax and the related power to spend for the public welfare, and the war power. It is largely in terms of these classifications of power that a dominant industrial nation and a major world power has taken form under a constitution framed to establish a restricted union of small and weak agricultural and commercial states.

It is under the commerce power that the federal government has undertaken much of its direct regulation of affairs in the United States. The Constitution provides that Congress shall have power "to regulate commerce with foreign nations, and among the several states, and with the Indian tribes." While we have no way to read the minds of the framers of the Constitution on this point, we can be perfectly sure that in phrasing this clause they did not even dream of authorizing the federal government to regulate the hours and wages of elevator operators, repairmen, and custodians in buildings wherein floor space was leased out to manufacturers of clothing, part of which after manufacture was shipped in interstate commerce.[3] Neither did they contemplate authorizing the federal government to exclude from interstate commerce wheat produced by a man whose only offense had been that he had grown on his own farm, and threshed and fed to his own livestock, a quantity of wheat in excess of a production quota allotted to him by a federal official.[4] No, the plans of the framers were much less ambitious. They were concerned primarily with eliminating barriers to interstate and foreign trade which the several states had erected for the purpose of collecting toll from business originating in other states or in foreign countries and for the purpose of reserving local business opportunities for the benefit of local businessmen. The commerce clause was one of a number of clauses in the Constitution by which the framers sought to remove local fetters from business and to keep them removed. If they had any intention to stimulate, or even to authorize, extensive regulation of enterprise by the federal government, that fact is not disclosed by the records.

As viewed by Daniel Webster in the argument of *Gibbons* v. *Ogden* in 1824, the purpose of the commerce clause was to protect as a single entity all that commerce which affected more than one state. What was it that was to be regulated, he asked. Not the commerce of the several states respectively but the commerce of the United States. "Henceforth," he declared, "the commerce of the states was to be an unit; and the system by which it was to exist and be governed, must necessarily be complete, entire and uniform. Its character was to be described in the flag which waved over it, *E Pluribus Unum*."[5] In that quotation Webster came close to the modern conception of commerce as a network of relationships extending over the business community—a community which includes the

[3] See *Kirshbaum* v. *Walling*, 316 U.S. 517 (1942).
[4] See *Wickard* v. *Filburn*, 317 U.S. 111 (1942).
[5] *Gibbons* v. *Ogden*, 9 Wheaton 1, 14 (1824).

several states and not just the area immediately affected by an individual transaction. The difference between the conceptions of Webster and of a spokesman of the Department of Justice who might today appear before the Supreme Court to defend the constitutionality of a broad regulatory statute based upon the commerce clause does not lie so much in a different conception of commerce as in the fact that Webster was, in general, opposed to regulation of private enterprise, whereas the spokesman in question would be called upon to defend regulation. In Webster's time, to say that "the commerce of the states was to be an unit" was to say that for the most part such commerce was to go unregulated. It should be remembered, however, that, when Webster spoke of the commerce of the states as a unit, he was arguing not in behalf of federal regulation but of something approaching laissez faire. Such was clearly the outlook of Chief Justice Marshall, who wrote the opinion of the Court in *Gibbons* v. *Ogden*, as well as Webster. Marshall was not facing the threat of a New Dealish expansion of power of the federal government under the leadership of James Monroe or John Quincy Adams but a condition which today would no doubt be called the Balkanization of the United States through the efforts of state legislatures. The states evidently knew and respected the intent of the commerce clause as it applied to traditional forms of commerce. Navigation by the newly invented steamboat, however, was such a novelty as to seem to justify a separate classification. In their efforts to conserve local business by steamboat for local enterprise, they re-created the conditions which in part had given rise to the adoption of the Constitution. Chief Justice Marshall wisely refused to permit the new instrument to escape from the category of commerce and insisted on integrating navigation and, incidentally, all forms of intercourse into the conception. In so doing, he broke up the shortsighted movement on the part of the states to interfere with commerce across state lines. The ultimate importance of the decision, however, extended beyond the immediate effect to provide justification for positive control of interstate commerce by the federal government, a type of control which was exercised only on an infinitesimal scale for many decades after this decision of basic importance was handed down.

Federal regulation of interstate commerce did not begin to assume its modern form until a century after the adoption of the Constitution, when Congress enacted the Interstate Commerce Act of 1887 and the Sherman Antitrust Act of 1890. In the meantime most judicial decisions on the commerce clause had dealt largely with questions about the beginnings and endings of interstate and foreign commerce. They were highly particularistic in character. Had the commodity shipped actually started its interstate or foreign journey? Had the commodity "come to rest"? Had the "original package" been broken? Had the transition from manufacture to commerce taken place? This judicial preoccupation with the beginnings and endings of particular shipments carried over into the modern period, but, with the growth of federal regulation, it gradually gave way to other considerations. For example, when interstate commerce consisted of a series of technically complete transactions many of which did not individually cross state lines, the Supreme Court was in certain cases persuaded, nevertheless, to regard the series as a flow or current of commerce, with the result that technically local parts of the flow might be regulated by the federal government as interstate commerce. The parent-case was *Swift* v. *United States*, which was decided in 1905. The Chicago beef trust was resisting enforcement of the Sherman Act on the ground that its activities were local and not interstate. The Supreme Court, however, found that the activities of the meat packers constituted a "current of commerce among the states." Said Justice Holmes for the Court:

Commerce among the states is not a technical legal conception, but a practical one, drawn from the course of business. When cattle are sent for sale from a place in one state, with the expectation that they will end their transit, after purchase, in another, and when in effect they do so, with only the interruption necessary to find a purchaser at the stockyards, and when this is a typical, constant and recurring course, the current thus existing is a current of commerce among the states, and the purchase of the cattle is a part and incident of such commerce.[6]

The effect of the Swift decision was to broaden substantially the area of commerce which the federal government might regulate. The area was further broadened by another line of decisions which began with the Shreveport case in 1914. In that case the Supreme Court held that the Interstate Commerce Act constitutionally authorized regulation of aspects of intrastate railroad business of which regulation was necessary to the effective regulation of interstate commerce.[7] In terms, therefore, of these two decisions, based on two important statutes, Congress might regulate, as interstate commerce, commerce which at first glance did not appear to be interstate, and it might regulate commerce which was not interstate at all if such regulation was necessary to effective control of interstate commerce.

The Interstate Commerce Act and the Sherman Act were followed by amending measures which extended their scope and by other regulatory measures based on the commerce power such as the Pure Food and Drug Act, the White Slave Act, the Federal Trade Commission Act, and the Packers and Stockyards Act. Although the Supreme Court restrained expansion of federal regulatory power in terms of due process of law and conceptions of the reserved powers of the states, the process of expansion continued. It was only natural, therefore, that when the New Deal administration set out in 1933

[6] *Swift v. United States*, 196 U.S. 375, 398–99 (1905).

[7] See *Houston E. & W. Texas Railway Co. v. United States*, 234 U.S. 342 (1914).

drastically to regulate almost the entire economic order for the purpose of defeating the depression, it relied heavily upon the commerce clause to justify its exercise of power. Illustration is to be found in the "Declaration of Policy" of the National Industrial Recovery Act, which reads as follows:

A national emergency productive of widespread unemployment and disorganization of industry, which burdens interstate and foreign commerce, affects the public welfare, and undermines the standards of living of the American people, is hereby declared to exist. It is hereby declared to be the policy of Congress to remove obstructions to the free flow of interstate and foreign commerce which tend to diminish the amount thereof; and to provide for the general welfare by promoting the organization of industry for the purpose of cooperative action among trade groups, to induce and maintain united action of labor and management under adequate governmental sanctions and supervision, to eliminate unfair competitive practices, to promote the fullest possible utilization of the present productive capacity of industries, to avoid undue restriction of production (except as may be temporarily required), to increase the consumption of industrial and agricultural products by increasing purchasing power, to reduce and relieve unemployment, to improve standards of labor, and otherwise to rehabilitate industry and to conserve natural resources.[8]

This declaration left little yet to be done in the way of translating the commerce of the United States into *E Pluribus Unum.*

The attempts under the National Industrial Recovery Act to regulate everything from the cutting of trees in the backwoods to the shining of shoes on the street corner represented by far the most comprehensive effort Congress had ever made to use the commerce clause as a source of power to regulate the economy of the country. For determination of constitutionality the statute was brought before a Supreme Court of which a majority was hostile to the extension of federal power over private enterprise and of which the entire membership was horrified at the blithe disregard of traditional procedure which char-

[8] 48 Stat. 195.

acterized administration under the New Deal. The Court held the statute unconstitutional as a delegation of legislative power and found that the regulations involved in this particular case, which had to do with the marketing of chickens in New York City, were not justified as an exercise of the power of Congress over interstate commerce.[9] Chief Justice Hughes, speaking for the Court, rejected the contention that in any event the transactions involved affected interstate commerce and were, therefore, subject to federal regulation whether or not they made up a part of the current or flow of interstate commerce. Relying upon decisions previously handed down in interpreting the Sherman Act, he drew a distinction between direct and indirect effects upon interstate commerce. While refraining from definition of the two terms, he held that the activities involved in this case only indirectly affected interstate commerce and were, therefore, not subject to federal regulation.

A few weeks after the Supreme Court held the National Industrial Recovery Act unconstitutional, Congress enacted the Bituminous Coal Conservation Act of 1935 to regulate the production and marketing of bituminous coal. In the enacting clause Congress stated the purpose of the act as in part to "stabilize the bituminous coal-mining industry and promote its interstate commerce." In the first section of the act, Congress attempted to control interpretation by the declaration that "practices prevailing in the production of bituminous coal directly affect its interstate commerce and require regulation for the protection of that commerce, and that the right of mine workers to organize and collectively bargain for wages, hours of labor, and conditions of employment should be guaranteed in order to prevent constant wage cutting and the establishment of disparate labor costs detrimental to fair competition in the interstate marketing of bituminous coal, and in order to

---

[9] *Schechter* v. *United States*, 295 U.S. 495 (1935).

avoid those obstructions to its interstate commerce that recur
in the industrial disputes over labor relations at the mines."[10]
The Supreme Court took notice of this declaration that the
labor activities dealt with in the statute "directly" affected interstate commerce, but it asserted its right to disagree, and,
in so doing, it held the statute unconstitutional.[11]

The majority of the Supreme Court appeared for a time un-
disturbed by President Roosevelt's wrathful suggestion that
the first of the two decisions cited grew out of thinking which
dated from the horse-and-buggy days and by public discussion
of various techniques for getting around benighted decisions
in these and other cases .When early in 1937 the President sent
to Congress a bill to reform the judiciary by adding new members to the Supreme Court and when it looked as if the bill
might be enacted into law, the Court seems to have realized
the seriousness of the situation involved in the fact that the
program of the administration and the judicial interpretation
of the Constitution were badly out of line. In *National Labor
Relations Board* v. *Jones and Laughlin Steel Corporation*,[12] decided April 12 , 1937, the Court, by a vote of five to four,
handed down the first of a series of decisions in which the
commerce clause was interpreted as an instrument of such
broad regulatory power as to justify almost any kind of statute
that Congress might see fit to rest upon it.

The Jones and Laughlin case had to do with the federal
regulation of labor relations in a steel plant which used materials from other states to manufacture steel products which
were in turn shipped in interstate commerce. Counsel for the
National Labor Relations Board contended that the steel plant
was but a "throat" of interstate commerce and sought to justify
regulation on the basis of the Swift case and other cases in
which the concept of the flow, or current, or throat of inter-

[10] 49 Stat. 991, 992.
[11] *Carter* v. *Carter Coal Co.*, 298 U.S. 238 (1936).   [12] 301 U.S. 1.

state commerce had been used. Chief Justice Hughes, speaking for the Court, referred back to the Shreveport case and declared, however, that use of the metaphor was not necessary to justify the regulation. The regulatory activity of the federal government was not limited to action upon interstate commerce itself.

> The congressional authority to protect interstate commerce from burdens and obstructions is not limited to transactions which can be deemed to be an essential part of a "flow" of interstate or foreign commerce. Burdens and obstructions may be due to injurious action springing from other sources. . . . . Although activities may be intrastate in character when separately considered, if they have such a close and substantial relation to interstate commerce that their control is essential or appropriate to protect that commerce from burdens and obstructions, Congress cannot be denied the power to exercise that control.[13]

Later decisions, also reflecting the changed attitude of the Supreme Court, enlarged upon the broad interpretation of the commerce power set forth in the Jones and Laughlin case. In connection with a new statute for the regulation of the coal industry the Court upheld the power of Congress to take positive measures toward industrial stabilization.

> Congress under the commerce clause is not impotent to deal with what it may consider to be dire consequences of laissez-faire. It is not powerless to take steps in mitigation of what in its judgment are abuses of cut-throat competition. And it is not limited in its choice between unrestrained self regulation on the one hand and rigid prohibitions on the other. The commerce clause empowers it to undertake stabilization of an interstate industry through a process of price fixing which safeguards the public interest by placing price control in the hands of its administrative representative.[14]

To the plea that the extension of regulation under the commerce power encroached upon the powers of the states, the Court replied as follows:

[13] *Ibid.*, pp. 36–37.
[14] *Sunshine Anthracite Coal Co.* v. *Adkins,* 310 U.S. 381, 396 (1940).

At the formation of the Union, the states delegated to the federal government authority to regulate commerce among the states. So long as the things done within the states by the United States are valid under that power, there can be no interference with the sovereignty of the state. It is the non-delegated power which under the Tenth Amendment remains in the state or the people.[15]

The doctrine that the very existence of the states stands as a limitation upon the exercise of the powers conferred upon the federal government had tremendous vitality, however. That doctrine, restated in many decisions, was best known in connection with the Child Labor case of 1918.[16] In spite of the breadth of his interpretation of the federal commerce power, Chief Justice Hughes had voiced the doctrine in the Jones and Laughlin case:

Undoubtedly the scope of this power must be considered in the light of our dual system of government and may not be extended so as to embrace effects upon interstate commerce so indirect and remote that to embrace them, in view of our complex society, would effectually obliterate the distinction between what is national and what is local and create a completely centralized government.[17]

In United States v. Darby,[18] however, which was decided February 3, 1941, the Supreme Court overruled the Child Labor case and went a long way toward rejecting the limitation on federal power as stated by Chief Justice Hughes. Said Chief Justice Stone:

Such regulation is not a forbidden invasion of state power merely because either its motive or its consequence is to restrict the use of articles of commerce within the states of destination and is not prohibited unless by other constitutional provisions. It is no objection to the assertion of the power to regulate interstate commerce that its exercise is attended

[15] United States v. Appalachian Electric Power Co., 311 U.S. 377, 428 (1941).

[16] Hammer v. Dagenhart, 247 U.S. 251 (1918).

[17] National Labor Relations Board v. Jones & Laughlin Steel Corp. 301 U.S. 1, 37 (1937).

[18] 312 U.S. 100.

by the same incidents which attend the exercise of the police power of the states. . . . . Whatever their motive and purpose, regulations of commerce which do not infringe some constitutional prohibition are within the plenary power conferred on Congress by the commerce clause.[19]

As to the generalizations here quoted and others phrased in the Darby case, however, a word of caution should be uttered. While they reject the contention that powers conferred upon the federal government are limited by the Tenth Amendment or by the very existence of the states, the conception of the fundamental duality of our system of government is so intrenched in the minds of judges as well as of the people generally that the exercise of powers granted to the federal government in such a way as to destroy that duality is unthinkable. The intellectual puzzle involved in making choices between the unrestricted grant of federal power over interstate commerce, on the one hand, and the dual character of our system, on the other, is revealed in the following statement of Justice Frankfurter in another important case:

To search for a dependable touchstone by which to determine whether employees are "engaged in commerce or in the production of goods for commerce" is as rewarding as an attempt to square the circle. The judicial task in marking out the extent to which Congress has exercised its constitutional power over commerce is not that of devising an abstract formula. Perhaps in no domain of public law are general propositions less helpful and indeed more mischievous than where boundaries must be drawn under a federal enactment between what it has taken over for administration by the central government and what it has left to the states. To a considerable extent the task is one of accommodation as between assertions of new federal authority and historic functions of the individual states. The expansion of our industrial economy has inevitably been reflected in the extension of federal authority over economic enterprise and its absorption of authority previously possessed by the states. Federal legislation of this character cannot therefore be construed without regard to the implications of our dual system of government.[20]

[19] *Ibid.*, pp. 114–15.
[20] *Kirshbaum* v. *Walling*, 316 U.S. 517, 520 (1942).

In spite of the general language of the several recent opinions, therefore, what we can be thoroughly certain about as to the extent of the federal commerce power is principally that the present membership of the Supreme Court finds the exercise of the power in certain specific ways to be constitutional. In order to prevent the clogging of the channels of interstate commerce, it is within the power of Congress to regulate the amount of goods to be shipped in interstate commerce and to exercise the regulatory power even to the extent of limiting production for local use when such production affects the sale of other goods which might be shipped in interstate commerce. Labor conditions are subject to federal regulation under whatever circumstances such regulation is deemed necessary to prevent interference with interstate commerce. Such regulation may extend even to the control of the hours, wages, and working conditions of elevator operators, porters, watchmen, and other employees employed in buildings in which space is rented out for the manufacture of clothing, part of which is shipped in interstate commerce. In the light of these illustrations it is clear that, although the states rise up to disturb the meditations of justices who are almost ready to say that the commerce clause gives to Congress complete power over everything in any way affecting such commerce, the disturbance seems unlikely to interfere seriously with the broad regulation of commerce of the several states which makes up the commerce of the United States—E Pluribus Unum!

Turning to taxation as a source of federal power, we start with the fact that the basic purpose of taxation is to provide the sustenance without which governments cannot survive. "A tax," says Justice Roberts, "in the general understanding of the term, and as used in the Constitution, signifies an exaction for the support of the government."[21] The taxing power is so

[21] United States v. Butler, 297 U.S. 1, 61 (1936).

essential to governments that the failure of the Articles of Confederation to confer it made necessary the amendment or replacement of the Articles as a constitution for the United States.

Although the provision of governmental sustenance has constituted the motive for the enactment of most of the tax measures of the federal government, some degree of incidental regulation of the economic order has also usually been implied. The tariff, even when collected nominally "for revenue only," has been recognized as having some effect upon the amount of goods imported and therefore upon goods locally produced. Although taxation which is so heavy as to destroy the enterprise upon which it is collected is not necessarily unconstitutional, the destruction of the source of revenue by protective tariffs is so obviously deprivation rather than provision of revenue that the Supreme Court has seen fit to uphold the power to collect protective tariffs on the basis not of the taxing power but of the power to regulate foreign commerce.[22] The levy provided for in the internal revenue measure which gave rise to the Whiskey Rebellion reflected a conception of the social value of the beverages affected. The same has been true as to most other excise taxes collected by the federal government.

It was not until 1894, however, with the enactment of a statute providing for collection of a graduated income tax with a broad base of exemptions, that the government undertook the sweeping exercise of regulatory power through the process of taxation. The interests most seriously affected, consisting primarily of wealthy people and corporations in certain eastern states, challenged this "assault upon capital" before the Supreme Court, contending, among other things, that the income tax was a direct tax and as such could be constitutionally collected only by apportionment among the several states

[22] See *University of Illinois* v. *United States*, 289 U.S. 48 (1933).

according to population. The purpose of the direct-tax provision of the Constitution, it will be recalled, had been to prevent Congress from discriminating against the property within some states or some minority group of states by levying taxes upon property found exclusively or principally within those states. In spite of many decisions in which it had been at least suggested that the direct tax provision of the Constitution applied only to poll taxes and to taxes on land and its appurtenances, the justices of the Supreme Court recognized the territorially discriminating effect of the income-tax statute; and, in addition—and perhaps more important—a number of them were firmly convinced that the leveling tendencies which found expression in the statute were calculated to destroy the vital order of developing capitalism in which they believed. A majority of the Court classified income taxes, or certain of them, as direct taxes which could be collected constitutionally only by apportionment among the several states according to population.[23] It thereby prevented the collection of such taxes—save as they were enacted deviously as excise taxes upon corporations until the Sixteenth Amendment became a part of the Constitution in 1913.

Since the adoption of the Sixteenth Amendment, the income tax has provided a steadily increasing proportion of federal revenue and, because of the way in which it is graduated, has become an increasingly important regulatory device. It is hard to overestimate the leveling effects of a tax measure in terms of which some individuals pay no tax at all and others at the opposite extreme pay a base tax plus a surtax of ninety-one per cent upon annual income of over two hundred thousand dollars, with the great mass of the American people graduated between these two extremes in terms of the amounts of their respective incomes.

[23] *Pollock v. Farmers' Loan & Trust Co.*, 157 U.S. 429; 158 U.S. 601 (1895).

Important as is the regulatory aspect of the income tax, however, that regulation is exercised, nevertheless, in subordination to the collection of revenue. In other fields the taxing device has often been used for regulatory purposes when the collection of revenue was quite incidental or a matter of no importance at all. In 1904 the Supreme Court upheld the constitutionality of a tax on colored oleomargarine which was clearly intended to bring to an end the sale of olemargarine in that form, with the result, of course, that no tax could be collected. However, persons who read the opinion of the Court and jumped to the conclusion that Congress could regulate any subject whatsoever by the device of levying a tax ignored the generalizations in the last paragraph of the opinion to the effect that "the manufacture of artificially colored oleomargarine may be prohibited by a free government without a violation of fundamental rights" and that, "where the abuse of the taxing power was so extreme as to be beyond the principles which we have previously stated, and where it was plain to the judicial mind that the power had been called into play, not for revenue, but solely for the purpose of destroying rights which could not be rightfully destroyed consistently with the principles of freedom and justice upon which the Constitution rests, that it would be the duty of the courts to say that such an arbitrary act was not merely an abuse of a delegated power, but was the exercise of an authority not conferred."[24] When in other cases, as, for example, that of the tax upon goods produced by child labor, Congress encroached upon judicial conceptions of fundamental rights, the Court refused to sustain the use of the taxing device for purposes of regulation.[25]

When Congress has the alternative of regulating by means

[24] *McCray* v. *United States*, 195 U.S. 27, 64 (1904).
[25] See *Bailey* v. *Drexel Furniture Co.*, 259 U.S. 20 (1922).

of the commerce power or by means of taxation under circumstances wherein the revenue collected is relatively unimportant, the Supreme Court has usually seemed to prefer use of the commerce power.[26] The most recent important distinction of that kind, however, probably grew as much out of a change in circumstances as out of the difference between constitutional clauses. In 1936, by a vote of six to three, the Supreme Court held in an opinion by Justice Roberts that the processing tax provided for in the Agricultural Adjustment Act for the regulation of agricultural production was not a true tax but was a device for the regulation of matters which belonged within the jurisdiction of the states, and was therefore unconstitutional.[27] In 1939, again speaking through Justice Roberts, with dissenting votes by two justices who had been with the majority in the earlier case, the Court upheld a regulation of interstate commerce which was intended to limit shipment in interstate commerce and would therefore have the effect of limiting production. Because the second case dealt with interstate commerce, however, and only indirectly with production, Justice Roberts made no mention of the relation between the two cases. It was left to the dissenting justices to point out the alleged inconsistency.[28] It has been suggested that the difference in the constitutional phrases involved in the two cases was less important in determining the difference between the two decisions than the threat to pack the Court in 1937 and the subsequent rejuvenation given to it by the appointment of new personnel. However that may be, the fact remains that the use of the taxing power and the commerce power for regulatory purposes has been more widely sanctioned as to the latter than as to the former.

[26] See *Hill* v. *Wallace*, 259 U.S. 44 (1922), and *Board of Trade* v. *Olsen*, 262 U.S. 1 (1923).

[27] *United States* v. *Butler*, 297 U.S. 1 (1936).

[28] *Mulford* v. *Smith*, 307 U.S. 38 (1939).

Deriving its vitality from the power to tax, and perhaps to a degree also from the power to borrow money on the credit of the United States, is the tremendously important spending power of the federal government. For more than a century constitutional lawyers speculated as to whether Congress had the power to spend money merely in exercise of the powers delegated by other language in the Constitution or whether a substantive power to spend for the general welfare apart from these grants was given by the power "to lay and collect taxes, duties, imposts, and excises, to pay the debts and provide for the common defense and general welfare of the United States." For almost as long a period, Congress considered and experimented with the granting of federal funds or federally owned property to the states to promote education, public health, the building of roads, and the performance of other civic functions which had traditionally been regarded as functions of the states rather than of the federal government. The making of such expenditures continued for many decades without anything like an effective constitutional challenge. When in 1923, in *Massachusetts* v. *Mellon*, the Supreme Court was asked to pass upon the constitutionality of an act providing for appropriations to the states of federal funds to be matched by other funds from the states in order to reduce maternal and infant mortality and to protect the health of mothers and infants, the Supreme Court avoided the constitutional question by holding that neither a state nor a federal taxpayer was sufficiently injured by the act to give a right to maintain a suit. The state was under no legal obligation to make the appropriation which was necessary to secure an allotment of federal funds; hence, there was no coercion. An individual taxpayer of the federal government lacked sufficient interest in undifferentiated funds in the Treasury of the United States to make him a legitimate party to a suit to contest the constitutionality of such an expenditure. Therefore, the Court could not pass on the constitutional question.[29] As a result of this decision, the federal government was able thereafter to pour a steadily increasing stream of funds into the states for expenditure in terms of federal conceptions of public welfare without reference to the constitutionality of such expenditures.

When Congress passed the Agricultural Adjustment Act of 1933, however, it made the tactical mistake of providing in the same statute for the expenditure of funds to secure the limitation of agricultural production and for the tax by which these particular funds were to be raised. This linkage between the expenditure and the tax enabled a resisting taxpayer to challenge the validity of the tax, and the statute was held unconstitutional on grounds of the illegitimacy of this particular expenditure. The case gave some support to regulation through spending, however, in bringing from the Supreme Court its first statement as to the breadth of the general welfare clause. The Court stated that "the power of Congress to authorize expenditure of public moneys for public purposes is not limited by the direct grants of legislative power found in the Constitution."[30] But power of taxation and appropriation, however, said Justice Roberts for the Court, "extend only to matters of national, as distinguished from local, welfare."[31] In a case involving the constitutionality of federal expenditures for old age benefits the Court, speaking this time through Justice Cardozo, further developed the doctrine as follows:

The line must still be drawn between one welfare and another, between particular and general. Where this shall be placed cannot be known through a formula in advance of the event. There is a middle ground or certainly a penumbra in which discretion is at large. The dis-

[29] *Massachusetts* v. *Mellon*, 262 U.S. 447 (1923).
[30] *United States* v. *Butler*, 297 U.S. 1, 66 (1936).
[31] *Ibid.*, p. 67.

cretion, however, is not confided to the courts. The discretion belongs to Congress, unless the choice is clearly wrong, a display of arbitrary power, not an exercise of judgment.[32]

As the situation now stands, therefore, Congress can still make expenditures out of the general funds in the Treasury which will have been accumulated either through general taxation or through borrowing, without challenge to the constitutionality of the expenditures, because of the fact that no taxpayer has sufficient interest in the funds to make him a party to such a suit. If, perchance, it is desired to spend funds raised by a particular levy, so that a taxpayer may have sufficient interest to be a party to a suit to contest the validity of the expenditure, the government has the support of decisions that Congress may spend for the general welfare and that discretion as to drawing the line between national and local welfare belongs to Congress. It seems improbable, therefore, that any constitutional barrier will be found to the expenditure of billions of dollars of federal funds upon highways, public health, education, and large numbers of other projects in terms of which federal policy is likely to be carried into execution. Government officials were for a long time uneasy about the constitutionality of federal expenditures on slum clearance and housing projects and sought to avoid judicial determinations of the question, but a recent Supreme Court decision in this field has apparently quieted all fears.[33] With the expenditure of federal funds may go the power of regulation, even if the expenditure covers only a fraction of the cost of the project involved. Says the Supreme Court through Justice Jackson: "It is hardly lack of due process for the government to regulate that which it subsidizes."[34]

[32] *Helvering* v. *Davis*, 301 U.S. 619, 640 (1937).

[33] *Cleveland* v. *United States*, 65 S. Ct. 280 (1945).

[34] *Wickard* v. *Filburn*, 317 U.S. 111, 131 (1942).

In summary as to the spending power, therefore, Congress, by the process of allotting funds for expenditure upon particular projects in chosen localities, is in a position drastically to remold most of the basic institutions of the United States. It is true that, when the making of federal appropriations is conditioned upon the matching of federal funds by appropriations from state treasuries, the states have the power to refuse to co-operate, but the power is oftentimes more theoretical than actual. Political pressure upon the legislature to make use of all available money for expenditure within the state may be well-nigh irresistible. Furthermore, the matching of federal funds by the states does not have to be made a condition of appropriation by the federal government. Congress may choose the projects on which it spends money as long as the purpose is for the general welfare and there is some plausible argument that the welfare is essentially national rather than local. Even if the expenditure is on a matter which would ordinarily be regarded as one of local welfare, furthermore, there may be no way of bringing the expenditure to a constitutional test. The powers of the federal government in this field, therefore, are tremendous, and they seem likely to be exercised hereafter on a tremendous scale.

The power to make war, by contrast with the other powers here discussed, has traditionally been considered an emergency power, one which is in abeyance most of the time. It has been our habit to think of it as important only in emergency periods. Those periods may be enormously important in them-selves, however, and they tend to become increasingly so. Furthermore, the exercise of war powers often establishes patterns for continued exercise, or the later resumption of exercise, of the same functions under some other constitutional authorization. The first World War, for example, provided much of the pattern of regulation of enterprise which was put into effect at the beginning of the New Deal period. The second World War, building upon the experience of its predecessor and the New Deal as well, will undoubtedly have provided a pattern for the continued exercise of power hitherto unknown in time of peace. The precedents established during the second World War include sweeping price controls in a great variety of fields, many of which had not previously been subject to regulation, the rationing of commodities not similarly dealt with in this fashion, a considerable degree of regimentation of civilian manpower, and measures restricting civil liberties in certain military danger zones—the latter to be discussed in another chapter. Exercise of the war power has given rise to a military machine and to a civilian establishment behind it which has had no parallel at any time in American history. Although the constitutionality of price control in certain fields has been upheld by the Supreme Court[35] and other measures have reached or are about to reach that tribunal for appraisal, the great mass of wartime activities has not been subject to judicial appraisal and may never have to submit to it. As a matter of fact, the American attitude toward the Constitution as a basis for the exercise of war powers has never been entirely clear. In suspending the privilege of the writ of habeas corpus during the Civil War, President Lincoln justified his action by saying that he believed it to be legal but intimating that, if it was not legal, it was better to violate a single legal provision than to permit the collapse of the entire structure upon which our legal system rested.[36] The attitude of some members of Congress during the Civil War and during the first World War was that the Constitution was more or less sus-

[35] *Bowles* v. *Willingham*, 321 U.S. 503 (1944), and *Yakus* v. *United States*, 321 U.S. 414 (1944).

[36] See James D. Richardson (ed.), *A Compilation of the Messages and Papers of the Presidents*, VI, 25.

pended during the period of the crisis. President Roosevelt's conception of the relation of the war power to the Constitution was by no means clear. War obviously appeared to him to justify the centralization of great power in the Executive. In his first inaugural address, delivered March 4, 1933, he proposed the following alternative in the event that Congress failed to cope adequately with the depression: "I shall ask the Congress for the one remaining instrument to meet the crisis—broad Executive power to wage a war against the emergency, as great as the power that would be given to me if we were in fact invaded by a foreign foe."[37] In September, 1942, in attempting to drive Congress to the enactment of a measure for the control of farm prices, he declared that he would act in the matter himself if Congress did not do so. "The President," he declared, "has the powers, under the Constitution and under congressional acts, to take measures necessary to avert a disaster which would interfere with the winning of the war." He could not tell what powers might have to be exercised in order to win the war:

> The American people can be sure that I will use my powers with a full sense of my responsibility to the Constitution and to my country. The American people can also be sure that I shall not hesitate to use every power vested in me to accomplish the defeat of our enemies in any part of the world where our own safety demands such defeat.
>
> When the war is won, the powers under which I act automatically revert to the people—to whom they belong.[38]

His assumption seemed to be that the Constitution and statutes already existing actually authorized him to take any steps which he might think necessary to the winning of the war. He never deemed it necessary to define specifically the sources of his general powers. His habit of lumping together a variety of sources without differentiation as justification for

[37] *Congressional Record*, LXXVII, 6.
[38] *Congressional Record*, LXXXVIII, 7044.

particular steps is illustrated by the following introductory sentence to the executive order establishing the Foreign Economic Administration:

By virtue of the authority vested in me by the Constitution and the statutes of the United States, as President of the United States and Commander-in-Chief of the Army and Navy, and in order to unify and consolidate governmental activities relating to foreign economic affairs, it is hereby ordered as follows: . . . .[39]

It is impossible from such a statement to tell whether President Roosevelt relied principally upon his peacetime powers as President or upon inherent powers as Commander-in-Chief or upon particular statutory grants. When special weight was to be given to a particular statute, but when it nevertheless seemed desirable to draw an aura of authority from other sources, he phrased executive orders somewhat as follows:

By virtue of the authority vested in me by the Constitution and laws of the United States, and particularly by Title I of the First War Powers Act, 1941 and Title XIII of the Second War Powers Act, 1942, as President of the United States and Commander-in-Chief of the Army and Navy of the United States, and in order to prevent the accumulation of unreasonable profits, to avoid waste of government funds, and to implement other measures which have been undertaken to forestall price rises and inflation, it is hereby ordered as follows: . . . .[40]

[39] Executive Order 9380, 8 F.R. 13081, 50 U.S.C.A. App. 601, p. 259.

[40] Executive Order 9127, 7 F.R. 2753, 50 U.S.C.A. App. 643, p. 282. For a similar order issued by President Truman see Executive Order 9599, issued August 18, 1945, which uses the following language: "By virtue of the authority vested in me by the Constitution and the statutes of the United States, and particularly the War Mobilization and Reconversion Act of 1944, the First War Powers Act of 1941, the Second War Powers Act of 1942, as amended, and the Stabilization Act of 1942, as amended, and for the purpose of fully mobilizing the resources of the Government in this final stage of the war emergency, in order to promote a swift and orderly transition to a peacetime economy of free independent private enterprise with full employment and maximum production in industry and agriculture and to assure the general stability of prices and costs and the maintenance of purchasing power which are indispensable to the shift of business enterprises from wartime to peacetime production and of individuals from wartime to peacetime employment, it is hereby ordered as follows: . . . ."(10 F.R. 10155).

This kind of strategy makes it next to impossible to demonstrate that a particular executive action is without authorization. This result, no doubt, is a part of the end and aim of administrative strategy.

In so far as it can be analyzed, the position of President Roosevelt seemed to be that war powers are exercised within the scope of the Constitution but that, under the Constitution, these powers loom up tremendously in the Executive and that the power to do particular things may rest upon an aggregate of many sources. He did not necessarily challenge the recent statement of the Supreme Court that "Congress and the President, like the courts, possess no power not derived from the Constitution."[41] Indeed, if one conceives of the war powers as representing the exercise of normal functions of government—and in the light of the frequency of exercise it ought to be considered as normal—there is no need to go outside the Constitution in search of justification. The difficulty arises from the fact that the exercise of war powers makes inroads upon our conventional ways of running our economy and encroaches upon civil liberties beyond the point at which they are deemed to be protected in time of peace by constitutional guaranties. Such guaranties are not absolutes, however, and are enforced subject to the necessities involved in the exercise of the powers granted. Because war occurs only intermittently and because we tend to regard the conditions of peace as determining the true norm wherein constitutional principles take shape, the unsettled conditions of wartime always appear to create a hiatus in the law. All this suggests the grim comment that if we live long enough under conditions of war, we shall adjust the law to wartime conditions, so that the law of wartime will seem more normal than the law of peace.

In the development of constitutional law in time of war

[41] *Ex parte Quirin*, 317 U.S. 1, 25-26 (1942).

there are two dangers. The first is that the passions and uncertainties of the moment will lead to decisions which do not reflect the sound and considered judgment of thoughtful men. The second is that the tremendous building-up of power in the hands of the Executive and of a military machine will subject the country to more of control by one of the three branches of government than is wise in the long run and that the military caste and the military machine will arrogate to themselves a measure of power which will constitute a menace to the welfare of a traditionally liberty-loving people.

In summary, the commerce clause of the Constitution and clauses dealing with taxation, spending, and war are potential sources of tremendous power for utilization by the federal government. Although that government is one of delegated powers, the passing years have brought increasingly broad interpretation of these powers so as to make possible the concentration of the forces of the nation both for the promotion of the general welfare in time of peace and for the waging of war. In the light of present interpretations, we have no problem of too little power in government—for the power available seems almost commensurate with the potentialities of all the resources of the nation. The unanswered question is rather whether with the expansion of governmental power we have adequately maintained our traditional restraints upon the exercise of governmental authority.

V

CONSTITUTIONAL BARRIERS TO THE EXERCISE OF POWER

✻

OUR forefathers had a healthy distrust of men in positions of power. When they drafted state constitutions, they hedged offices and agencies with restrictions. When they drafted the Constitution of the United States, they assumed that the power of the federal government would be limited by the fact that it would have only those powers conferred upon it by the Constitution, but, even so, as a matter of precaution, they included a number of limiting statements to prevent unjust discrimination. As to the basically important powers of taxation, for example, they required that direct taxes should be apportioned among the several states according to population and that indirect taxes should be uniform. They forbade discrimination among the ports of the United States and declared that no taxes should be levied on exports. Members of certain of the ratifying conventions felt that the inclusion of these prohibitions in the Constitution and others, such as those dealing with the rights of the accused in the courts of the United States, was not sufficient, and they brought about the subsequent adoption of amendments to the Constitution which have been commonly known as the Bill of Rights. These amendments dealt further with the rights of the accused and protected individuals against the government by guaranteeing certain fundamental rights such as freedom of speech, freedom of the press, and freedom of religion, and gave protection to property through due process and just compensation clauses. New amendments adopted immediately after the Civil War outlawed slavery, identified citizens of the United States and of the states, set up various safeguards against the states, and protected the right to vote against discrimination based on race, color, or previous condition of servitude. A later amendment outlawed discrimination as to voting on the basis of sex.

The protection of civil rights is a subject of such importance in our constitutional history that it must be set apart for separate discussion. Protection of property rights against the federal government has been accorded down through the years in terms of the prohibitions in the Constitution and by means of restrictive interpretations on the powers granted to the federal government, such as the power to regulate commerce and the power to tax. Much has already been said about judicial limitation of federal powers on the basis of the contention that the powers granted to the federal government were not intended to interfere with spheres of activity which traditionally belonged to the states. This contention was originally used by lawyers and judges who, in part at least, were sincerely attempting to protect the powers of the states against attrition resulting from broad interpretation of federal powers. The later use of this type of argument for the restriction of the interpretation of federal powers, however, was not attributable to hearts throbbing with filial affection for the Prairie State of Illinois or the Old Line State of Maryland but to the desire of particular interests to escape from the tentacles of federal control. It was not counsel for the Tar Heel State of North Carolina who in 1918 challenged the federal Child Labor Act as a legitimate exercise of the commerce power, contending that if Congress could regulate everything and everybody touched by interstate commerce, there remained nothing upon which it might not for all practical purposes impose its will "and the states have lost their police power."[1] Nominally the argument was on behalf of a North Carolina farmer who objected to federal interference with the right of his two sons, one under the age of fourteen and the other between the ages of fourteen and sixteen years, to work in a cotton mill at Charlotte, North Carolina. One who naïvely accepted the appearance for the reality would be entitled to inquire whether, if the farmer involved could afford the expense of costly litigation, he could not also afford to keep his minor sons in school instead of hiring them out to a cotton mill. Actually, of course, this particular farmer and his sons were merely instruments of employers who wished to preserve to themselves the economic benefits of the cheap labor of children.

The case of *United States* v. *Butler*,[2] in which the processing tax provisions of the Agricultural Adjustment Act of 1933 were held unconstitutional, should be viewed in a similar light. In arguing the case before the Supreme Court for Calvin Coolidge's friend, William M. Butler, receiver of the Hoosac Mills Corporation, George Wharton Pepper, although he declaimed passionately, was probably not actually deeply stirred by federal encroachments upon the rights of Mr. Butler's state of Massachusetts or potentially upon those of his own state of Pennsylvania. Rather his true sentiments were revealed by the following paragraphs of his peroration:

I have tried very hard to argue this case calmly and dispassionately, and without vehement attack upon things which I cannot approve, and I have done it thus because it seems to me that this is the best way in which an advocate can discharge his duty to this Court.

But I do not want your Honors to think that my feelings are not involved, and that my emotions are not deeply stirred. Indeed, may it

[1] *Hammer* v. *Dagenhart*, 247 U.S. 251 (1918). See the summary of arguments of counsel, 62 L. Ed. 1103.

[2] 297 U. S. 1 (1936).

please your Honors, I believe I am standing here today to plead the cause of the America I have loved; and I pray Almighty God that not in my time may "the land of the regimented" be accepted as a worthy substitute for "the land of the free."[3]

In other words, Mr. Pepper was concerned with the substitution of the land of the regimented for the land of the free rather than with the line of demarcation between the powers of the federal government and the powers of the states. He did not wish to curb the exercise of federal power in order that the states might regulate enterprise more adequately, but, rather, he wished to prevent the regulation altogether. Such has usually been the motivation of counsel when advancing this type of argument and such, it is safe to assume, has usually been the philosophy of the judiciary when it has yielded to this argument. All this is not to suggest that a valid argument is vitiated by the fact that individuals or corporations may profit by advancing it. It is merely to suggest that, when the argument is made the tool of a vested interest for use in its own behalf, the validity of the argument should be keenly scrutinized and that, when judicial decisions seem to turn actually not on the legal issues involved but on philosophical conceptions not vital to the legal issues, the reasoning of the judges must be suspect. At any rate, this type of argument, although much and effectively used in times past, seems not to be popular with the present membership of the Supreme Court. There may be difference of opinion as to whether the change is the product of improved judicial logic or whether it merely signifies a shift in the economic and political philosophy of the Court.

Apart from cases turning on the narrow interpretation of the powers granted to the federal government and from cases involving civil liberties and the rights of the accused, the great body of restrictions on the exercise of power by the federal

[3] *Ibid.*, p. 4.

government has been based on the provision in the Fifth Amendment that no person shall "be deprived of life, liberty, or property, without due process of law." The phrase had its origin in English constitutional development as far back or further back than Magna Carta.[4] The American history of its interpretation falls into three periods. During the first period, covering roughly the first century of government under the Constitution, due process was interpreted principally as a restriction upon procedure—and largely the judicial procedure —by which the government exercised its powers. During the second period, which, again roughly speaking, extended through 1936, due process was expanded to serve as a restriction not merely upon procedure but upon the substance of the activities in which the government might engage. During the third period, extending from 1936 to date, the use of due process as a substantive restriction has been largely suspended or abandoned, leaving it principally in its original status as a restriction upon procedure. Our concern here is primarily with the second and third periods. So important is the part played by due process in the history of constitutional barriers to the exercise of power, indeed, that this discussion might appropriately be entitled "The Rise and Decline of Substantive Due Process."

In the study of due process as a restriction on the substantive activities of the federal government it is necessary to consider at length the use of the same term in the Fourteenth Amendment, where, in 1868, it became a constitutional restriction on the states; for it received its expansion as an instrument of substantive restriction through broad interpretation of the provision that no state shall take life, liberty, or property without due process of law, whereafter the expanded meaning was

---

[4] See Robert E. Cushman, "Due Process of Law," *Encyclopaedia of the Social Sciences*, V, 264–68, and materials there cited.

fed back into the Fifth Amendment as a restriction upon the federal government.

Adoption of the Fourteenth Amendment, it will be recalled, constituted one of the many steps taken to restore order within the jurisdictions of both the state and federal governments after the Civil War and to protect the newly acquired rights of the liberated colored people. The provisions relevant to this discussion are found in Section 1. That section answers the controversial question as to who are citizens of the United States and of the states. It forbids states by law to abridge the privileges or immunities of citizens of the United States, to deprive any person of life, liberty, or property without due process of law, and to deny to any person within its jurisdiction the equal protection of the laws. While the records of the adoption of the Fourteenth Amendment do not disclose the exact meaning attributed to the separate phrases, it seems clear that leaders among the framers intended to restrain the states from interference with all the several rights which citizens under a free government might be expected to have under the conditions of normal living. The most direct support of this conception is found in the so-called "privileges and immunities clause" providing that no state "shall make or enforce any law which shall abridge the privileges or immunities of citizens of the United States."

Aggrieved persons of the white race quickly resorted to the amendment for protection against restrictive state laws. Among them were butchers in the city of New Orleans who complained of a state zoning law which restricted and regulated the slaughtering of livestock in the city. In deciding the so-called Slaughterhouse Cases,[5] a majority of the Supreme Court in 1873 held that the privileges and immunities protected were not all those possessed by a citizen of the United States

[5] 16 Wallace 36 (1873).

but merely those which were attributes of his federal citizenship as distinguished from his state citizenship. The great bulk of the rights of the citizen, the Court declared, were attributes of his state citizenship and were, therefore, not protected by the privileges and immunities clause.

By this interpretation, the privileges and immunities clause was effectively devitalized as an instrument for the protection of most of the rights connected with the conditions of daily living. Whatever the future yet may hold in the way of a new interpretation of that clause, the majority of the Court in almost every case decided since 1873 has adhered rather closely to the original interpretation. In the original case, however, and in many later cases a minority has insisted on a broader interpretation of the clause. Or, rather, it is perhaps more accurate to say that the original minority insisted on the interpretation of the Fourteenth Amendment, as distinguished from the particular clauses within it, in such a way as to give broad protection to all the rights of the citizen. Indeed, the mention of particular clauses in the minority opinions in the early cases seems to be more or less incidental to the argument that the amendment as a whole is calculated to give such broad protection.

However, although the minority remained a minority as far as interpretation of the privileges and immunities clause was concerned, it had back of it a strong body of sentiment for resistance to drastic governmental curbs upon business. When resort to the Fourteenth Amendment in general and to the privileges and immunities clause in particular failed to provide those curbs, the minority of the Court, including particularly Justices Field and Bradley, began to insist upon a broadened interpretation of the due process clause, hitherto principally a procedural safeguard, to give protection against statutes which state legislatures might enact. For a time the majority held its ground, declaring that "for protection against abuses by legislatures the people must resort to the polls, not to the courts."[6] The shadow of coming events can be discerned, however, by comparing this statement made by Chief Justice Waite in 1877 with another made by him in 1886:

> From what has thus been said it is not to be inferred that this power of limitation or regulation is itself without limit. This power to regulate is not a power to destroy, and limitation is not the equivalent of confiscation. Under pretense of regulating fares and rates, the state cannot require a railroad corporation to carry persons or property without reward; neither can it do that which in law amounts to a taking of private property for public use without just compensation, or without due process of law.[7]

With changing personnel on the Supreme Court the trend continued, through determinations that railroad rates and other charges fixed by government must be subject to judicial review, and that they must be reasonable, and that in order to be reasonable they must allow the earning of a fair return upon a fair value, and that the discovery of fair value must be made by giving an undefined weight to each of a great variety of factors named and unnamed, and that the fair return upon the value of the property varied with the circumstances. In short, by means of an expanded interpretation of the due process clause, the Supreme Court set itself up as a restraining agent upon the entire field of rate-fixing activities of the state governments. A parallel body of doctrine held that states could not fix rates at all in businesses other than those which were "affected with the public interest." Although the passing years brought reluctant expansion of the list of businesses so affected, the Court tended to restrict the list to those businesses which in times past had been held to be so affected. To rephrase and expand the generalization as to due process, that

---

[6] *Munn* v. *Illinois*, 94 U.S. 113, 134 (1877).

[7] *Stone* v. *Farmers Loan & Trust Co.*, 116 U.S. 307, 331 (1886).

clause immunized from state regulation prices in almost all
fields except a few traditionally subjected to regulation, and
the judiciary made itself the final judge of the validity of regulations in fields where regulation was permitted at all. This
body of interpretation could be and was transferred in full
from the Fourteenth Amendment, where it stood as a restriction upon the powers of the states, to the Fifth Amendment,
where it was used in similar fashion as a restraint upon the
power of the federal government.

While the Supreme Court was developing this line of doctrine, it was also reading into due process the concept of freedom of contract. Important implications of the doctrine that
the due process clause of the Fourteenth Amendment forbids
the state to interfere with the freedom of people to make contracts are brought out in the case of *Lochner* v. *New York*,[8]
which the Supreme Court decided in 1905. That case had to
do with the offense of Joseph Lochner, who, in violation of a
New York statute forbidding the employment of persons in
certain fields of activity for more than sixty hours a week, was
indicted for having "wrongfully and unlawfully required and
permitted an employee working for him in his biscuit, bread,
and cake factory and confectionary establishment, at the City
of Utica . . . . to work more than sixty hours in one week."[9]
Justice Peckham, speaking for five of the nine members of the
Supreme Court, cited the due process clause of the Fourteenth Amendment and declared that "the right to purchase or
to sell labor is part of the liberty protected by this Amendment, unless there are circumstances which exclude the
right."[10] Since the occupation of a baker was not shown to be a
particularly unhealthful one and since there was no evidence
that bakers were less able to take care of themselves than men

[8] 198 U.S. 45 (1905).
[9] *Ibid.*, p. 46.   [10] *Ibid.*, p. 53.

in other occupations, he held that the state was forbidden by the Constitution to restrict labor contracts made with them.

The words of one of the minority justices are important at this point, not because they had any effect upon the case then decided or upon other cases decided for many years thereafter, but because they marked as early as 1905 the beginning of the disintegration of the doctrine that due process of law stood as a sweeping guaranty of the perpetuation of laissez faire. Said Justice Holmes:

> This case is decided upon an economic theory which a large part of the country does not entertain. . . . . The Fourteenth Amendment does not enact Mr. Herbert Spencer's Social Statics. . . . . A constitution is not intended to embody a particular economic theory, whether of paternalism and the organic relation of the citizen to the state or of laissez-faire. . . . . I think that the word "liberty," in the Fourteenth Amendment, is perverted when it is held to prevent the natural outcome of a dominant opinion, unless it can be said that a rational and fair man necessarily would admit that the statute proposed would infringe fundamental principles as they have been understood by the traditions of our people and our law. It does not need research to show that no such sweeping condemnation can be passed upon the statute before us. A reasonable man might think it a proper measure on the score of health. Men whom I certainly could not pronounce unreasonable would uphold it as a first installment of a general regulation of the hours of work.[11]

Justice Holmes was again in the minority when in 1908, in *Adair* v. *United States*,[12] the Supreme Court carried the doctrine of freedom of contract from the due process clause of the Fourteenth Amendment over into that of the Fifth Amendment. In the Adair case the Court used the doctrine, along with a restricted interpretation of the commerce clause, to strike down a provision of an act of Congress forbidding the making of yellow-dog contracts with railroad workers. Justice Holmes argued in dissent that "the right to make contracts at

[11] *Ibid.*, pp. 75–76.
[12] 208 U.S. 161 (1908).

will that has been derived from the word 'liberty' in the Amendments has been stretched to the extreme by the decisions," declaring that "where there is, or generally is believed to be, an important ground of public policy for restraint, the Constitution does not forbid it, whether this Court agrees or disagrees with the policy pursued."[13]

The battle between the reserved powers of the states and the delegated powers of the federal government, on the one hand, and the restrictions of due process of law, on the other, continued thereafter in many Supreme Court decisions, with victory now to one side and now to the other. In 1917, for example, in spite of the peculiar sanctity which continued to be attributed to wages and prices, a bare majority of the Court upheld the Adamson Act, which represented an attempt to avert a nation-wide railroad strike by adoption of the eight-hour day, with the requirement that for a limited period daily compensation should equal that previously given for ten hours. In spite of the public interest involved in the settlement of the dispute, three of the four dissenting justices found that the regulation of wages took property without due process of law and declared that "if the Constitution is not to become a dead letter the protection of the due process clause must be given to all entitled to this safeguard of rights which the Amendment intended to secure."[14] In 1921 a bare majority of the Court held that the business of housing had become affected with a public interest in an emergency which grew out of the first World War and that the federal government might fix rents in the District of Columbia without violation of due process of law.[15]

In 1923, however, the advocates of freedom of contract and

[13] *Ibid.*, p. 191.

[14] *Wilson* v. *New*, 243 U.S. 332, 366 (1917).

[15] *Block* v. *Hirsh*, 256 U.S. 135 (1921).

a minimum of governmental interference with private enterprise again came into ascendancy. After the decision in the Lochner case in 1905 the Supreme Court had upheld a number of state restrictions on hours of labor in such a way as to create the impression that the Lochner case had in effect been overruled. That case was revived as a precedent, however, when in 1923, in *Adkins* v. *Children's Hospital*,[16] five members of the Supreme Court found unconstitutional an act of Congress establishing or providing for the establishment of a scale of minimum wages for women in the District of Columbia. Justice Sutherland admitted that there was no such thing as absolute freedom of contract. "But freedom of contract is, nevertheless, the general rule and restraint the exception; and the exercise of legislative authority to abridge it can be justified only by the existence of exceptional circumstances."[17] He contended that the power to fix high wages connoted by like course of reasoning the power to fix low wages. "If, in the face of the guaranties of the Fifth Amendment, this form of legislation shall be legally justified, the field for the operation of the police power will have been widened to a great and dangerous degree."[18] In reply to the contention that legislation of the kind now under review was required in the interest of justice, he replied piously that

to sustain the individual freedom of action contemplated by the Constitution is not to strike down the common good, but to exalt it; for surely the good of society as a whole cannot be better served than by the preservation against arbitrary restraint of the liberties of its constituent members.[19]

Three justices dissented, and one did not sit in the case. Chief Justice Taft stated his belief that the Lochner case had been overruled *sub silentio* and contended that wages were no

[16] 261 U.S. 525 (1923).
[17] *Ibid.*, p. 546.
[18] *Ibid.*, pp. 560–61.
[19] *Ibid.*, p. 561.

more immune to regulation than hours. A boundary of the police power beyond which its exercise became an invasion of the guaranty of liberty under the Fifth and Fourteenth amendments, he said, was not easy to mark. The Supreme Court had been laboriously engaged in pricking out a line in successive cases. The members should follow that line as well as they could and not depart from it by suggestion of a distinction that was formal rather than real.

Justice Holmes wrote a vigorous dissent, in which he pointed out that objection to the statute was not found in a specific provision of the Constitution such as that forbidding the taking of private property for public use without just compensation. The only objection that could be urged against it was found "within the vague contours of the Fifth Amendment, prohibiting the depriving of any person of liberty or property without due process of law." As for reliance upon that prohibition,

the earlier decisions upon the same words in the Fourteenth Amendment began within our memory, and went no farther than an unpretentious assertion of the liberty to follow the ordinary callings. Later that innocuous generality was expanded into the dogma, Liberty of Contract. Contract is not specially mentioned in the text that we have to construe. It is merely an example of doing what you want to do, embodied in the word "liberty." But pretty much all law consists in forbidding men to do some things that they want to do, and contract is no more exempt from law than other acts.[20]

While the critical phrases of Holmes and Taft had no effect upon the case at hand or upon other cases in the field of minimum wages until well down into the New Deal period, they had an effect in developing sentiment against excessive restrictions upon the exercise of governmental power through judicial decisions.

[20] *Ibid.*, p. 568.

The development of such sentiment also received encouragement through minority opinions in other fields in which the majority made restrictive use of due process clauses. This was particularly true in connection with the regulation of the rates of public utilities. In controversies over the valuation of property on which rates were to be based the Supreme Court continued to talk about the so-called rule in *Smyth* v. *Ames* which required that the valuing authorities take into account original investment, reproduction cost, and other items mentioned and unmentioned without prescribing a scale of weights to be allotted to each. Furthermore, although successive decisions indicated that the return on the value which the Supreme Court would accept as fair was probably someplace between five and eight per cent, this concept provided another variable in each case. Because of the uncertainties involved, utility companies were often able to fight off restrictions for years at a time by securing injunctions against regulatory measures pending the determination of their constitutionality in the courts and then by keeping the litigation alive by interminable series of legal maneuvers. The irony of the situation was further disclosed by the fact that, as far as the rate base was concerned, utility companies sought to measure value largely in terms of the original investment if that investment happened to be high whereas current costs were low, while, on the other hand, if current prices happened to be high so that reproduction costs would be greater than the original cost had been, they sought to have present value measured by such reproduction costs. It at least takes nothing from the irony of the situation to note that certain members of the Supreme Court followed utility counsel back and forth as they maneuvered to show the highest possible value in the property and, therefore, to secure a maximum return for their clients.

In the Southwestern Bell case,[21] decided in 1923, Justice
Brandeis, with the supporting vote of Justice Holmes, wrote a
concurring opinion in which he characterized the so-called
rule of *Smyth* v. *Ames* as in his opinion "legally and economically unsound," and proposed a substitute. He proposed to
find value for rate-making purposes in large part by discovering the amount that had been prudently invested in the property. Resort to this device would eliminate much of the insta-
bility in the rate base and would bring to an end an enormous
amount of litigation which was detrimental to the public interest. Justice Brandeis had the support of Joseph B. Eastman,
who was a member of the Interstate Commerce Commission
and who had expressed the opinion in 1920 that "the valuation
doctrines which are prevalent in railroad and public utility cir-
cles and which have been urged upon us are fundamentally
unsound in many respects and subversive of the public welfare."[22] Some two weeks after the decision in the Southwestern
Bell case, Eastman wrote a dissenting opinion as an Interstate
Commerce commissioner in which he likewise sponsored the
prudent investment scheme.[23] Evidently under Eastman's
leadership, although not acting through an opinion written by
him, the Interstate Commerce Commission in 1927 went a
long way toward committing itself to adoption of the prudent
investment scheme. When in 1929 the case reached the Supreme Court, however, that tribunal, taking the position that
the statute governing the Interstate Commerce Commission
required it to apply legal concepts as they had been judicially
determined, reversed the decision of the Commission on the
ground that it had not given consideration to reproduction

[21] *Missouri* ex rel. *Southwestern Bell Telephone Co.* v. *Public Service Commission*, 262 U.S. 276 (1923).

[22] *Ex parte* 74, 58 I.C.C. 220, 256 (1920).

[23] *San Pedro, Los Angles & Salt Lake Railroad Co.* v. *Public Service Commission*, 75 I.C.C. 463 (1923).

costs.[24] Although Justices Holmes, Brandeis, and Stone continued to chip away at the assurance with which this use of the concept of due process was voiced, this controversy, like that over due process in relation to the fixing of wages, continued into the New Deal period.

In the meantime, in a number-of decisions the Supreme Court had continued to restrict the areas in which prices might be regulated by keeping the category of business affected with a public interest almost completely closed. When in 1927 the Court held that the resale of theater tickets was not subject to price regulation because the business was not affected with a public interest, Justice Stone remarked in dissent that "to say that only those businesses affected with a public interest may be regulated is but another way of stating that all those businesses which may be regulated are affected with a public interest."[25] Justice Holmes remarked in apparent disgust that "the notion that a business is clothed with a public interest and has been devoted to the public use is little more than a fiction intended to beautify what is disagreeable to the sufferers." The truth seemed to him to be that, "subject to compensation when compensation is due, the legislature may forbid or restrict any business when it has a sufficient force of public opinion behind it."[26] In dissenting from an opinion of the Court holding that the rates charged by employment agencies were not subject to regulation because the business was not affected with a public interest, Justice Stone attacked the attempt of the Court to differentiate between reasonable regulations of price and reasonable regulations of the use of property.

[24] *St. Louis & O'Fallon Railway Co.* v. *United States*, 279 U.S. 461 (1929).

[25] *Tyson & Brother* v. *Banton*, 273 U.S. 418, 451 (1927).

[26] *Ibid.*, p. 446.

To say that there is constitutional power to regulate a business or a particular use of property because of the public interest in the welfare of a class peculiarly affected, and to deny such power to regulate price for the accomplishment of the same end, when that alone appears to be an appropriate and effective remedy, is to make a distinction based on no real economic difference, and for which I can find no word in the Constitution itself nor any justification in the opinions of this Court.[27]

Dissenting in the Oklahoma Ice case,[28] which was decided in 1932, when the people were "confronted with an emergency more serious than war," Justice Brandeis delivered still another attack upon the use of the due process clause and the concept of businesses affected with a public interest to restrain the exercise of governmental power. The Supreme Court held unconstitutional an Oklahoma statute requiring a license of persons desiring to manufacture, sell, and distribute ice and directing the corporation commission of that state to withhold licenses wherever adequate service of this kind was already provided. Justice Brandeis commented in part as follows:

There must be power in the states and the nation to remold, through experimentation, our economic practices and institutions to meet changing social and economic needs. I cannot believe that the framers of the Fourteenth Amendment, or the states which ratified it, intended to deprive us of the power to correct the evils of technological unemployment and excess productive capacity which have attended progress in the useful arts.[29]

He warned of the dangers of denying the right of experimentation.

This Court has the power to prevent an experiment. We may strike down the statute which embodies it on the ground that, in our opinion, the measure is arbitrary, capricious or unreasonable. We have power to do this, because the due process clause has been held by the Court applicable to matters of substantive laws as well as to matters of procedure. But in the exercise of this high power, we must be ever on our

[27] *Ribnik* v. *McBride*, 277 U.S. 350, 374 (1928).

[28] *New State Ice Co.* v. *Liebmann*, 285 U.S. 262 (1932).

[29] *Ibid.*, p. 311.

guard, lest we erect our prejudices into legal principles. If we would guide by the light of reason, we must let our minds be bold.[30]

The break in the use, or the misuse, of the doctrine of businesses affected with a public interest to prevent regulation of prices came in 1934 with the decision of the Supreme Court in *Nebbia* v. *New York*.[31] The case had to do with the constitutionality of a New York statute which fixed minimum prices for the sale of milk in order to curb destructive price-cutting under the conditions of the depression. No claim was made that the business was affected with a public interest in the sense that monopoly conditions existed or that it was a public utility. Counsel for the price-cutter involved in the litigation contended that the fixing of prices was a type of regulation absolutely forbidden by the due process clause of the Fourteenth Amendment. Justice Roberts, speaking for a majority consisting of five members of the Supreme Court, rejected this contention.

We think there is no such principle. The due process clause makes no mention of sales or prices any more than it speaks of business or contracts or buildings or other incidents of property. The thought seems nevertheless to have persisted that there is something peculiarly sacrosanct about the price one may charge for what he makes or sells, and that, however able to regulate other elements of manufacture or trade, with incidental effect upon price, the state is incapable of directly controlling the price itself.[32]

Justice Roberts set out to show that this view had been negatived in the Munn case,[33] the original public interest case decided by the Supreme Court. It was clear, he said, that "there is no closed class or category of businesses affected with a public interest, and the function of courts in the application

[30] *Ibid.*

[31] 291 U.S. 502 (1934).

[32] *Ibid.*, p. 532.

[33] 94 U.S. 113 (1877).

of the Fifth and Fourteenth Amendments is to determine in each case whether circumstances vindicate the challenged regulation as a reasonable exertion of governmental authority or condemn it as arbitrary or discriminatory."[34] Price control, he declared, "like any other form of regulation, is unconstitutional only if arbitrary, discriminatory, or demonstrably irrelevant to the policy the legislature is free to adopt, and hence an unnecessary and unwarranted interference with individual liberty."[35]

Although the spokesman for the four dissenting justices in the Nebbia case had an easier task in writing a well-organized and acceptable opinion than did Justice Roberts, because of the fact that most of the recent cases seemed to be on their side, the decision of the majority has continued to express the view of the public interest doctrine held by the Supreme Court during the decade which has passed since that decision was handed down. It did not completely destroy the concept of a business affected with a public interest, but it showed that the question whether or not a business was so affected and the question whether or not price could be regulated depended not upon classification in a closed category but upon the extent to which public interest was actually involved. In other words, the dissenting opinions of Justices Holmes, Brandeis, and Stone had now come to represent the law of the land. It is now possible to regulate the price of bituminous coal,[36] the fees charged by employment agencies,[37] and prices in other fields whenever it can be shown that the promotion of the public welfare provides a plausible justification for such regulation.

The immunity of minimum wages for women from governmental regulation was maintained by the Supreme Court as

---

[34] 291 U.S. 536.   [35] *Ibid.*, p. 539.

[36] *Sunshine Anthracite Coal Co.* v. *Adkins*, 310 U.S. 381 (1940).

[37] *Olsen* v. *Nebraska*, 313 U.S. 236 (1941).

late as 1936,[38] but in 1937 this bastion of due process also collapsed.[39] Said Chief Justice Hughes for the Court:

> In each case the violation alleged by those attacking minimum wage regulation for women is deprivation of freedom of contract. What is this freedom? The Constitution does not speak of freedom of contract. It speaks of liberty and prohibits the deprivation of liberty without due process of law. In prohibiting that deprivation the Constitution does not recognize an absolute and uncontrollable liberty. Liberty in each of its phases has its history and connotation. But the liberty safeguarded is liberty in a social organization which requires the protection of law against the evils which menace the health, safety, morals and welfare of the people. Liberty under the Constitution is thus necessarily subject to the restraints of due process, and regulation which is reasonable in relation to its subject and is adopted in the interests of the community is due process.[40]

In terms of this revised statement of principle, the Supreme Court has found it possible not merely to uphold the regulation of minimum wages for women but also to uphold the federal Fair Labor Standards Act of 1938, by which Congress sought to establish minimum wages for both men and women.[41]

The last of the due process barriers to be swept away was the requirement that the rates fixed by government must be high enough to yield a fair return on the fair value of the property as measured by the so-called rule of *Smyth* v. *Ames*. Early in 1939 Justice Frankfurter, accompanied by Justice Black, criticized a decision of the Court because it seemed to give new vitality to that "mischievous formula." "The force of reason," Frankfurter declared, "confirmed by events, has gradually been rendering that formula moribund by revealing it to be useless as a guide for adjudication."[42] Without direct mention of any kind, that formula was apparently discarded in

---

[38] *Morehead* v. *New York* ex rel. *Tipaldo*, 298 U.S. 587 (1936).

[39] *West Coast Hotel Co.* v. *Parrish*, 300 U.S. 379 (1937).

[40] *Ibid.*, p. 391.   [41] *United States* v. *Darby*, 312 U.S. 100 (1941).

[42] *Driscoll* v. *Edison Light & Power Co.*, 307 U.S. 104, 122 (1939).

1942, when Justice Stone, speaking for the Court, declared that "the Constitution does not bind rate-making bodies to the service of any single formula or combination of formulas."[43] Once a fair hearing had been given, he continued, and proper findings made and other statutory requirements satisfied, the courts could not intervene "in the absence of a clear showing that the limits of due process have been overstepped."[44] Even the cautious device, reflected in the words just quoted, of keeping a tentative judicial hand upon the subject of rate regulation via the due process clause, seemed to Justices Black, Douglas, and Murphy to represent unjustifiable judicial interference. "Price fixing," they declared, "like others forms of social legislation, may well diminish the value of the property which is regulated. But that is no obstacle to its validity."[45] They parted company with their brethren in so far as the latter assumed that, regardless of the statute, the due process clause of the Fifth Amendment gave the Court power to invalidate an order as unconstitutional when it found the charges to be unreasonable.[46]

When such utterances could be seriously made by members of the Supreme Court, it was clear that substantive due process had indeed fallen upon evil times. Supporting statements appeared elsewhere to the effect that "an act of Congress is not to be refused application by the courts as arbitrary and capricious and forbidden by the due process clause merely because it is deemed in a particular case to work an inequitable result";[47] and "it is hardly lack of due process for the government to regulate that which it subsidizes";[48] and again—

[43] *Federal Power Commission* v. *Natural Gas Pipeline Co.*, 315 U.S. 575, 586 (1942).

[44] *Ibid.*, p. 586.

[45] *Ibid.*, p. 603.   [46] *Ibid.*, p. 599.

[47] *Wickard* v. *Filburn*, 317 U.S. 111, 129–30 (1942).

[48] *Ibid.*, p. 130.

in a dissenting opinion by Justice Black—"the chief weapon in the arsenal of restriction, only recently falling into disrepute because of overuse, is the due process clause."[49]

Finally, in 1944, Justice Douglas was able to say for a majority of the Supreme Court that "rate making is indeed but one species of price fixing" and that "the fixing of prices, like other applications of the police power, may reduce the value of the property which is being regulated. But the fact that the value is reduced does not mean that the regulation is invalid."[50] He apparently demolished the concept of fair value as the basis for legitimate rates by holding that "the heart of the matter is that rates cannot be made to depend upon 'fair value' when the value of the going enterprise depends on earnings under whatever rates may be anticipated."[51] The statute involved in the case, the Natural Gas Act, provided that the rates fixed must be just and reasonable. The Court found this requirement highly flexible, with ample room for the exercise of administrative judgment. As spokesman for the Court, Justice Douglas did not directly say, as he had said with a minority group, that the Constitution, as distinguished from the statute, did not require that rates be reasonable, but people who thought otherwise could draw little comfort from the language which he did use.

All this indicates that due process, as a substantive restriction on governmental control of property, is largely a thing of the past or, at any rate, is not a thing of the present. Although it could be revived in the future without gross distortion of the current line of decisions, evidence of such a revival is not in sight. Due process remains in good standing in its orginal

[49] *Magnolia Petroleum Co.* v. *Hunt*, 320 U.S. 430, 462 (1944).

[50] *Federal Power Commission* v. *Hope Natural Gas Co.*, 320 U.S. 584, 601 (1944).

[51] *Ibid.*, p. 601.

procedural meaning, particularly as a check upon betrayal of the rights of the accused. There is no evidence that processes of erosion are operating in this field. There is evidence of erosion as far as the use of due process to insure judicial review of administrative rulings affecting property is concerned—a subject which will be discussed in the following chapter.

Superficially, and perhaps actually, even the substantive as well as the procedural characteristics of due process remain vital for the protection of civil liberties. On that point suffice it to say at the moment, however, that there may be design in the tendency of justices, when weighing the protection of civil liberties, to talk not specifically of due process of law but of the Fourteenth Amendment generally. It is possible that we shall eventually see the protection of civil liberties against state interference rested not upon the due process clause of the Fourteenth Amendment but upon a revived privileges and immunities clause or upon a composite of clauses, just as such protection against the federal government depends not upon due process of law but primarily upon the language of the First Amendment.

However that may be, we can say, by way of summary, that in the exercise of federal power over property the government is not now seriously handicapped by narrow judicial interpretation of federal powers for the purpose of protecting the jurisdiction of the states or by the restrictive power of substantive due process, which for a time constituted a formidable barrier, or by incidental restrictions, such as those requiring that direct taxes be apportioned and that indirect taxes be uniform and that private property should not be taken for public use without just compensation. As far as judicial restriction is concerned, the way is open, within the scope of the powers granted, to the exercise of such breadth of power as Congress and the President may deem necessary for the protection of the public welfare. The current changes in the process of judicial interpretation do not represent current distortions of the Constitution or efforts on the part of the justices to escape from their legitimate responsibilities. Instead, in a very real sense, particularly as far as the due process clauses of the Constitution are concerned, the Supreme Court is merely reverting to earlier conceptions of constitutional phraseology and of the place of the judiciary in the federal system. The judiciary has not been completely withdrawn from the picture. It remains for the enforcement of the clear mandate of the Constitution, but, to a large extent, a court is, and by its very nature must be, a restrictive institution. If such an institution not merely performs its legitimate powers but so exercises its power to obstruct as in effect to determine the course of exercise of positive power, it has ceased to perform the type of function for which it has been created and has made itself a positive agency of government. It has assumed responsibility for the performance of functions which it is not equipped to perform. The withdrawal of the Supreme Court from the excessive exercise of restraining power has the effect of restoring the proper relations among the three branches of the federal system. Under these circumstances it becomes possible for the legislative and executive branches of the government to exercise the powers conferred by the Constitution in terms of the will of the people as that will is expressed by electoral machinery and discovered by collateral devices for the measurement of public opinion.

It is true, of course, that the powers of government may be abused in spite of the legitimate checks which the three branches of government exercise upon one another. The exercise of all governmental power may develop into abuse. It is one of the prerogatives of democracy that the people, through their government with its constitutional safeguards, may exercise power wisely or with a lack of vision and judgment and receive the rewards or suffer the penalties of their action. It is a delusion of political thought that machinery of government can be so devised that it will operate adequately in the public interest even when run by men lacking in intelligence, sound judgment, and concern for the public welfare. Our constitutional problem is that of providing machinery which, when operated by carefully selected officials under the constant scrutiny of watchful people, will develop the political capacity of a participating citizenry and achieve a reasonably high degree of public service. Our present government, in terms of current interpretations of the judiciary, has tremendous power for exercise in the public interest. Whether, apart from the basic issue of the validity of the doctrine of the separation of powers, our system of government erected upon the Constitution is capable of adequate operation in the public interest and whether the needs for such scope of power can be justified in terms of the opposition to be met and the tasks to be performed are topics for further discussion.

VI

THE GROWTH OF ADMINISTRATIVE JUSTICE

"WE FEAR to grant power," Justice Holmes once said, "and are unwilling to recognize it when it exists."[1] The history of tyranny has been too well implanted in the minds of the American people and their awareness of the intoxicating effects of the possession of power upon their fellows is too immediate to permit facile delegation of broad powers to men by whom they might thereafter be oppressed. Hence we divide the powers which we reluctantly give and allocate them according to the principle of federalism. On a broad base we separate legislative, executive, and judicial departments and set them up as checks one upon the other. We directly elect our federal legislative officers for limited terms and indirectly elect our principal executive officer for a similarly limited term. We place constitutional and statutory restrictions upon the conduct of our so-called public servants and discuss, criticize, and castigate their official conduct as a further means of keeping them in the path of official rectitude. So well intrenched, indeed, are our attitude of suspicion and our habits of carefulness in such matters that we tend to forget that government exists not for the purpose of being kept in a straight jacket but for the purpose of exercising the powers conferred upon it.

The difficulty in harmonizing our feelings about the exercise of governmental power shows itself particularly in con-

[1] *Tyson* v. *Banton*, 273 U.S. 418, 445 (1927).

nection with the varied activities of many administrative agencies. Such agencies are not to be classified by means of the terms in which we portray the traditional three branches of government. Rather they incorporate in varying proportions characteristics of the three branches into integrated instruments for execution of the policies and programs which have run the gauntlet of consideration and criticism by at least the legislative and executive branches. As a rule, we do not greatly concern ourselves about the classification of administrative activities which are highly specialized and limited in scope. If a physician in a United States Marine Hospital diagnoses cases as patients arrive, directs their placement in particular wings of the hospital, gives instructions as to their care, performs operations on them, and subsequently releases them from the hospital, we do not attempt to segregate the legislative, executive, and judicial aspects of his duties. We assume that he has carried out policy determined by the legislative and executive branches of the government by an integration of conduct which may incidentally have legislative, executive, and judicial aspects. We do not demand the separation of the several aspects of conduct. We do not insist that the physician who makes a rule should have nothing to do with its enforcement. We do not assume that a physician who has made a diagnosis will, in doing so, have acquired a prejudice which unfits him for participation in treatment.

Our acceptance of the integration of functions in an administrative agency might well be the same even when the scale is larger. Congress, in enacting and amending the Interstate Commerce Act, and the President, in making, with senatorial approval, appointments to the Interstate Commerce Commission, have agreed upon a policy of regulating the operation and the rates of interstate railroads. The statute with varying degrees of definiteness indicates the kind of regulation desired and the general considerations in terms of which particular things are to be done. The Interstate Commerce Commission, through its hundreds of employees, keeps in touch with ever changing conditions and issues such orders and takes such steps to enforce them as are necessary to the execution of the policy which Congress has outlined. The fact that the Commission has to make rules in order to execute policies, that in many respects its activities resemble those of any executive office, and that it has to determine questions of right much as courts have to determine them does not make it a substitute for the legislative, executive, or judicial branches of the government. Rather it is the instrument of those branches, or of one or more of them, for the doing of those things which could be done less well or could not be done at all in the event of absolute separation of those functions which seem legislative, executive, and judicial.

Much the same generalization could be made as to large numbers of administrative agencies in the federal government which have a degree of immunity from control or which make up the several executive departments. If we look at only those which are smaller and more highly specialized or if we look singly at the larger ones, the integration of legislative, executive, and judicial characteristics does not seem disturbing. If, on the other hand, we group them together and, particularly, if we get involved in an attempt to discover or perhaps to protect private rights by making contact in the right way with the right officials of the right organizations, we are quickly impressed with what has been called the wonderland of American bureaucracy and with the apparent fact that legislative, executive, and judicial powers, instead of being separated in the federal government as the textbooks tell us, are entangled in a seemingly hopeless maze. Congress seems often to have abdicated important legislative powers in favor of agencies unknown to the electorate; the Executive seems threatened with obstruction and defeat by commissions not subject to its control; and the judiciary seems to have been short-circuited out of the system. Because of the confusion in our thinking on these matters, it is important that we appraise the success of the operators of our constitutional system in evolving machinery for the execution of the powers given by the Constitution without violating the basic safeguards of the separation of powers.

Examples of merging in one office or agency powers which had at least two of the three types of governmental characteristics can be found all the way back to the beginning of our national history. Few questions seem to have been raised about such mergers except as to the power of the President to interfere with executive officers in their performance of duties laid upon them directly by Congress. On this point, although the power of the President to remove any executive officer has been upheld,[2] the power of Congress to impose duties with which the President cannot interfere has also been upheld.[3]

American consciousness of the problems of administrative justice was developed largely in connection with the independent regulatory commissions. In appraising the Interstate Commerce Commission, which was established in 1887, and the Federal Trade Commission, which was established in 1914, the Supreme Court seems to have viewed the agencies as necessary, if somewhat anomalous, instruments for achievement of governmental ends and not to have concerned itself greatly, in the early years at least, with the exact nature of the powers allotted to them. For many years neither the Supreme Court nor anyone else in authority gave much atten-

[2] *Myers* v. *United States,* 272 U.S. 52 (1926).

[3] *Kendall* v. *United States* ex rel. *Stokes,* 12 Peters 524 (1838).

tion to theoretical diagnosis. Robert E. Cushman has picked out at random the following conflicting characterizations of the Interstate Commerce Commission. It is "in essence a judicial tribunal." It is "not a court. It is an administrative body." It is "not a part of the executive branch of this government; but is really the arm of Congress." It is "an executive body." It is "a purely administrative body." Its function "is wholly legislative." It has "only executive power."[4] Because reference to the powers of the independent regulatory commissions as legislative or judicial seemed to imply violation of the principle of the separation of powers and hence violation of the Constitution, the custom was gradually evolved of referring to those powers as quasi-legislative and quasi-judicial. Commissioner Joseph B. Eastman declared that the duties performed by the Interstate Commerce Commission were "primarily quasi-legislative. It is the procedure which is judicial. We exercise very few strictly judicial functions."[5]

While it is clear that for many years the Supreme Court tolerated these novel agencies reluctantly, it showed its distrust largely by narrow interpretations of their powers and by asserting broad power of judicial review over their activities. By the time the New Deal President and his "brain trust" had infiltrated the executive branch of the government with a great variety of types of new agencies which were subject directly to presidential control, the older independent regulatory commissions had won a degree of judicial tolerance and were much less subject to judicial suspicion than the aggregation of new executive offspring. This fact was probably quite as important as were principles of law or constitutionality in

[4] See Robert E. Cushman, *The Independent Regulatory Commissions* (1941), p. 418.

[5] *Reorganization of Government Agencies: Hearings of the Senate Select Committee on Government Organization on S. 2700* (75th Cong., 1st sess.), p. 178.

leading the Supreme Court to protect personnel of the commissions against removal by the President.

It will be recalled that, in establishing the independent regulatory commissions, Congress had devised the scheme of securing continuity of policy and minimizing "political" interference by arranging that appointments should be for relatively long periods, usually for seven years, and that the dates of their expiration should be staggered and that members should be subject to removal by the President only for specified causes. Republican Presidents had fretted under this restraint but had been unable directly to escape it. Even so, by the making of a series of appointments to the Federal Trade Commission over a period of years, Presidents Harding and Coolidge are said so to have changed the attitude of that agency that its drive against monopoly "dwindled into a mere campaign against false advertising."[6] One of the commissioners chosen to make the Federal Trade Commission safe for business was William E. Humphrey, who was appointed by President Coolidge and reappointed by President Hoover. His sympathies, naturally enough, were completely out of line with the New Deal program. President Roosevelt asked Humphrey for his resignation, saying that "I feel the aims and purposes of the administration with respect to the work of the Commission can be carried out most effectively with personnel of my own selection."[7] Humphrey refused to resign. Thereupon the President's advisers impressed upon him the language of the Supreme Court in the Myers case, decided in 1926, wherein, in holding that the President had power to remove a postmaster in spite of congressional restriction, the Court had gone beyond the case at hand to say that the President was not debarred from removing members of executive

---

[6] James M. Landis, *The Administrative Process* (1938), p. 113.

[7] *New York Times*, October 8, 1933.

tribunals even though duties of a quasi-judicial character were imposed upon them. "Otherwise," wrote Chief Justice Taft, "he does not discharge his own constitutional duty of seeing that the laws be faithfully executed."[8] Fortified by this opinion, the President removed Humphrey from office, and Humphrey contested the removal by bringing suit for his salary. When the Supreme Court decided the case in 1935, at a time when the chaos of New Deal administration was uppermost in the minds of the judiciary, it held unanimously that the President had no constitutional power to remove a member of the Federal Trade Commission in violation of an act of Congress. Said Justice Sutherland for the Court:

> The Federal Trade Commission is an administrative body created by Congress to carry into effect legislative policies embodied in the statute, in accordance with the legislative standard therein prescribed, and to perform other specified duties as a legislative or as a judicial aid. Such a body cannot in any proper sense be characterized as an arm or an eye of the executive. Its duties are performed without executive leave and, in the contemplation of the statute, must be free from executive control.[9]

And again:

> The authority of Congress, in creating quasi-legislative or quasi-judicial agencies, to require them to act in discharge of their duties independently of executive control, cannot well be doubted; and that authority includes, as an appropriate incident, power to fix the period during which they shall continue, and to forbid their removal except for cause in the meantime. For it is quite evident that one who holds his office only during the pleasure of another cannot be depended upon to maintain an attitude of independence against the latter's will.[10]

This decision is probably less illuminating as to the principle of the separation of powers than as to the determination of the Supreme Court in this particular period to exert all possible checks upon a President who was accused of yearning for dic-

[8] *Myers* v. *United States*, 272 U.S. 52, 135 (1926).

[9] *Humphrey's Executor* v. *United States*, 295 U.S. 602, 628 (1935).

[10] *Ibid.*, p. 629.

tatorship and whose administration was probably justly condemned for a lack of proper concern about the orderly processes of law. If the President recognized this fact, however, he showed no inclination to bow to the will of the judiciary. He and his advisers took the position that the successful operation of the government of the United States required the integration of all policy-making agencies or, rather, the integration of all executive action which reflected the policy of the government. He admitted, at least privately, that the chaotic organization of the government during the early years of his administration was a legitimate ground of attack, and he sought to remove the defects by the appointment of what came to be known as the President's Committee on Administrative Management to make recommendations for streamlining the government. In making its report, the Committee wrote as follows concerning the independent regulatory commissions:

They are in reality miniature independent governments set up to deal with the railroad problem, the banking problem, or the radio problem. They constitute a headless "fourth branch" of the Government, a haphazard deposit of irresponsible agencies and uncoordinated powers. They do violence to the basic theory of the American Constitution that there should be three major branches of the Government and only three. The Congress has found no effective way of supervising them, they cannot be controlled by the President, and they are answerable to the courts only in respect to the legality of their activities.[11]

And again:

It would be more accurate to call them the "irresponsible" regulatory commissions, for they are areas of unaccountability.[12]

This attack upon the independent regulatory commissions brought a response only less vigorous than that brought by the

[11] President's Committee on Administrative Management, *Report of the Committee with Studies of Administrative Management in the Federal Government* (1937), p. 39.

[12] *Ibid.*, p. 40.

challenge to the independence of the judiciary which was embodied in the plan to appoint new justices of the Supreme Court to sit alongside incumbent justices who had reached the age of retirement but had failed to retire. The position of the President and of his Committee on Administrative Management was probably not generally understood. A healthy suspicion of too much concentration of power in a few hands was sufficient to counterbalance the logic of the argument that administration needed to be systematized and co-ordinated if the government was to perform adequate service to society. At any rate, not only did Congress refuse to strip away from the commissions for lodgment in the executive branch of the government all except their judicial functions, but it also postponed action on clearly legitimate recommendations which had been vitiated by association with the attack upon the commissions. Most of the several commissions, therefore, retained their integrity as far as the grouping of their functions is concerned, and their personnel remained immune from presidential removal except for causes specified by statute. Another fact is significant, however. Although a number of additional independent regulatory commissions were created during the early years of the New Deal, that type of development, for the time being at least, has come to an end. President Roosevelt and his advisers had seen fit to bring about the necessary expansion of governmental organization not by means of independent agencies but of agencies which are fully subject to executive control.

Even before the New Deal clash over the independence of the regulatory commissions, the merging of functions was taking place on a large scale in agencies lodged within executive establishments where personnel was subject to executive control. To give one of scores of examples, the Packers and Stockyards Act of 1921 authorized the Secretary of Agriculture to fix maximum rates to be charged by market agencies for buying and selling livestock. Under the statute, therefore, the Secretary performed a mixture of rule-making and adjudicatory functions. Even though the Secretary was a politically selected officer whom the President had the legal power to remove at any time, the constitutionality of the allotment of mixed functions to him was not seriously questioned. Serious questions were involved, however, as to the reviewability of the decisions made by him. Clearly the rates fixed by the Secretary were limited by the restriction of due process that the rates fixed must be reasonable—that is, they were then so limited to the extent to which that rule prevailed. It may be questioned, indeed, whether the restrictions as to rate-making, which have already been discussed, did not derive a considerable amount of impetus from suspicion of the anomalous character of the various state and federal regulatory agencies. While there was too general a belief in the desirability of freedom from regulation to justify the conclusion that, had Congress and the state legislatures themselves been able to fix schedules of rates, the courts would have refrained from the exercise of restrictive power, we are probably justified in believing that the situation was much aggravated by the fact that it was necessary to delegate rate-fixing powers to agencies which had no proper progenitors in our governmental system.

The distrust of regulatory agencies, which are neither legislatures nor courts but which, nevertheless, make rules and adjudicate, has many facets. These unholy combinations are said to violate the principle of the separation of powers and therefore to invite tyranny. Their use is said to deny the right of access to an impartial tribunal. As far as judicial action is concerned, the conviction of many people and of almost all lawyers is that such impartiality is possible only in a tribunal made up of lawyers and organized as a court. The tradition of the judiciary and the watchfulness of the bar, it is said, insure a degree of rectitude which cannot be assumed in an agency of any other kind. Agencies which are not courts are said to lack the tradition of impartiality which characterizes the courts, and they are not coerced into adherence to standards of impartial conduct by the watchfulness of a profession which they represent. The courts are said to be freed from the temptation to bias by the divorcement of adjudication from the controversial task of prosecution, whereas administrative agencies combine within themselves the functions of fact-finding, prosecution, and adjudication, with consequent perversion of the course of justice. The harsher critics of administrative agencies, therefore, argue for the curtailment of their powers and insist upon judicial review of their proceedings at every possible point. The courts have sought to chart a middle path between complete redetermination of the work of administrative agencies, on the one hand, and the complete acceptance of that work, on the other. The rule which seems most nearly to satisfy them is that the courts will not seek to redetermine the law and facts in a given case if there seems to be reasonable evidence upon which the determinations might be based but that, as specialists in law, they will examine administrative determinations of legal questions. In other words, they have applied to the administrative-judicial relationships the principle of differentiating between facts and law which has traditionally been applied within the courts themselves, in which juries are accepted as authorities upon facts and questions of law are left to the judge. If the principle is clear, however, the application is often difficult. Facts and law are often inextricably entangled. Judges who have a profound distrust of what they regard as undisciplined and dangerous mongrel agencies have no great difficulty in manipulating review of law in such a way as to substitute their own judgment of the facts for that of the administrative agency. The result may be the loss of benefit of action by an agency that can move more expeditiously than a court and loss of the benefit of the specialized knowledge and understanding of the specialists who make up or who serve administrative agencies.

A watchful Supreme Court has hedged with further restrictions the principle as to the division of authority between courts and administrative agencies by holding that facts are immune to judicial redetermination when the very jurisdiction of the court in the particular case turns on questions of fact. This restriction provided the occasion for an important clash between opposing groups on the Supreme Court in the decision of *Crowell* v. *Benson*[13] in 1932. The case involved an award made to Benson by Crowell, an administrator under a federal workmen's compensation law. The application of the statute, and hence the jurisdiction of the lower federal court, turned upon the questions of fact as to whether Benson was on board ship or ashore when he was injured and whether he was in good standing as an employee at that time. The Supreme Court, speaking through Chief Justice Hughes, took the position that, since the jurisdiction of the Court depended upon these questions of fact, their final determination did not have to be left to the administrator but rather was subject to redetermination by the Court. Justice Brandeis, with the concurrence of Justices Stone and Roberts, made such a powerful attack upon this position in a dissenting opinion that the validity of this judicial inroad upon the area of administrative responsibility has been widely challenged.

An even broader ground for judicial interference with administrative findings of fact is the principle that a court may redetermine the facts when a constitutional right depends upon them. During the long period in which it was held that the

[13] 285 U.S. 22 (1932).

Constitution required rates fixed by government to be high enough to yield a fair return on a fair value, the facts concerning value were, in terms of this principle, left open to redetermination by the judiciary. This principle brought another clash between Chief Justice Hughes as spokesman for the Supreme Court and Justice Brandeis as spokesman for a liberal minority in 1936 in the St. Joseph Stock Yards case.[14] Once more the powerful blows of the dissenting justices had the effect of highlighting the majority as unfairly limiting the legitimate powers of administrative agencies.

Early in the New Deal period the Supreme Court also had to decide important cases affecting the powers of administrative agencies in terms of the principle that legislative power may not be delegated. As far as the federal government is concerned, the principle is not derived from specific language in the Constitution. Rather it is an importation out of the dim regions of antiquity. Although the Supreme Court had long paid lip service to the principle, it had not, prior to 1935, held any act of Congress unconstitutional on this ground. Instead it had recognized the practical necessity for the delegation of rule-making power and had sanctioned such delegation by avoiding the classification of the rules made by subordinate bodies as legislation.

Some of the early New Deal statutes, however, went much further than Congress had ever gone before in delegating to the President or to some administrative agency broad discretion as to the rules which were to be made. Although the *Congressional Record* reveals only one instance wherein a member of Congress proclaimed "In Roosevelt I trust," and boasted of the fact that he was voting for a bill submitted by the White House without having read it, it is clear that many legislators became for a time little more than rubber stamps of the Pres-

---

[14] *St. Joseph Stock Yards Co. v. United States,* 298 U.S. 38 (1936).

ident for sanctioning whatever measures he chose to propose. Many of the administrative agencies set up under the broad grants of power which were enacted during this period showed a lack of consideration for careful procedure which was shocking to the orderly minds of Supreme Court justices. The first important test of the constitutionality of the delegation of legislative power under the New Deal was made in the so-called Hot Oil cases,[15] the argument of which disclosed disgracefully slipshod procedure in the process of administrative rule-making.[16] The case had to do with a provision of the National Industrial Recovery Act which authorized the President at his discretion to prohibit the shipment in interstate commerce of oil which had been produced in excess of production quotas set up by the producing states. The statute did not define the circumstances under which the President was to act or require that he state the facts which led to action on his part. The Supreme Court held that this provision of the statute provided for an unconstitutional delegation of legislative power to the President, taking the position, apparently, that due process of law required adherence to a specific type of procedure when the delegated power was exercised:

To repeat, we are concerned with the question of the delegation of legislative power. If the citizen is to be punished for the crime of violating a legislative order of an executive officer, or of a board or commission, due process of law requires that it shall appear that the order is within the authority of the officer, board or commission, and, if that authority depends on determinations of fact, those determinations must be shown.[17]

Only Justice Cardozo dissented, arguing that the context of the provision of the statute provided adequate standards to

[15] *Panama Refining Co.* v. *Ryan*, 293 U.S. 388 (1935).

[16] See Carl B. Swisher, *American Constitutional Development* (1943), pp. 925-26.

[17] *Panama Refining Co.* v. *Ryan*, 293 U.S. 388, 432 (1935).

ward off a conclusion that legislative power was unconstitutionally delegated.

In May, 1935, after the disclosure of additional embarrassing information as to slipshod procedure on the part of New Deal administrators, the Supreme Court decided the Schechter case,[18] in which it held unconstitutional the provisions of the National Industrial Recovery Act which delegated broad legislative power to code-making authorities. Without explaining what was meant by "fair competition," the statute authorized the adoption of codes of fair competition which were to have the force of law and it outlawed as unfair whatever methods of competition were not in harmony with the codes. While admitting the necessity of adapting legislation to complex conditions involving a host of details with which Congress could not deal directly, Chief Justice Hughes, again speaking for the Court, insisted that Congress was not permitted to abdicate or transfer to others the essential legislative functions with which it was vested. "Congress cannot delegate legislative power to the President to exercise an unfettered discretion to make whatever laws he thinks may be needed or advisable for the rehabilitation and expansion of trade or industry."[19] Justice Cardozo wrote a concurring opinion, in which he analyzed the delegation made by the statute and declared: "This is delegation running riot. No such plenitude of power is susceptible of transfer."[20]

A year later, in May, 1936, in *Carter* v. *Carter Coal Company*,[21] the Supreme Court condemned as an unconstitutional delegation of legislative power a provision of the Bituminous Coal Conservation Act of 1935 by which producers of more than two-thirds of the coal mined in an area were authorized

[18] *Schechter* v. *United States*, 295 U.S. 495 (1935).

[19] *Ibid.*, pp. 537–38.

[20] *Ibid.*, p. 553.   [21] 298 U.S. 238 (1936).

to fix maximum hours and minimum wages for all mining done within respective areas. Said Justice Sutherland:

> The power conferred upon the majority is, in effect, the power to regulate the affairs of an unwilling minority. This is legislative delegation in its most obnoxious form; for it is not even delegation to an official or an official body, presumptively disinterested, but to private persons whose interests may be and often are adverse to the interests of others in the same business.[22]

Since 1936, no act of Congress has been held unconstitutional because of its delegation of legislative power. The explanation probably lies in three factors. The first is that changes in personnel on the Supreme Court have brought a more tolerant judicial attitude toward the exercise of administrative discretion. The second is that, until the beginning of the recent war, Congress exercised greater care in circumscribing its delegations of power as a result of judicial criticism. The third factor is the war itself, with the flexible conduct of which the Supreme Court was most reluctant to interfere.

Delegation during the war period will be discussed further along. An illustration of the change in the character of legislation and the corresponding change in the attitude of the Supreme Court toward delegation in the pre-war period is to be found in *Currin* v. *Wallace*,[23] which was decided in 1939. The case involved application of the Tobacco Inspection Act of 1935 which authorized the Secretary of Agriculture to investigate the handling, inspection, and marketing of tobacco and to establish standards by which types, grades, prices, and conditions of tobacco shipped in interstate commerce could be determined. This grading of tobacco was intended to make it easier for growers to estimate the value of their tobacco and

[22] *Ibid.*, p. 311.
[23] 306 U.S. 1 (1939).

hence easier for them to estimate the value of their product. The rules worked out by the Secretary of Agriculture were to apply only to those markets in which their application was favored by two-thirds of the growers of the market area who voted at a prescribed referendum. The statute was challenged as providing for an unconstitutional delegation of legislative power to the Secretary of Agriculture and to those growers upon whose votes the application of the statute depended. As to the Secretary, Justice Roberts held for the Court that his discretion was limited by the prescription of adequate standards so that the delegation was not unconstitutional. The question of the delegation to two-thirds or more of the growers voting at a prescribed referendum may have seemed more difficult because of the language of the Supreme Court in the Carter case denouncing delegation of power to fix maximum hours and minimum wages to only part of the operators and miners in a particular area. In the tobacco case, however, the growers did not fix marketing standards but merely took action in terms of which it was decided whether the standards fixed by the Secretary of Agriculture should apply. Said Justice Roberts:

So far as growers of tobacco are concerned, the required referendum does not involve any delegation of legislative authority. Congress has merely placed a restriction upon its own regulation by withholding its operation as to a given market "unless two-thirds of the growers voting favor it."[24]

Many other cases arose between 1936 and the beginning of the second World War in which the delegation of legislative power was challenged; but more careful legislative draftsmanship, coupled with changed judicial attitudes, gave protection to the delegations in question. The Supreme Court continued to exert an important influence, however, by decisions in

[24] *Ibid.*, p. 15.

which it sought to coerce administrative procedure into the channels of essential fairness to the regulated interests. As a result of the much-discussed Morgan cases[25] and others, it began to appear that the requirements of notice and hearing were constitutional requirements for administrative rule-making to the extent that administrative rules had to take shape out of procedure which was virtually judicial in character. In other words, the area of conflict over the delegation of legislative power shifted from the question of the constitutionality of the delegation itself to that of the constitutionality of the procedure by which administrative rules were evolved and given the force of law.

This change in the relation of the Supreme Court to administrative agencies suggests the change in attitude toward such agencies which has taken place widely among their critics. Whereas in earlier years attempts were made either to prevent the development of such agencies or to curtail their powers to the point of ineffectiveness, the tendency now is to accept them and build them in such a way that they can perform their functions without the perpetration of serious abuses. Some such change has characterized the attitude even of the American Bar Association, which, since the beginnings of the New Deal, has been deeply concerned about the growth of the power of administrative agencies. The attitude of the first chairman of the Association's Committee on Administrative Law is reflected in his characterization of an administrative tribunal as "something that looks like a court and acts like a court but somehow escapes being classified as a court whenever you attempt to impose any limitations on its power."[26] For a number of years the committee worked on a

[25] See *Morgan v. United States*, 298 U.S. 468 (1936); 304 U.S. 1 (1938); and *United States v. Morgan*, 307 U.S. 183 (1939); 313 U.S. 409 (1941).

[26] *Report of the Fifty-sixth Meeting of the American Bar Association* .... *1933*, LVIII, 197.

plan to develop in Washington an administrative court or courts to which would be transferred the great mass of adjudicating functions hitherto performed by the great variety of administrative agencies in the federal government. Failing to get adequate support for such a project, the committee then shifted its ground and supported what came to be known as the Walter-Logan Bill, which was intended to systematize procedure in administrative agencies, curtail their powers, and provide broadly for judicial review of their activities. The Senate committee on the judiciary explained the bill in the following language:

> The basic purpose of this administrative-law bill is to stem and, if possible, to reverse the drift into parliamentarism which, if it should succeed in any substantial degree in this country, could but result in totalitarianism with complete destruction of the division of governmental power between the federal and the state governments and with the entire subordination of both the legislative and judicial branches of the federal government to the executive branch wherein are included the administrative agencies and tribunals of that government. This drift has become very pronounced during the past fifty years with the increasing complexity of social and economic problems.[27]

When Congress passed the bill in December, 1940, the President returned it with an indignant veto message in which he defended administrative agencies and denounced lawyers who saw the administrative tribunal encroaching upon their exclusive prerogatives and powerful interests which were opposed to reforms that could be made effective only through the use of the administrative tribunal. A large part of the legal profession, he declared, had never reconciled itself to the existence of the administrative tribunal.

> Many of them prefer the stately ritual of the courts, in which lawyers play all the speaking parts, to the simple procedure of administrative hearings which a client can understand and even participate in. Many

[27] *Senate Report No. 442* (76th Cong., 1st sess.), p. 5.

of the lawyers prefer that decision be influenced by a shrewd play upon technical rules of evidence in which the lawyers are the only experts, although they always disagree. Many of the lawyers still prefer to distinguish precedent and to juggle leading cases rather than to get down to the merits of the efforts in which their clients are engaged. For years such lawyers have led a persistent fight against the administrative tribunal. . . . . The very heart of modern reform administration is the administrative tribunal. Great interests, therefore, which desire to escape regulation rightly see that if they can strike at the heart of modern reform by sterilizing the administrative tribunal which administers them they will have effectively destroyed the reform itself.[28]

The bill was not passed over the President's veto.

In the meantime a committee known as the Attorney-General's Committee on Administrative Procedure had been making a thorough study of the operation of diverse administrative agencies of the federal government. Early in 1941 it made a comprehensive and illuminating report on the subject,[29] with recommendations as to legislation which would bring about a certain amount of order without defeating the purposes for which administrative agencies were established. Preoccupation with national defense, however, and then with the second World War brought indefinite postponement of general legislation on the subject.

In spite of the failure of Congress and of the President to agree on legislation for sweeping administrative reform, however, some improvement had been taking place since the chaotic period of the early years of the New Deal. Reacting to the charge that it was virtually impossible to discover the content of the great body of law being made from day to day in administrative agencies, Congress provided for the establishment of the *Federal Register*, wherein orders and rules of general applicability which had the force of law were to be pub-

[28] *Congressional Record*, LXXXVI, 13942–943.

[29] *Administrative Procedure in Government Agencies* (Senate Doc. 8 [77th Cong., 1st sess.]).

lished as they were issued. In addition, Congress provided for the compilation of a *Code of Federal Regulations*, which was to be compiled after the fashion of the *United States Code* and kept up to date by the issue of periodic supplements. Under the lash of criticism from the Supreme Court, Congress prescribed more carefully the procedure of new administrative agencies as they were established.

Furthermore, a number of administrative agencies of their own initiative sought to improve procedure in the interest of more adequate justice. The Secretary of Agriculture made it known that, without waiting for criticism from the Supreme Court, the Department of Agriculture, in the administration of the Packers and Stockyards Act, had worked out careful procedure as to the use of examiners' reports and had brought about segregation of prosecuting and judicial functions.[30] In its annual report for 1941, the Securities and Exchange Commission stated that it was an invariable rule that an attorney assigned to prepare an opinion for the Commission must not have had any connection with any previous phase of the case with which the opinion dealt. Furthermore, the writer of the opinion was subject to the following instructions:

In no cases assigned for the preparation of opinions should the attorney confer with the attorneys who have been responsible for the preparation or prosecution of the proceeding. . . . . It is just as improper to consult employees of the Commission who have taken part in the proceedings as it would be to consult attorneys for the respondent. Even on formal or procedural matters not concerned with the merits of the case, attorneys should consult the supervising attorney and allow him to make any inquiries from other divisions of the Commission which may be necessary. The same inflexible rule must apply to consultation with the trial examiner.[31]

[30] See the letter of Henry A. Wallace to the Editor, *New York Times*, May 8, 1938.

[31] *Seventh Annual Report of the Securities and Exchange Commission* . . . . *1941*, p. 225.

So many agencies, indeed, have adopted procedure for the separation of prosecuting and judicial functions that a careful student of administration could say in 1941 that the commingling of these functions in a single pair of hands in a literal sense "practically never exists in the federal administrative machine."[32]

Many regulatory agencies, including particularly some of the independent regulatory commissions, have established traditions of careful and fair operations and have developed internal discipline comparable to that of the courts. When Congress directs the Federal Power Commission to fix rates for the interstate sale of natural gas which are "just and reasonable," and prescribes in a general way standards which include approximately the requirements that a fair return shall be provided on the basis of the prudent investment scheme of valuation, the Commission may be expected to exercise a scrupulousness in its search for what is "just and reasonable" comparable to that which would be exercised by a court. No necessary disregard of private rights is involved, therefore, when the Supreme Court says with seeming casualness that "since there are no constitutional requirements more exacting than the standards of the act, a rate order which conforms to the latter does not run afoul of the former."[33]

Another type of limitation on the scope of judicial review which has recently been upheld offers no necessary shock to our traditions. Congress authorized the National Mediation Board to take certain steps toward the settlement of disputes between railroad employers and employees. As the Supreme Court interpreted the statute, "the dispute was to reach its last terminal point when the administrative finding was made.

[32] Walter Gellhorn, *Federal Administrative Proceedings* (1941), p. 20.

[33] *Federal Power Commission* v. *Hope Natural Gas Co.*, 320 U.S. 591, 607 (1944).

There was to be no dragging out of the controversy into other tribunals of law."[34] Since no right of judicial review had been provided by Congress, the Supreme Court would not furnish it in a case of this kind, even though questions of law might be involved.

It seems clear that many of the problems of the establishment and control of administrative agencies in such a way that they can fit properly into our system of government, and perform without serious abuse the many functions to be performed by them, were on their way toward constructive solutions when the outbreak of the second World War once more precipitated something approximating governmental chaos in Washington. To facilitate the conduct of the war, Congress once more made sweeping delegations of power to the President and to subordinate agencies without careful prescription of the condition under which the powers were to be exercised. The President delegated his own power or redelegated that given by Congress—usually failing to distinguish between the two sources—with a similar lack of concern for standards. Agencies which, under the pressure of the reform movement, had made use of the *Federal Register* to keep the public informed as to their procedure and activities in many instances took advantage of the war situation to justify withholding such information. "The mimeograph has superseded the *Federal Register*," said the American Bar Association's reconstituted special committee on administrative law in its 1943 report, "and the Office of War Information has attempted to limit both the output of professed information and the maintenance of mailing lists."[35] The committee described the situation in Washington in part as follows:

[34] *Switchmen's Union* v. *National Mediation Board*, 320 U.S. 297, 305 (1943).

[35] *Annual Report of the American Bar Association . . . . 1943*, LXVIII, 250.

At present, particularly with wartime or emergency agencies but affecting also the regular establishments, there is a maze of interrelated and interlocking organizations, independent and departmental agencies, presidential and statutory offices, coordinators and conciliators, committees and boards, agencies "in" but not "of" departments, general delegations of broad statutory powers, and enlarged agency staffs which change daily in their internal organization.

As a result the citizen often not only does not know where to go or what to do but, even if he does go some place and do something, the problem of getting an authoritative decision is often appalling and results impossible. The system too frequently operates to prevent action and it thus is the very antithesis of that flexibility and adaptation which is cited as a basic reason for the existence of administrative justice. The frustration of the citizen in this condition is reflected in public agencies themselves. One agency is pitted against another. It is difficult for Congress itself to discover the precise administrative set-ups which it attempts to investigate on many fronts.[36]

While the traditional attitude of the American Bar Association toward administrative agencies has been such as to suggest the inevitability of bias in the committee's report, evidence from many quarters indicates that the report is well substantiated in fact. Even though the defense may be offered that what has been done is largely justified in terms of the over-all success of the government in running the war, the fact remains that, for the preservation of the rights of individuals and groups, it will be necessary as quickly as possible to reestablish orderly government as it existed before the war and to continue thereafter with efforts further to improve our administrative mechanism.

Few decisions of the Supreme Court have dealt as yet with administrative activities connected directly with the war. Those that can be cited uphold broad delegations of legislative power, curtailment of the right of judicial review, and great flexibility in the process of making administrative rules which have the force of law. Two of them require mention. In

[36] *Ibid.*

Yakus v. *United States*,[37] the Supreme Court gave its sanction to the Emergency Price Control Act, which sought to prevent inflation by authorizing an administrator to fix maximum prices which should be "fair and equitable" and which should "in his judgment" effect the purposes of the act. The right of judicial review of the orders of the administrator was limited to delayed action, without the right of injunction, before an Emergency Court of Appeals for which the act provided. Judicial approval of the discretionary exercise of governmental power over prices, as given in this case, was breathtaking in its sweep, by contrast with decisions of even merely a decade earlier, when five of the nine judges had daringly upheld the power of a state to fix minimum prices for the sale of milk.[38]

In the other case, *Bowles* v. *Willingham*,[39] the Supreme Court upheld the provisions of the Emergency Price Control Act which authorized the administrator to fix maximum rents in areas which he was empowered to determine and to designate as defense-rental areas. Little was said in the statute to limit the discretion of the administrator in designating the areas or in fixing the rents. The Court held that the general language of the statute gave sufficient guidance to the activities of the administrator to protect the delegation of legislative power against the charge of unconstitutionality. It held that the statute did not violate due process in authorizing the administrator to fix rents without first providing a hearing to landlords, particularly in view of the fact that the right of judicial review was provided. It held that price control did not constitute a "taking" of property, that it might reduce the value of the property without being unconstitutional for that

[37] 321 U.S. 414 (1944).

[38] See *Nebbia* v. *New York*, 291 U.S. 502 (1934).

[39] 321 U.S. 503 (1944).

reason, and that "a nation which can demand the lives of its men and women in the waging of that war is under no constitutional necessity of providing a system of price control on the domestic front which will assure each landlord a 'fair return' on his property."[40]

This brief statement about the content of these two decisions indicates the extent of the power which the present Supreme Court is willing to sanction in the hands of administrators in time of war. Much of the language of the two opinions of the Court, furthermore, indicates that it is not the war power alone but a revised judicial attitude generally toward the exercise of administrative power that is now determining the course of Supreme Court decisions. If this is true and if the functions of the federal government continue to expand in the future as the course of events seems to promise and if Congress and the President continue to establish and expand administrative agencies and endow them with sweeping powers, the task of disciplining such agencies and keeping their conduct in line with our fundamental conceptions of justice will be one of the most difficult and important that the government and the people have to face. If the functions which we allocate to them are to be performed, the agencies are essential, but we must use them and not be used by them. Like the industrial mechanism which provides us with the material good things of life, they must be made our servants and not our masters. The solution calls for wisdom and skill on the part of our chosen representatives and for eternal watchfulness and criticism on the part of the people. To put the matter in other language, Congress and the President must have arms and hands of the sort of the agencies which we have been discussing, if they are to perform the functions which we demand of them. But the arms and the hands are not to be

[40] *Ibid.*, p. 519.

permitted to become independent centers of power and to make war one upon the other or upon the central agencies of government or to transform themselves from the category of servants of the people into that of the people's masters. Nor are agencies or aggregations of agencies to be permitted to transform themselves into lethargic obstructions to intelligent efforts to promote the public welfare. They must be kept animated, humble, and under control. Under other circumstances they become a menace to the welfare which they exist to promote and to preserve.

VII

THE TRAVAIL OF LIBERTY

*

OVER a period of some centuries of Anglo-American history the word "constitution" has had peculiarly close association with concepts of liberty, freedom, and rightness. This association grew out of the fact that the English people, as might be expected, were particularly aware of those features of their constitution which were undergoing important change and that the course of English constitutional development was that of erecting barriers against the royal executive for the protection of the rights and liberties of the people. The founders of government in the United States brought with them from England a liberty-loving heritage and a consciousness of the ever looming threat of governmental tyranny. In the atmosphere of frontier freedom they pushed restraint upon royalty to its logical outcome of abolishing royalty altogether. They incorporated in our Constitution restrictions upon the exercise of governmental power which the English Constitution had contained and still others which had at that time achieved in the mother-country the status only of nebulous aspirations.

In the presence of resources of unparalleled richness, and largely isolated from the menace of attack by external enemies, the American people prospered for a century or more after the adoption of the Constitution under a regime of restricted government and growing business enterprise. Then, with a steadily increasing momentum, the exercise of governmental power expanded to place checks upon gigantic

155

business interests, to promote the welfare of individuals in a society now dominated by mass-production enterprise, and to wage war as war can be waged only in a highly industrialized world. The changed and changing position of government in society and the regimentation of life in traditional areas of freedom offer a challenge to old conceptions of liberty and call for re-examination of the essential values which we seek to preserve under our constitutional system.

In the interest of perspective, it should be repeated that the principal function of the Constitution of the United States, as, indeed, of any constitution, is to give power. Government exists for the purpose of exercising power. But for that purpose, the existence of government could not be justified. Having provided for the exercise of power, however, it is a secondary but nevertheless a tremendously important function of our Constitution, and of other constitutions representing ideals similar to our own, so to channel and limit the exercise of power that government shall be prevented from doing things which it ought not to do and from doing legitimate things in illegitimate ways. As to the latter, the Constitution provides, for example, that, in taking life, liberty, or property, the procedure of both state and federal governments shall be in terms of due process of law and that in federal courts trials shall be by jury, etc. As to the former, Congress is forbidden to prohibit the free exercise of religion and to abridge the freedom of speech or of the press or the right of assembly; while the same prohibitions operate against the states through the more general language of the Fourteenth Amendment.

Since the powers delegated to the federal government were assumed to be limited to those given by the grants phrased in the Constitution, it was originally assumed that few constitutional prohibitions needed to be laid upon the federal government. It will be recalled that, in the judgment of many reputable statesmen, there was no point at all in including a bill of rights in a document which conferred only the powers specified and which certainly did not include authority to do the things which were customarily forbidden in bills of rights. The first ten amendments were added to the Constitution, therefore, only to soothe the fears of an uneasy minority.

Caught, however, in the tide of expansion of population, territory, and economic enterprise, the constitutional system, with its broad grants of authority, expanded with the growth of the social and economic order. The powers delegated to the federal government grew from rivulets to rivers and became the constitutional sources for the exercise of such sweeping governmental power as the world has seldom seen. Against this expansion of power have stood the interests which sought to avoid regulation by the use of any and all constitutional arguments, including those based on the constitutional amendments. Particularly through the concept of freedom of contract, which is not mentioned in the Constitution but which was judicially derived from the guaranty that life, liberty, and property should not be taken without due process of law, enterprise, threatened with regulation, sought to fight off the controlling hand of government. By restricted interpretations of powers granted and by broad interpretations of constitutional restrictions, the judiciary helped to restrain the course of governmental expansion. Within the decade just passed, however, the Supreme Court itself has been forced to give way and to sanction such uses of governmental power as have been referred for its appraisal.

In the face of the Gargantuan appearance of the federal government today, many people honestly believe that the ancient traditions of liberty which have characterized our national life are on their way to dissolution. Others who are less fearful are nevertheless convinced that the time has come when we must seek to discover the essentials of the things that are good in the concept of liberty so that we may more adequately protect them in a regime where the rule is the comprehensive exercise of governmental power. The feeling is not that we should profit greatly by additional hair-splitting on the part of professional political theorists as to the content of liberty and freedom and rights, but rather that the intelligent American citizen, who is not necessarily a master of fine verbal distinctions, needs carefully to appraise the factors which in his belief represent the essential ingredients of the good society.

Sound thinking on the subject is impeded by attitudes which are the product of conditions of a dead past. Because our pioneer forefathers needed but little that government could provide, they could afford to insist on a high degree of freedom from control simply because they did not like to take orders. Since the government was their own, with changes in personnel largely subject to their command, they seldom found it necessary to seek philosophical justification beyond the range of their emotional dislike of authority. At a time and amid conditions wherein the well-being of the people demands a great deal of governmental control, however, we need to seek deeper for the criteria of freedom than our own individual dislike of authority.

If for the rootage of our thought we dig back into the philosophy of the Founding Fathers, we find an inseparable mixture of conceptions which, in varying degrees of strength, have probably seeped through the intervening years to mold subconsciously the attitudes which now characterize us. Some of the early pioneers sought on American shores escape from governmental regimentation because their religious and political ideas were out of harmony with those then dominating the government which had jurisdiction over them. They were not so much opposed to governmental control as to what they regarded as control to the wrong end. Someone has said with more than a grain of truth that they sought freedom to worship God in their own way—and to compel everybody else to do the same! Such an attitude has little direct relation to genuine beliefs in liberty or freedom. It belongs within the category of the attitudes of all minorities which seek, by transforming themselves into majorities or by other methods, to enforce their own will upon the group as a whole. Its principal value for liberty lies in the fact that the ferment of change helps to maintain an awareness that the status quo of the exercise of governmental authority is not something which is necessarily fixed for all time.

Beyond the range of this pragmatic desire merely to change specific measures of governmental control, however, lies the belief of many thoughtful people over the centuries that only through preserving broad areas of liberty for the individual can the "good life" be achieved either for the individual or for the society of which he is a part. Development of the finer qualities of human life derives not from paternalism but from the exercise of the capacities of the individual on behalf of himself and his fellows. A regime which converts the individual into an unthinking and irresponsible private in a gigantic civilian army however powerful, and into an industrial robot in an economic system of whatever degree of prosperity, is headed inevitably for the disaster of human decay. Men must make decisions for themselves, with the opportunity of reaping the just reward both of those which are good and those which are bad, if they are to grow individually and achieve the stature even of their ancestors.

In the areas in which it is to be permitted to operate, therefore, government performs not a single broad function but two functions. The first is that of protecting the persons of individuals, of protecting property if the regime is one in which property is legitimatized, and of providing order within the economic system if the regime is of such a character that governmental supervision of the economic order is required. The second function which, in the long run, may be even more important than the first is that of developing the capacities of the members of society through their efforts to operate the government. The justification of political liberty does not rest upon canonization of the individual whim or the aggregate of individual whims; for undisciplined responses to situations at times seem to symbolize all that is ignorant, selfish, and asinine. It does not rest upon assumptions as to the comparative efficiency of democratic government; for democracy can fumble and procrastinate and display inconsistency and shortsightedness to shame its most enthusiastic apologists. No, the justification of political liberty lies in the fact that democracy takes men and women as it finds them and demonstrates through its operation that they get government, whether good or bad, in terms of the intelligent effort which they put into it. It disciplines citizens by making them their own disciplinarians. It educates them in a political "school of hard knocks." To the defenders of genuine political liberty the development of the judgment, the creative capacities, and the self-control of the members of society is basically important. Most liberty-loving Americans, for example, while admitting some admiration for the industrial and military efficiency of our recently defeated German enemies, feel a profound contempt for the aggregation of automatons who recognize no obligation but to do the will of self-imposed masters and have no sense of responsibility for the deeds of the state which they deem themselves born to serve.

It should be emphasized that political liberty does not imply freedom from the exercise of the coercive power of government, but rather the liberty of the people to govern themselves at their own discretion, with the responsibility for such government, whether good or bad and with range wide or narrow, resting upon themselves. It is true, however, that, having taken this position, we find ourselves under the necessity of limiting it by the proviso that self-goverment imposed by the people must not go so far as to cut off the facilities of expression and self-education so as to make it impossible for the people to continue to govern themselves. In other words, no tenable principles of political liberty will permit political liberty to decree its own execution. We are driven, then, to a discussion of those elements of liberty which are so vital to the preservation of liberty itself that, even in terms of liberty, they may not be impaired.

Important as they are, we are not here primarily concerned with procedural rights, such as immunity from search except upon the presentation of search warrants, the requirement that criminal trials shall take place only after indictment by grand jury, the requirement of trial by jury, etc. Apart from procedural rights, freedom of religion, freedom of speech, freedom of the press, and freedom of assembly have been regarded traditionally as so fundamental to the preservation of the essentials of personal and political liberty in a democratic society that their integrity must be fully preserved. No group can ever truly govern itself without freedom to believe and to express belief, without the freedom to proclaim ideas and persuade others to accept them. In the light of this fact, protection of this area of freedom against encroachment by the federal government was incorporated into the First Amendment. The point is well made in a recent statement by Justice Black:

> I view the guaranties of the First Amendment as the foundation upon which our governmental structure rests and without which it could not continue to endure as conceived and planned. Freedom to speak and write about public questions is as important to the life of our government as is the heart to the human body. In fact, this privilege is the heart of our government. If that heart be weakened, the result is debilitation; if it be stilled, the result is death.[1]

[1] Dissenting, *Milk Wagon Drivers Union* v. *Meadowmoor Dairies*, 312 U.S. 287, 301–2 (1941).

As stated in the language of Justice Jackson:

> The very purpose of a Bill of Rights was to withdraw certain subjects from the vicissitudes of political controversy, to place them beyond the reach of majorities and officials and to establish them as legal principles to be applied by the courts. One's right to life, liberty, and property, to free speech, a free press, freedom of worship and assembly, and other fundamental rights may not be submitted to vote; they depend on the outcome of no elections.[2]

Yet sweeping as is the language of these constitutional guaranties, they are not to be interpreted as absolutes. Although the practice of polygamy was sanctioned by the Mormon church, the Supreme Court long ago held that the practice was not protected by the First Amendment.[3] The Court recently held that when one of Jehovah's Witnesses denounced a municipal officer as "a goddamned racketeer" and "a damned Fascist" he had gone beyond the protective pale of constitutional provisions. Said Justice Murphy for the Court:

> There are certain well-defined and narrowly limited classes of speech, the prevention and punishment of which have never been thought to raise any Constitutional problem. These include the lewd and obscene, the profane, the libelous, and the insulting or "fighting" words—those which by their very utterance inflict injury or tend to incite an immediate breach of the peace. It has been well observed that such utterances are no essential part of any exposition of ideas, and are of such slight social value as a step to truth that any benefit that may be derived from them is clearly outweighed by the social interest in order and morality.[4]

Under the pressure of war conditions the Supreme Court was forced to admit not only that freedom of speech and the press was not an absolute but also that the same utterance might be entitled to constitutional protection under one set of circumstances and not entitled to it at all under other circumstances. Justice Holmes, speaking for the Court shortly after

---

[2] *West Virginia State Board of Education* v. *Barnette*, 319 U.S. 624, 638 (1943).

[3] *Church of Jesus Christ* v. *United States*, 136 U.S. 49 (1890).

[4] *Chaplinsky* v. *New Hampshire*, 315 U.S. 568, 571–72 (1942).

the end of the first World War, attempted to state a guiding principle through what has come to be known as the clear-and-present-danger doctrine.

The question in every case is whether the words used are used in such circumstances and are of such a nature as to create a clear and present danger that they will bring about the substantive evils that Congress has a right to prevent. It is a question of proximity and degree. When a nation is at war many things that might be said in time of peace are such a hindrance to its effort that their utterance will not be endured so long as men fight, and that no court could regard them as protected by any constitutional right.[5]

The clear-and-present-danger doctrine has been much buffeted by the winds of controversy which have blown against it. Justice Holmes first phrased the doctrine in a case in which a clear and present danger was found to exist. It was applied in other cases growing out of the first World War in which such a danger was also found to exist. In still other cases, however, Justice Holmes parted company from a majority of the Court, contending that he could see no such danger. Because the doctrine was utilized so often in dissenting opinions rather than in opinions of the Court, doubt was raised as to whether it was any longer valid as a guiding principle. In 1937 the doctrine reappeared in the opinion of Justice Roberts as spokesman for the Court, however,[6] and in 1941 Justice Black, speaking for the Court, phrased so strongly the necessity for the existence of a clear and present danger in order to justify abridgment of freedom of speech and of the press as almost to suggest that that freedom was protected by an absolute guaranty:

What finally emerges from the "clear and present danger" cases is a working principle that the substantive evil must be extremely serious and the degree of imminence extremely high before utterances can be punished. Those cases do not purport to mark the furthermost constitu-

[5] *Schenck* v. *United States*, 249 U.S. 47, 52 (1919).
[6] *Herndon* v. *Lowry*, 301 U.S. 242, 255 (1937).

tional boundaries of protected expression, nor do we here. They do no more than recognize a minimum compulsion of the Bill of Rights. For the First Amendment does not speak equivocally. It prohibits any law "abridging the freedom of speech or of the press." It must be taken as a command of the broadest scope that explicit language, read in the context of a liberty-loving society, will allow.[7]

In the eyes of Justice Black, therefore, and in those of the other four justices for whom he spoke, interference with freedom of speech and of the press can be justified only by a danger that is very great and very clear and very imminent. Yet, for some purposes at least, this criterion still has validity as a guide to restrictions which may be legitimate only under extreme circumstances. Again speaking for the Court, this time in a Japanese relocation case, Justice Black declared that "nothing short of apprehension by the proper military authorities of the gravest imminent danger to the public safety can constitutionally justify" nocturnal confinement of loyal citizens of Japanese ancestry to their homes or their deportation from West Coast areas.[8] Clearly the Supreme Court operates in a zone of thoroughly mixed values when it attempts to segregate the powers forbidden to government from powers which are given. The exercise of legitimate and essential governmental powers, whether in time of war or peace, involves directly or indirectly some control over speech and press and assembly and, more often than casual reflection would lead us to suspect, over religion.

An unusually large number of decisions handed down by the Supreme Court since 1937 reflect intense concern on the part of the justices for preservation of the fundamentals of liberty. The number is undoubtedly due in part to the activities of a persistent religious sect, Jehovah's Witnesses, first, in getting itself involved with law enforcement officers and,

[7] *Bridges* v. *California*, 314 U.S. 252, 263 (1941).

[8] *Korematsu* v. *United States*, 65 S. Ct. 193 (1944).

second, in forcing cases up to the Supreme Court both as a matter of its own defense and as a means of continuing its propaganda. To explain in this manner alone, however, all that the justices have said and the concern which they have shown about the issues involved is greatly to oversimplify interpretation of an important current judicial trend. While heeding a warning against the tendency of critics of the courts to read into judicial minds ideas and conceptions which have never entered them, we may legitimately view groups of decisions in their broad context and speculate upon the relation of one group to another. It may well be that the earnestness with which members of the Supreme Court have considered problems of civil liberties in connection with the tribulations of Jehovah's Witnesses, to which they are undoubtedly tired of listening, is due largely to the fact that decisions in this field parallel other and still more numerous decisions in which the Court has given the go-ahead signal to the exercise of sweeping governmental power. At a time when the commerce clause is being interpreted as a source of power almost without limit, when the power to tax and spend for the public welfare is coming into its own as an independent source of authority, when the war powers are looming up as powers overlapping almost all others for the period of the emergency, and when conventional restrictions upon the exercise of power over property such as that of substantive due process are fading into the limbo of lost things, it is indeed time for earnest judicial consideration of the essentials of liberty which must be preserved in the face of sweeping extensions of the exercise of governmental power. That the Supreme Court is deeply preoccupied with this fundamental question is indicated by the uniform carefulness with which the justices have analyzed problems of civil liberties, whether, as in many cases, they involved Jehovah's Witnesses or, in lesser numbers, other religious sects, or labor in the process of defending itself through peaceful picketing or through criticism of judicial decisions, or the ordeal of Americans of Japanese ancestry who were restrained within or expelled temporarily from their homes as a result of the vicissitudes of war.

In other words, the Supreme Court has recognized the right of the American people to commit themselves to a regime of mass-production industrialism wherein our entire economy is so interknitted and interrelated as to require broad governmental supervision with a mixture of restraining and promotional governmental activities. The Court has departed from many of its decisions of earlier years to interpret the constitutional powers of the federal government with such breadth as to sanction those uses of power which the government is now making. To the protest that such sweeping exercise of governmental power narrows the area of individual freedom far beyond such limits as were thought out in the minds of the Founding Fathers, the Court might well make two answers. It might say, first of all, that whatever the conceptions of freedom and control which existed in the minds of the Founding Fathers, the Constitution authorized the people to govern themselves to the extent of their desire to do so as long as they acted within the scope of the powers granted. If they choose to set other limits to freedom than those which would have satisfied the framers, they are acting within their rights as long as they limit governmental action to the area of the powers granted. The Court might say, in the second place, that, our economic system being what we have made it or permitted it to become, the choice of the American people is not between genuine freedom, on the one hand, and submission to governmental control, on the other. The choice rather is, in a high degree, one between control by government, on the one hand, and control by the business instruments of our economy, on the other. It is in the light of this fact that we can explain particularly the position of Justice Murphy, who, in language which reflects a veritable passion for justice, demands as against government, protection for religious and racial minorities and at the same time demands as against employers, protection for the rights of workers even to the extent of transforming peaceful picketing into the freedom of speech which is protected by the Constitution.

To put the matter still another way, both the expressed desires of the people through their governmental organs and the momentum of our economic system have determined that individuals shall be largely subject to group control to the extent to which their lives are molded by economic matters. To the extent to which the Supreme Court is a molder of national policy and a guardian of the essence of human welfare, it may well feel that governmental activity represents at least an approximate expression of the liberty of the people, by contrast with the infinitesimal elements of popular choice reflected by the activities of gigantic business units, the great corporations of the country. If men have the benefits of liberty as long as, but only as long as, they exercise conscious choice and reap the rewards and penalties of that choice, then to a large extent it is government and not privately organized industry which preserves the essentials of liberty for the masses of the people. Yet it must be admitted that even the acceptance of governmental control as a device of escape from industrial dictatorship becomes a council of despair if, in order to achieve its end, it must be carried to such an extreme that conscious choice on the part of the people ceases to be a vital factor in government.

To discuss liberty more directly in terms of constitutional provisions and recent decisions—protection of freedom of religion and freedom of speech and the press against the federal government rests upon the fairly specific language of the First Amendment. No such specific language is included in the Constitution as a restraint upon the states. In 1925, however, in the Gitlow case, the Supreme Court assumed that "freedom of speech and of the press—which are protected by the First Amendment from abridgment by Congress—are among the fundamental personal rights and 'liberties' protected by the due process clause of the Fourteenth Amendment from impairment by the states."[9] That assumption created difficulties of interpretation. The due process clauses of the Fifth and Fourteenth amendments are supposed to be identical in meaning except that one stands as a restriction upon the federal government and the other as a restriction upon the states. Yet, in view of the fact that freedom of religion, speech, and press are protected by the First Amendment, it is not assumed that they are substantively protected by the due process clause of the Fifth Amendment. If they are so protected, then there is excess verbiage in the First and Fifth amendments, while, if they are protected by the due process clause of the Fourteenth Amendment and not by the same clause in the Fifth Amendment, there seems so satisfactory way of explaining the difference.

Another cause of judicial embarrassment in basing substantive protection of liberty upon due process of law lies in the inconsistency of giving substantive protection to civil liberties in terms of this clause while quietly withdrawing it as to the rights of property. This inconsistency, quite as much as the desire to take a verbal short cut, may account for the fact that in a number of recent decisions the spokesmen for the Supreme Court have avoided mention of the due process clause altogether and have talked instead of the larger concept of the Fourteenth Amendment. As the several clauses of the Fourteenth Amendment have been thus far officially interpreted, only the due process clause lends itself reasonably well to the inclusion of the substance of the First Amendment.

[9] *Gitlow* v. *New York*, 268 U.S. 652, 666 (1925).

There may be significance, however, in the fact that four members of the Supreme Court recently went on record as favoring the revitalization of the provision that "no state shall make or enforce any law which shall abridge the privileges or immunities of citizens of the United States."[10] In terms of such revitalization, it might be possible to read the content of the First Amendment into that clause or, at any rate, into the aggregate of clauses which make up Section 1 of the Fourteenth Amendment. Certain members of the Court may or may not have in mind such a strategic move. There may be significance in the fact that shortly after the date of the decision just mentioned, Justice Frankfurter, in a dissenting opinion, took occasion to criticize a majority opinion written by Justice Black because of its failure to state the specific constitutional clause upon which the protection of civil liberties was to be rested:

To say that the protection of freedom of speech of the First Amendment is absorbed by the Fourteenth does not say enough. Which one of the various limitations upon state power introduced by the Fourteenth Amendment absorbs the First? Some provisions of the Fourteenth Amendment apply only to citizens, and one of the petitioners here is an alien; some of its provisions apply only to natural persons, and another petitioner here is a corporation. . . . . Only the Due Process Clause assures constitutional protection of civil liberties to aliens and corporations. Corporations cannot claim for themselves the "liberty" which the Due Process Clause guarantees. That clause protects only their property. . . . . The majority opinion is strangely silent in failing to avow the specific constitutional provision upon which its decision rests.[11]

In a sense it makes no great difference in terms of what constitutional clause protection is given to liberty. On the other hand, however, straight thinking in connection with issues that arise in other cases may call for careful discrimination in the phrasing of constitutional arguments. Illustration of the

[10] See *Edwards* v. *California*, 314 U.S. 160 (1941).
[11] *Bridges* v. *California*, 314 U.S. 252, 280–81 (1941).

point is found in Justice Jackson's concurring opinion in *Edwards* v. *California*, in which the majority of the Supreme Court held that California had unconstitutionally encroached upon the federal commerce power by its efforts to exclude indigent persons from the state:

> The migrations of a human being, of whom it is charged that he possesses nothing that can be sold and has no wherewithal to buy, do not fit easily into my notions as to what is commerce. To hold that the measure of his rights is the commerce clause is likely to result eventually either in distorting the commercial law or in denaturing human rights.[12]

And again:

> This Court has not been timorous about giving concrete meaning to such obscure and vagrant phrases as "due process," "general welfare," "equal protection," or even "commerce among the several states." But it has always hesitated to give any real meaning to the privileges and immunities clause lest it improvidently give too much.[13]

This fact, at any rate, is to be kept in mind as vitally important: the essence of the liberty which is to be protected at all costs is not merely the right of property, is not merely that which within any legitimate meaning of the word is commerce. Neither is it merely process of law, however much emphasis we may place upon the descriptive term "due." The term "liberty" plumbs to the depths of human aspirations, judgment, and endeavor. It finds its justification in its own being and not in its commercialization or in its relation to things commercial or in its relation to the procedure of the law. The need for straight judicial thinking on the subject of liberty, therefore, suggests the desirability of a more adequate basis for judicial protection than clauses dealing either with commerce or with procedure. Fortunately, we have such language in the First Amendment as far as the protection of liberty against the federal government is concerned. But it

---

[12] 314 U.S. 160, 182 (1941).   [13] *Ibid.*, p. 183.

would be well if the somewhat swampy underpinning provided by past interpretations of the Fourteenth Amendment
to give protection against the states could in some way be
strengthened.

The difficulty of detecting encroachments on the fundamentals of liberty varies from situation to situation and in
terms of the tactics of government in exercising restrictive
power. Detection is likely to be easier when the government
involved has merely prohibited conduct of a particular kind,
without making the prohibition appear to be an integral part
of a program of legitimate positive action. On the other hand,
the judicial task is much more difficult when the restriction is
imbedded in a traditional device for protecting the independence of the courts, or when it is an integral part of a program
for developing attitudes of loyalty toward the United States,
or when it is an incident to the waging of war.

The first example mentioned is represented by *Bridges* v.
California,[14] in which the Supreme Court divided five to four,
with Justices Black and Frankfurter as spokesmen for the majority and minority, respectively. The case involved the action
of a California judge in punishing for contempt of court public
discussion of the outcome of a labor case in which a decision
was pending. One of the critics predicted dire results if the
judge was severe in his application of penalties, and the other
predicted dire results if the judge was lenient. Regarding both
types of utterances as attempts to determine the action of the
court, the judge imposed sentences for contempt on both
parties.

Justice Black used the case as a medium for the delivery of
sentiments already quoted as to the compulsions of the Bill
of Rights and as to the scope of the clear-and-present-danger
doctrine. He declared that "the only conclusion supported by

[14] 314 U.S. 252 (1941).

history is that the unqualified prohibitions laid down by the framers were intended to give to liberty of the press, as to the other liberties, the broadest scope that could be countenanced in an orderly society."[15] As for the right to forbid discussion of a controversial topic at the time of deepest public interest in it as, in this case, when a trial had been held and action of the judge was being awaited, he remarked caustically that "no suggestion can be found in the Constitution that the freedom there guaranteed for speech and the press bears an inverse ratio to the timeliness and importance of the ideas seeking expression."[16] As for the necessity of refraining from discussion of the case in such a critical period as a mark of respect for the court, he remarked that "an enforced silence, however limited, solely in the name of preserving the dignity of the bench, would probably engender resentment, suspicion, and contempt much more than it would enhance respect."[17] Justice Frankfurter, on the other hand, remarking that "the administration of justice by an impartial judiciary has been basic to our conception of freedom ever since Magna Carta,"[18] found the restriction of liberty involved a legitimate device for protecting a court against public pressure at a time when such pressure was peculiarly dangerous.

We cannot read into the Fourteenth Amendment the freedom of speech and of the press protected by the First Amendment and at the same time read out age-old means employed by states for securing the calm course of justice. The Fourteenth Amendment does not forbid a state to continue the historic process of prohibiting expressions calculated to subvert a specific exercise of judicial power. So to assure the impartial accomplishment of justice is not an abridgment of freedom of speech or freedom of the press, as these phases of liberty have heretofore been conceived even by the stoutest libertarians. In fact, these liberties

[15] *Ibid.*, p. 265.   [17] *Ibid.*, p. 270.

[16] *Ibid.*, p. 269.   [18] *Ibid.*, p. 282.

themselves depend upon an untrammeled judiciary whose passions are not even unconsciously aroused and whose minds are not distorted by extrajudicial considerations.[19]

The purpose of this discussion is not to indicate that one justice was wrong and the other right but rather to suggest the difficulty of the judicial task. A reading of the two opinions leaves one convinced that important principles were in danger on both sides and that the decision, whatever it might be, involved the possibility of injury to the public welfare by neglect of the principle which in this case it must refrain from supporting. It so happened that five judges aligned themselves on the side of protecting the liberty involved, whereas only four deemed the protection of the judiciary as involved in this case to be more important. Clearly the case stands at the frontier of the liberties protected by the Constitution, and reasonable men might well disagree as to the drawing of the line.

The requirement of a state that children participate in the familiar ceremony of saluting the American flag as a condition of attendance at the public school seemed initially to have such plausible justification that only one member of the Supreme Court found it an unconstitutional invasion of the religious freedom of children whose religious convictions it flouted. Justice Frankfurter, speaking for the Court in the Gobitis case, took the position that a legislature might at its discretion use its coercive power to create in young people the sentiment upon which national unity depends

The ultimate foundation of a free society is the binding tie of cohesive sentiment. Such a sentiment is fostered by all those agencies of the mind and spirit which may serve to gather up the traditions of a people, transmit them from generation to generation, and thereby create that continuity of a treasured common life which constitutes a civilization.

[19] *Ibid.*, p. 284.

"We live by symbols." The flag is the symbol of our national unity, transcending all internal differences, however large, within the framework of the Constitution.[20]

Justice Frankfurter refused to commit himself as to the desirability of this particular device for developing patriotic sentiment. He declared, however, that to the legislature no less than to the courts was committed the guardianship of deeply cherished liberties. Where all the effective means of inducing political changes were left free from interference, education in the abandonment of foolish legislation was itself a training in liberty.

Justice Stone, however, standing alone, found the invasion of liberty so obvious as to justify holding the statute unconstitutional. It did more than suppress freedom of speech and prohibit the free exercise of religion, he protested, for by it the states sought to coerce children to express a sentiment which they did not entertain and which violated their deepest religious convictions.

The publicity given to the decision and the use which was thereafter made of the requirement of saluting the flag as a device for persecuting Jehovah's Witnesses seemed to certain of the justices sufficient ground for rethinking the decision in which they had participated. Other states enacted statutes of the same kind and used them as devices for prosecuting children of Jehovah's Witnesses as incorrigible delinquents. Furthermore, the two-year period following the decision was one of widespread persecution of the sect involved in a great variety of ways both with and without the excuse of statutory authorization. While not all that took place could be attributed to the decision of the Supreme Court, there was good circumstantial evidence for believing that the failure of the Court to look to the heart of the liberty involved was in part responsible for the abuses which took place. At any rate, in

[20] *Minersville School District* v. *Gobitis*, 310 U.S. 586, 596 (1940).

June, 1942, in a case involving the requirement of a license for the sale of religious books, three members of the Court took occasion to announce their belief that the position which they had taken in the Gobitis case was wrong.[21] Finally, in the Barnette case,[22] decided in June, 1943, after certain changes in personnel on the Supreme Court, the Court overruled the Gobitis decision with only three justices dissenting. As to coercing acceptance of symbols, said Justice Jackson speaking for the Court:

Symbols of State often convey political ideas just as religious symbols come to convey theological ones. Associated with many of these symbols are appropriate gestures of acceptance or respect: a salute, a bowed or bared head, a bended knee. A person gets from a symbol the meaning he puts into it, and what is one man's comfort and inspiration is another's jest and scorn.[23]

He declared that the very purpose of a bill of rights was to withdraw certain subjects from the vicissitudes of political controversy, to place them beyond the reach of majorities and officials, and to establish them as legal principles to be applied by the courts. Perhaps in reply to Justice Frankfurter's contention in the Gobitis case that the legislature as well as the courts was a guardian of our liberties and should be permitted some discretion subject to the restraining power of the electorate, Justice Jackson declared that "one's right to life, liberty, and property, to free speech, a free press, freedom of worship and assembly, and other fundamental rights may not be submitted to vote; they depend on the outcome of no elections."[24] In spite of Justice Frankfurter's eloquent dissenting opinion, the reader is left with the feeling that the majority of the Court, educated perhaps by the experience of state activity

[21] *Jones* v. *Opelika*, 316 U.S. 584, 623–24 (1942).

[22] *West Virginia State Board of Education* v. *Barnette*, 319 U. S. 624 (1943).

[23] *Ibid.*, pp. 622–23.

[24] *Ibid.*, p. 628.

after the date of the Gobitis decision, had come closer to a correct understanding of the essence of the liberty protected by the Constitution.

Liberty suffered heavy buffeting under the military program of the federal government upon our entry into the second World War. This was particularly true as to the treatment accorded American citizens of Japanese ancestry living along the exceedingly vulnerable Pacific Coast of the United States. Citizenship alone was no proof of attachment to the United States rather than to Japan, even though it was acquired by birth and not by naturalization. It seemed inevitable that a minority would go to any extremes to aid Japan. In the absence of any feasible technique for discovering and isolating that minority, it was deemed necessary to issue restrictive regulations affecting the entire group, even though the group was made up largely of persons who were completely and oftentimes intensely loyal to the United States. The American people were still feeling the cold chills produced by the attack on Pearl Harbor when, in June, 1943, the Supreme Court decided the Hirabayashi case[25] involving a military curfew order upon all persons of Japanese ancestry within a specified area. Quoting a speech of Chief Justice Hughes to the effect that "the power to wage war is the power to wage war successfully," Chief Justice Stone, speaking for the Court, upheld the order. Military authorities had deemed such an order necessary to safeguard the United States against the enemy, and the Court found plausible support for this belief. As for the discrimination involved in the segregation of all persons of Japanese ancestry without evidence as to individual loyalty to the United States, Chief Justice Stone pointed out that no provision in the Fifth Amendment forbade the federal government to deny equal protection of the law. While the decision

[25] *Hirabayashi* v. *United States*, 320 U.S. 81 (1943).

was unanimous, however, Justice Douglas deemed it worth while to write a concurring opinion in which he stated that "loyalty is a matter of mind and of heart not of race."[26] Justice Murphy, remarking that for the first time, so far as he was aware, the Court had sustained a substantial restriction of the personal liberty of citizens of the United States based upon the accident of race or ancestry, declared that in his opinion this went "to the very brink of constitutional power."[27]

When in December, 1944, the Supreme Court passed on the more drastic military order for the complete evacuation of American citizens of Japanese ancestry from certain areas, fear of Japanese attack on our shores had greatly diminished. A majority of the Court, speaking through Justice Black, upheld the constitutionality of the order,[28] but three justices dissented. Justice Roberts saw the order as a clear violation of constitutional rights, declaring that "it is the case of convicting a citizen as a punishment for not submitting to imprisonment in a concentration camp, based on his ancestry, and solely because of his ancestry, without evidence or inquiry concerning his loyalty and good disposition toward the United States."[29] Justice Murphy declared that racial discrimination was unattractive in any setting but was utterly revolting among a free people who had embraced the principles set forth in the Constitution of the United States.[30] Justice Jackson objected to determination of the constitutionality of a military order by a judicial estimate as to the military reasonableness of the order. He came close to taking the position that the waging of war was extra-constitutional and not to be measured by constitutional tests. He declared that it would be imprac-

---

[26] *Ibid.*, p. 107.

[27] *Ibid.*, p. 111.

[28] *Korematsu* v. *United States*, 65 S. Ct. 193 (1944).

[29] *Ibid.*, p. 198.   [30] *Ibid.*, p. 206.

ticable and dangerous idealism to expect or insist that each specific military command in an area of probable operation would conform to conventional tests of constitutionality. A military commander, he said, issued orders which might have a certain authority as military commands, "although they may be very bad as constitutional law." He said further, however, that "if we cannot confine military expedients by the Constitution, neither would I distort the Constitution to approve all that the military may deem expedient. That is what the Court appears to be doing, whether consciously or not."[31] He took the position that, in the very nature of things, military decisions were not susceptible of intelligent judicial appraisal. He declared:

A judicial construction of the due process clause that will sustain this order is a far more subtle blow to liberty than the promulgation of the order itself. A military order, however unconstitutional, is not apt to last longer than the military emergency. Even during that period a succeeding commander may revoke it all. But once a judicial opinion rationalizes such an order to show that it conforms to the Constitution, or rather rationalizes the Constitution to show that the Constitution sanctions such an order, the Court for all time has validated the principle of racial discrimination in criminal procedure and of transplanting American citizens. The principle then lies about like a loaded weapon ready for the hand of any authority that can bring forward a plausible claim of an urgent need. Every repetition imbeds that principle more deeply in our law and thinking and expands it to new purposes. All who observe the work of courts are familiar with what Judge Cardozo described as "the tendency of a principle to expand itself to the limit of its logic." A military commander may overstep the bounds of constitutionality, and it is an incident. But if we review and approve, that passing incident becomes the doctrine of the Constitution. There it has a generative power of its own, and all that it creates will be in its own image. Nothing better illustrates this danger than does the Court's opinion in this case.

Even more drastic than the removal of citizens of Japanese ancestry from certain areas was their subsequent detention in

[31] *Ibid.*, p. 207.

relocation centers. The Supreme Court decided unanimously that the War Relocation Authority had no power to enforce such detention.[32] It did so not by holding that such detention was unconstitutional but by the thinly veiled device of interpreting the relevant statute, or the executive orders based upon it, in the light of the prohibitions of the Constitution and finding that the statute and orders as so interpreted did not authorize the detention in question. While the Court did not say that if the statute clearly provided for detention in relocation camps it would violate the Constitution, this implication seemed clear. Justices Murphy and Roberts insisted on saying as much in concurring opinions.

These civil liberties cases arising out of the war disclose the desire of the majority of the Supreme Court to rationalize military activity in time of war in terms of the Constitution and to interpret military power with such breadth as to leave the military unhampered judicially in time of war and at the same time to hope that somewhere exists an area of liberty which can be preserved even in the face of military necessity. No very distinguished work has been done in the way of defining that area of liberty. Only Justice Jackson takes the position that war is to be treated as a constitutional aberration not measured by principles of law known to the judiciary; but the device of the majority in technically avoiding the constitutional question as to the detention of American citizens of Japanese ancestry suggests a pretty general desire on the part of the justices to keep constitutional interpretation off the path of military necessity. The justification of such canniness in avoiding the placement of a constitutional check upon the administration in time of war is a matter for debate.

Shifting back to liberty under conditions not related to war, let us consider what might be called a positive program of the

[32] *Ex parte Endo*, 65 S. Ct. 208 (1944).

present administration with respect to labor. Labor is to have such support from government as to its own organization and as to its methods of bargaining with employers as to put it in a position of equal, if not superior, bargaining power with employers. The intervention of government is justified in part on the ground that governmental support is needed to counterbalance the power held by employers by virtue of their control of the means of production. While upholding the rights of workers to the extent of classifying peaceful picketing as exercise of the freedom of speech guaranteed by the Constitution, the Supreme Court has limited the freedom of speech of employers on labor issues where such speech is a part of the pattern of employer activities intended to interfere with the freedom of action of a labor union. The apparent partiality of the Supreme Court toward the constitutional rights of employees as against those of employers was evidently a subject of hot discussion among the justices in arriving at a decision in *Thomas* v. *Collins*,[33] which was decided early in 1945. The case involved the constitutionality of a Texas statute which required that all labor-union organizers operating in the state should secure an organizer's card from the secretary of state before soliciting members for a labor organization. The Court held by a vote of five to four that the mere requirement of registration as a condition of speaking represented an unconstitutional interference with liberty. As spokesman for the majority, Justice Rutledge declared that the employer had the same right of free speech on the subject of unionization as the employee except that "when to this persuasion other things are added which bring about coercion, or give it that character, the limit of the right has been passed."[34] Justice Jackson, however, said in a concurring opinion: "I must admit that in

[33] 65 S. Ct. 315 (1945).
[34] *Ibid.*, p. 326.

overriding the findings of the Texas court we are applying to
Thomas a rule the benefit of which in all its breadth and vigor
this Court denies to employers in National Labor Relations
Board cases."[35] Evidently in the light of this comment, on the
other hand, Justice Douglas, with Justices Black and Murphy
concurring, made the following statement:

> No one may be required to obtain a license in order to speak. But once
> he uses the economic power which he has over other men and their jobs
> to influence their action, he is doing more than exercising the freedom
> of speech protected by the First Amendment. That is true whether he
> be an employer or an employee. But as long as he does no more than
> speak he has the same unfettered right, no matter what side of an issue
> he espouses.[36]

Justice Roberts, speaking for the minority of four, could see
no essential difference between the constitutionality of the
requirements of registration as a prerequisite to the soliciting
of funds—which had been upheld—and the constitutionality of
such a requirement as to soliciting membership in a union.
Whether or not the solicitation involved payment of initiation
fees or dues to the solicitor, he declared,

> it involves the assumption of business and financial liability by him who
> is persuaded to join a union. The transaction is in essence a business one.
> Labor unions are business associations; their object is generally business
> dealings and relationships as is manifest from the financial statements
> of some of the national unions. Men are persuaded to join them for
> business reasons, as employers are persuaded to join trade associations
> for like reasons. Other paid organizers, whether for business or for
> charity, could be required to identify themselves. There is no reason why
> labor organizers should not do likewise. I think that if anyone pursues
> solicitation as a business for profit, of members for any organization, re-
> ligious, secular or business, his calling does not bar the state from re-
> quiring him to identify himself as what he is—a paid solicitor.[37]

[35] *Ibid.*, p. 330.

[36] *Ibid.*, p. 329.   [37] *Ibid.*, pp. 334–35.

The decision seems to reveal a tenderness of judicial feeling toward the constitutional rights of workers which does not apply to the same rights of employers. Whether or not a certain amount of hardness of heart toward employers is justified in the light of their past use of their economic power to encroach upon the rightful liberties of workers is a difficult question. The language of the First Amendment—which is said to be carried over into the Fourteenth Amendment as a restriction upon the states—prescribes no limitations upon the guaranties of freedom of religion, speech, and press, yet the Supreme Court has held that even these constitutional prohibitions are relative and not absolute. It has said that they are limited by the clear-and-present-danger doctrine, and, whether the Court takes the trouble to say so or not, they are probably to be interpreted also in the light of an over-all conception of the purposes of the Constitution. For the time being at least it appears that Congress, the President, and the Supreme Court have gone a long way toward erecting equality of bargaining power into a constitutional principle. If such a principle exists in the minds of the justices, it can be used to justify governmental discrimination between employers and employees. As to the areas of constitutional freedom which shall be allotted to each, the greater the power—that is the greater the economic power—the more limited the area of constitutional liberty. It remains to be seen whether the principle is flexible enough for use as a curb upon the liberty of workers to the extent to which they acquire overwhelming power, not through ownership and control of the instruments of production but through united and organized action.

As these recent decisions demonstrate, the periphery of liberty, as constitutionally guaranteed and judicially protected, is enshrouded in a haze of uncertainty. The same is true in the procedural field where due process of law is used to protect the rights of the accused, where the constitutional provisions as to treason are applied,[38] etc. Encroachments upon liberty which are allowed at certain points may seem to be compensated by the giving of protection elsewhere. For example, while natural-born citizens were suffering under the holding that they might be subjected to curfew laws and to deportation from their homes without investigation of their loyalty to the United States, the Supreme Court gave much-needed protection to the rights of naturalized citizens. The Department of Justice had started a crusade to cancel the naturalization certificates of naturalized citizens whose conduct after the date of naturalization was such as to indicate that their oath of allegiance to the United States had not been taken in good faith. Such a procedure if upheld would have subjected every naturalized citizen to investigation and what in effect was punishment for utterances and acts in which natural-born citizens might indulge with impunity. Acting not in terms of the Constitution but of the statute involved, the Supreme Court prohibited this whip of administration over naturalized citizens.[39] While citizenship certificates proved to have been acquired by fraud can, of course, be canceled, the decision of the Court goes far toward holding that for naturalized citizens as well as for those that are natural-born the principle of "once a citizen always a citizen" prevails.

The limits of many areas of freedom are unclear because of the difficulty or impossibility of securing judicial determinations. In the field of freedom of the press, for example, the Postmaster-General, through the control which statutes give him over the classification of mail, exercises tremendous power over publication. Publishers without adequate financial resources are seldom in position effectively to challenge his de-

[38] See *Cramer* v. *United States*, 65 S. Ct. 918 (1945).

[39] *Schneiderman* v. *United States*, 320 U.S. 118 (1943).

cisions. It may well be that only prosperous publishers like the sponsors of the magazine *Esquire* can afford to make a judicial challenge.[40]

Invasions may take place in other ways. While employment by government is not yet so fully a practice of our economy as to justify a pretense that any man has a right to be employed by the federal government, dismissal of employees to satisfy prejudices of men in power may work gross injustice. This is particularly true where, as in recent instances, Congress, exercising its power over appropriations, refuses to allow government funds to be used for the salaries of men whom particular legislators dislike but who have been convicted of no offense and have been given no fair hearings. Other abuses take place in the process of congressional investigation, when investigating committees of Congress unnecessarily invade privacy, browbeat witnesses, make public statements on the basis of inadequate evidence to the detriment of private reputations, and in other ways demonstrate themselves unfit custodians of the powers of government intrusted to them. Such tyranny, of course, is not limited to the legislative branch of the government. It is found here and there throughout the swollen executive establishment. Evidence of it will undoubtedly be revealed on a large scale as soon as preoccupation with the war gives way to a more careful examination of internal affairs.

It can be said in conclusion that now, as at the time of origin of the Constitution, potential tyrants are always with us, in the form both of those who love tyranny as such and those who sincerely profess a love of liberty but whose convictions as to what ought to be done are so dogmatic as to make them little less of a menace than are those who deliberately set them-

[40] *Esquire, Inc.* v. *Walker*, 55 F. Supp. 1015 (1944).

selves up as dictators. For the preservation of liberty adequate machinery of government is essential, but machinery alone is not enough. Fair-minded and self-controlled leaders are necessary, but leadership is not enough. The survival of liberty depends not merely upon these things but upon the abiding faith of the people that liberty represents a prime value of life which must be defended at all costs. Beyond even this point we can say that its survival depends not merely upon the devotion of the people but upon an intelligent awareness on the part of the people that the essentials of liberty are not to be measured as a static concept but in terms of the changing conditions of an ever changing society. Without perennial struggles to recapture the essential values for which liberty is to be preserved, we shall be in danger of losing the substance and finding ourselves left with the valueless husks which bear nothing but the name. Our conception of liberty, as has already been said, if it is to remain vital, must be in constant process of rethinking in terms of our conceptions of the life which man is to lead in the world. Liberty, in effect, is an article of faith. It symbolizes the belief that man can be trusted to work out for himself a high destiny—a destiny higher than that which other men could achieve for him. It involves the assumption that life itself has richness and takes on meaning in proportion to the extent to which men develop the capacity to shape their own destiny. Perhaps it can be said that thus far, on the whole, our defense of liberty has not been badly made. But, if so, we are in no position to rest content on the basis of past achievements. Now, as always, the price of liberty is eternal vigilance.

VIII

THE CONSTITUTION AND WORLD AFFAIRS

✢

THE Founding Fathers drafted the Constitution solely as an instrument of government for the United States. They did not contemplate direct or indirect control of other sections of the world. To do so would have been ambitious, indeed, on the part of men concerned primarily with solving knotty problems for a thin line of agricultural settlements along the Atlantic Coast. Their plans as to foreign affairs extended only to the establishment of a government strong enough to regulate foreign commerce, to make binding treaties with other nations, and to defend the United States against all enemies. When considerable areas of additional territory later fell under the jurisdiction of the federal government, such acquisition was regarded as a part of a normal process of assuming control of that which was properly our own. It did not reflect any doubt as to the right of other nations to exercise absolute sovereignty within their own spheres. What those nations did was for the most part their own affair. We recognized their right to immunity from interference by us and claimed the same right for ourselves.

The industrialization of many sections of the world, however, the development of rapid communication and transportation, and the increased dependence of each section upon many others has at least begun the development of something which might be called world-mindedness—a state of mind or mental attitude which a garrulous congresswoman has unsympathetically characterized as "globaloney." Industrialization has molded the world into a compact neighborhood. Any neighborhood which lacks government with authority throughout its entire area and which must rely completely upon rival governments territorially divided must be prepared for trouble in the keeping of the peace and in the preservation of order in its economy.

In the light of these facts it is time to rethink principles of government and interpretations of the Constitution as they apply to the United States in relation to the rest of the world. This rethinking is no easy task. Difficulty arises particularly from the fact that we lack a sound and popular tradition in support of it. Protected on the east and west by two broad oceans and bounded on the north by an always friendly power and on the south by relatively weak ones, our eyes for many generations, except for sporadic intervals, have turned inward rather than outward. The field of foreign affairs, instead of receiving the thoughtful attention of the great mass of the American people, has been left too largely to overspecialized, biased, or incompetent individuals and groups. These include the professional diplomat with the prejudices and restricted outlook of his profession, the generous campaign contributor who seeks to end his career amid glamorous scenes of intriguing if mystifying diplomacy, the businessman with an interest at stake which may be at variance with the national interest, the sentimentalist who idealizes foreigners progressively as to their distance from his native land and as to their difference from its inhabitants, and the missionary, whether religious, social, or political, who is raptly convinced that the great mission of the United States is to save the rest of the world and, usually, to remold it in the image of the United States. As distinguished from the internal affairs of this nation, about which the masses of the American people have a great deal of information and of which they have some understanding, they have a tragic lack of knowledge and understanding of the ethnic, geographic, political, and economic conditions and affairs of other sections of the world which today have an impact upon conditions and affairs in the United States. Because of this lack of knowledge and understanding and lack of a tradition for acquiring it, public reactions in this field tend to be unstable and highly emotional in character. The United States is, therefore, peculiarly at the mercy of its own lunatic fringes in the handling of its foreign affairs. These fringes range all the way from isolationists with heads buried in the sands of earlier generations to sentimental internationalists who believe that all major problems can be solved merely by the creation of some particular kind of international agency or by wholesale secretion of sentiment about the spirit of international brotherhood.

The point involved is that, in the field of foreign as of domestic affairs, the Constitution as a democratic instrument, however adequate its provisions, can function properly only in a setting of informed public opinion. It cannot function in an intellectual vacuum or, at any rate, in a vacuum as to forceful and stable public sentiment. Government in the absence of such a body of sentiment lacks the positive support which gives it validity and falls prey to the erratic influences which beat upon it. It is like a ship without either rudder or anchor. Intelligent conduct of foreign affairs under the Constitution must depend not merely upon constitutional provisions and the machinery resting thereon but upon judgment derived from broad factual knowledge and a substratum of informed popular attitudes toward the whole subject. Therefore, in the appraisal of our constitutional system as it relates to foreign affairs, care must be taken to differentiate between those defects, if any, which inhere in the Constitution itself and those which, on the other hand, merely reflect the absence of the necessary lubricant of public understanding and conviction.

In drafting the Constitution, the framers provided for the normal international functions which are performed through ambassadors and other public ministers and consuls, through exercise of the power to make treaties, and through the waging of war. Their goal was the establishment of prosperous foreign trade and the preservation of peace as far as the United States was concerned. Indeed, the desire for a government strong enough to win the respect of foreign nations and to make favorable and binding trade agreements with them provided a major incentive to the adoption of the Constitution. Fulfilment of this desire was thought to call for no real intimacy of contact with foreign nations or involvement in their internal affairs. Indeed, when in 1796 the president of the Constitutional Convention issued a farewell address as President of the United States, he warned against "the insidious drive of foreign influence" and declared that "the great rule of conduct for acts, in regard to foreign nations, is, in extending our commercial relations, to have with them as little *political* connection as possible."[1] Europe, he declared, had a set of primary interests which had little or no relation to our own and must, therefore, be engaged in frequent controversies the causes of which were essentially foreign to our concern. It would be unwise for us to implicate ourselves in the vicissitudes of European politics or in the ordinary combinations of European friendships and intimacies. If we remained aloof as one people under an efficient government, the period was not far off when we might defy material injury from external annoyance. Our neutrality would then be respected by belligerent nations, and we might choose peace or war as our interests guided by justice should counsel.

President Washington wrote his farewell address at a time when American fanatics on both sides, in disregard of the

[1] From George Washington's "Farewell Address," *Annals of Congress* (4th Cong., 2d sess.), p. 2878.

welfare of the United States, were threatening to embroil us in the conflict between Great Britain and France. He based his argument for American avoidance of European quarrels upon our temporary weakness as a newly established nation and upon the contention that those quarrels were not our concern. The address became a part of American thinking about foreign affairs, and it continued to be read as the key to our foreign policy even after the United States had become one of the most powerful nations in the world and after it had become obvious to thoughtful observers that serious international conflicts anywhere in the world were likely to make themselves felt in terms of American welfare. Since the doings of distant nations were not our affair, it was in general not thought necessary to be informed about them. In the light—or darkness—of this attitude most Americans who, as a matter of course, seek to know something of our own agricultural problems, labor problems, industrial problems, etc., feel little obligation to discover in detail what is happening in Soviet Russia or Spain or India or China or the Dutch East Indies for the purpose of promoting the world welfare of which the welfare of the United States and of the nations and possessions mentioned are component parts. There is, or until recently there has been, little awareness that those welfares are inseparably linked and that the condition of the part depends ultimately upon the condition of the whole.

As a result of the absence of an adequate substratum of popular information and interest, the people are not in a position to mold and to stabilize American foreign policy by supporting and restraining the political leaders and technical experts whose function it is to act in terms of democratic sentiment. Furthermore, because of the inadequacy of such a body of sentiment and the consequent tendency of the people to react variously in terms of highly emotional symbols, those leaders and experts have plausible grounds for denouncing popular interference in matters which only they can pretend to understand; and they are in a position to engage in interdepartmental strife over the control of policy which would not be tolerated if the people were competent to make leaders and experts what they ought to be, namely, largely the purveyors of popular sentiment as to the shaping of American foreign policy.

Much of the controversy which takes place over the provisions of the Constitution concerning foreign affairs derives from the efforts of the framers to apply the principle of the separation of powers in the foreign as in the domestic field. Indeed, the substance of much criticism of existing constitutional machinery is that the separation of powers provides an unwarrantable obstruction to what ought to be the largely unrestricted powers of the Executive. In other words, in foreign as in domestic affairs, men seeking speedy results in the solution of problems immediately at hand tend to forget or deny the need for the safeguards which our system of checks and balances is intended to provide.

Impatience with the separation of powers wins a certain amount of sympathy from the fact that the line of division of powers between the legislative and executive branches of the government is by no means clear. The framers of the Constitution seem to have kept vaguely in mind the principle that power for action should be allocated to the executive branch, while power to determine policy should be given to the legislative branch. Unfortunately, however, the line between policy and action and between the constitutional functions of the legislative and executive branches is exceedingly hard to draw. It is a baffling assignment, for example, to determine how far the constitutional power of the President to "make" treaties is limited by the phrases "by and with the advice and consent of the Senate," and "provided two-thirds of the Senators present concur." Again, the text of the Constitution throws little light on the question whether the provision that the President shall be Commander-in-Chief of the Army and Navy means that he shall have a free hand to wage as he sees fit a war declared by Congress or whether in his military capacity it is his duty to serve in terms of instructions given by Congress. The exercise of the treaty-making power has been the focal point of bitter battles between the President and the Senate almost from the time when the Constitution went into effect, and the division of war powers has been a subject of controversy during every major war fought by the United States. Although controversy is inevitable whenever power is divided, it is most unfortunate that the constitutional line of division in the instances mentioned, and particularly as to the treaty-making power, could not have been more sharply drawn.

Our foreign affairs therefore are carried on under the handicap of highly indefinitely divided powers and of a lack of informed public opinion about such matters, under circumstances such that much of what happens in lands distant from our own, although once largely irrelevant to our welfare, is now becoming increasingly relevant. Because the stakes of power are high, the menace of tyranny must be heeded in spite of the fact that confidence in negotiation and speed and decisiveness of action are important as never before. Yet only sporadically does public understanding and conviction express itself through Congress or the Senate in such a way as to provide constructive support for the President or checks upon him which represent something at a higher level than that of departmental jealousy.

In the light of these facts, it is not surprising that most action in foreign affairs consists not only of executive action under the direction of the President but also of policy developed by him. His influence over policy is attributable in part to the fact that he is the spokesman of the nation when it communicates with other nations. True, the Senate has the power to reject appointments as ambassadors and ministers, but the power is only negative. Furthermore, the President may work through subordinates whose appointments do not require senatorial confirmation, or in important matters he may see fit to negotiate directly with foreign powers without employment of intermediaries. The evolution and the modification of policy—as, for example, the phrasing of the Atlantic Charter and the tentative acceptance of the border between Poland and Russia largely as dictated by the latter—occur as part of the process of international negotiation and are announced without consultation with the legislative branch of the government.

Even apart from the processes of negotiation, which must naturally be in the hands of the Executive, the voicing of a national position falls more naturally to the office of President than to a Congress of 531 members or to a Senate of 96. Even as to earlier years when Congress was much smaller than it now is, we accept as perfectly natural the fact that it was President Monroe who voiced the doctrine which bears his name and not Congress or the Senate. Never in a lifetime would the legislators of the period of the first World War have evolved and given world notoriety to the Fourteen Points announced by President Wilson. The task is one not merely of phrase-making but also of integration of ideas and personalization of statement to secure the maximum impact. The effectiveness of a legislative body in this field is so limited that the Senate can seldom do more than defiantly declare what it will not do, or perhaps indicate that it is not opposed to some policy under discussion, as, for example, the joining of an international organization for the preservation of world peace.

Even when particular senators do attempt to take the lead in voicing policy along lines likely to be followed by the President, observers do not jump to the conclusion that leadership is passing from the President to the Senate but conclude merely that the Senate or particular senators are not to be feared as obstructionists of presidential policy.

It is true that from time to time the President has sought the advice of the Senate prior to the negotiation of treaties.[2] Yet in the main, since the day in 1789 when the Senate refused to discuss openly and informally with President Washington the provisions of a treaty then under consideration, the strategy of the Executive in handling foreign affairs has been colored by the desire to find a way to avoid senatorial obstruction, much more than by any genuine desire for senatorial advice. The strategy of avoiding obstruction has usually included presenting to the Senate a *fait accompli* in the form of a draft of a treaty representing an achievement in negotiation which it would seem folly to reject. For example, it would doubtless have been extremely bad politics for the Senate to reject or even long to delay action in approving the treaty for the acquisition of Louisiana, even though the purchase had been arranged without consultation with the Senate. Success, it is true, requires a careful estimate of public sentiment in support of the treaty in question. President Wilson tried to use the weight of popular desire for a treaty of peace at the end of the first World War to secure acceptance of the League of Nations, but unfortunately he miscalculated both the popular desire for completion of a treaty and the intensity of senatorial opposition to the League and to his political strategy. A minority group of Republican senators, including more than a third of the total membership, publicly stated a preference

[2] For a summary discussion of the treaty-making power and the citation of other sources see George H. Haynes, *The Senate of the United States* (1938), Vol. II, chap. xii.

for the immediate conclusion of terms of peace with Germany prior to taking up the proposal for the establishment of a League of Nations to insure the permanent peace of the world. Wilson defiantly answered the group of senators in a public address by the declaration that when the treaty of peace was eventually submitted "gentlemen on this side will find the Covenant not only in it, but so many threads of the treaty tied to the Covenant that you cannot dissect the Covenant from the treaty without destroying the whole vital structure."[3] It is a familiar story that the Senate successfully ran the political risk of refusing to approve the Treaty of Versailles without changes so drastic as to make it unacceptable to the President.

Since the coercive power of public sentiment is the most potent weapon which the President can employ to secure desired action by the Senate or by Congress as a whole, the lack of that weapon brings a serious handicap. President Wilson's experience with the Treaty of Versailles well illustrates the point. To illustrate further, the difficulty in securing from the Senate approval of treaties which have been negotiated has resulted oftentimes from the fact that the treaties dealt with subjects upon which the people had no clear judgment or upon which they were sharply divided. The difficulty in securing approval of arbitration treaties, for example, or in securing their approval without wholesale changes by the Senate, may be explained in large part by the fact that the American people have arrived at no clear judgment as to the proper method of settlement of international disputes.[4]

On two occasions when a President was unable to secure the two-thirds majority necessary for Senate approval of treaties for the annexation of territory, the President changed his

---

[3] *New York Times*, March 5, 1919.

[4] On this and related points see Royden J. Dangerfield, *In Defense of the Senate* (1933).

strategy and persuaded party leaders in Congress to introduce joint resolutions for achievement of the same end, because joint resolutions, although requiring action by both houses rather than merely by the Senate, required only majority votes for enactment. It was possible to get authorization in this way. Furthermore, after the Senate refused to give its approval to the Treaty of Versailles, Congress enacted a joint resolution terminating the war with Germany prior to the working-out of a separate treaty of peace. This strategy calls into question the desirability of the constitutional arrangement whereby the Senate, rather than both houses, is used for the making of treaties and whereby, when the Senate alone represents the legislative branch, the larger majority is required. The framers of the Constitution seem to have believed that the important function of making treaties should be allocated to an élite group, and they seem to have expected that the Senate, of which the members were to be elected by the several state legislatures, would constitute such an élite body, as distinguished from the House of Representatives, of which the members would be elected directly by the voters for shorter terms. As for the requirement of a two-thirds vote for the approval of treaties, it was evidently recognized that every treaty represents in some sense a foreign entanglement, and it was felt that the status quo ought not to be abandoned unless that degree of unanimity could be secured. The framers clearly did not have in mind an insidious arrangement whereby representatives of very small or very thinly populated states might combine to defeat the will of the aggregate of the more populous states—of which horrible but altogether hypothetical examples have been provided in recent discussions of the treaty-making power.[5] As a matter of fact, combinations of

[5] See, e.g., Kenneth Colegrove, *The American Senate and World Peace* (1944). For adverse comment see Herbert Wright, "The Two-thirds Vote of the Senate in Treaty-making," *American Journal of International Law,* XXXVIII (October, 1944), 643–50.

that kind never take place except in the bad dreams of critics of existing institutions. Furthermore, the argument, if it proves anything, proves too much. Because of the inequalities of population in the several states, a skilful juggler of figures can easily show that the guardianship of two-thirds or more of the senators is necessary to prevent the President and wilful representatives of thinly populated states from using the treaty-making power to impose their will upon the millions of people residing in the large and the thickly settled states.

The weakness of this conventional argument against the two-thirds requirement, however, should not be permitted to obscure the validity of other arguments. If we once had a choice between entanglement and nonentanglement with foreign nations, that choice no longer remains. We are entangled whether we like it or not, and events in foreign countries, apparently of slight significance, have indirect and varied impact upon our own welfare. The choice is no longer one between entanglement and nonentanglement but between action and inaction or between types of action in dealing with entanglements. It is possible, therefore, that the negation involved in the status quo has now lost the positive value which it once possessed and that the arrangement of governmental machinery to give it support has now become antiquated.

Furthermore, although differences of tenure, size, and tradition continue to distinguish the Senate from the House of Representatives, resort to popular election of senators has eliminated one of the principal characteristics in terms of which the Senate was designated as a select body to which the appraisal of treaties should be allocated. The Senate, at any rate, is not so different from the House of Representatives as to justify the drawing of any sharp line of distinction between the capacities of the two bodies. Again, without denying and, indeed, while emphasizing the fact that both houses of Congress demonstrate a lamentable lack of statesmanship in their consideration of foreign affairs, we may differ from the Founding Fathers to the extent of doubting whether the élite, as distinguished from the representatives of a thinking populace, should constitute our leadership in the shaping of American foreign policy. For the proper functioning of our constitutional machinery, it is possible that the great need is not for the shielding of the people and their representatives from responsibility in the conduct of foreign affairs but rather for education through the carrying of responsibility. It is true that in the development of capacity there is no complete substitute for experience, with the result that senators with their longer terms have an advantage over representatives, and it is also true that extreme size in governmental bodies tends to unwieldiness and inefficiency. There is, therefore, probably some argument for the use of the Senate, rather than the two houses jointly, for the handling of certain aspects of foreign affairs, but the argument is by no means overwhelming.

The current tendency on the part of the Executive is to seek to avoid the restraining power of the Senate by making international agreements in the form of executive agreements which either require no sanction from a legislative agency or can be made on the basis of a general congressional authorization and need not be submitted in the form of a treaty for Senate approval. It is clear that agreements such as those of armistice in wartime which are temporary in character, which must be negotiated speedily and which govern matters constitutionally submitted to executive discretion, can be validly made without direct congressional approval in any form. It is clear also that Congress can express national policy through a statute affecting foreign affairs, even though enforcement of the statute requires the making of executive agreements authorized by the statute. The making of reciprocal trade agreements to implement congressional policy as to foreign trade provides a clear example. Authorities tear their own and sometimes one another's hair, however, over the question whether executive agreements can, at the discretion of the President or of Congress and the President, be substituted for all those kinds of international compacts which have in the past been made in the form of treaties through the co-operation of the President and the Senate. In view of the fact that the Constitution provides no adequate guidance to interpretation of this field, it is not surprising that commentators take positions largely in terms of the answers at which they hope to arrive. Members of the executive branch of the government, and particularly State Department officials and others who have suffered frustration of their efforts at the hands of the Senate, find in the Constitution ample authorization for the substitution of executive agreements for treaties.[6] The same position is taken by many professional students of international relations who, at the moment, are more concerned about the achievement of the particular ends sought to be achieved by the Executive than about careful adherence to the mandate of the Constitution or to the preservation of the separation of powers.[7] By contrast, others who distrust the Executive in the unrestrained exercise of power in this field find in the Constitution evidence that the larger part of the field of international negotiation is covered by the requirement as to the making of treaties.[8]

Although partly or even largely in terms of obiter dicta, the

[6] See, e.g., Wallace McClure, *International Executive Agreements* (1941).

[7] See, e.g., Edward S. Corwin, *The Constitution and World Organization* (1944), and Quincy Wright, "The United States and International Agreements," *American Journal of International Law*, XXXVIII (July, 1944), 341–55.

[8] See, e.g., Edwin Borchard, "Shall the Executive Agreement Replace the Treaty?" *American Journal of International Law*, XXXVIII (October, 1944), 637–43.

Supreme Court has given support in recent years to the argument of the advocates of the use of executive agreements. Speaking for the Court in *United States* v. *Curtiss-Wright Export Corporation*,[9] Justice Sutherland declared that the power of the government over foreign affairs was not limited to the grants specified in the Constitution but included also authority derived from the position of the United States as a sovereign nation, and that the President was peculiarly spokesman and representative of the United States in this field. The powers of external sovereignty, he contended, passed not from Great Britain to the colonies individually but directly to the colonies in their collective and corporate capacity as the United States of America.

It results that the investment of the federal government with the powers of external sovereignty did not depend upon the affirmative grants of the Constitution. The powers to declare and wage war, to conclude peace, to make treaties, to maintain diplomatic relations with other sovereignties, if they had never been mentioned in the Constitution, would have vested in the federal government as necessary concomitants of nationality.[10]

Not only was the federal power over external affairs different in origin and essential character from that over internal affairs, he declared, but participation in the exercise of the power was significantly limited.

In this vast external realm, with its important, complicated, delicate and manifold problems, the President alone has the power to speak or listen as a representative of the nation. He *makes* treaties with the advice and the consent of the Senate; but he alone negotiates. Into the field of negotiation the Senate cannot intrude; and Congress itself is powerless to invade it.[11]

[9] 299 U.S. 304 (1936).

[10] *Ibid.*, p. 318.   [11] *Ibid.*, p. 319.

Legislative delegations of power to the President in the field
of foreign affairs were to be interpreted in the light of the
parallel existence of

the very delicate, plenary and exclusive power of the President as the
sole organ of the federal government in the field of international relations—a power which does not require as a basis for its exercise an act of
Congress, but which, of course, like every other governmental power,
must be exercised in subordination to the applicable provisions of the
Constitution. It is quite apparent that if, in the maintenance of our international relations, embarrassment—perhaps serious embarrassment—is
to be avoided and success for our aims achieved, congressional legislation which is to be made effective through negotiation and inquiry
within the international field must often accord to the President a degree
of discretion and freedom from statutory restrictions which would not
be admissible were domestic affairs alone involved.[12]

In *United States* v. *Belmont*,[13] Justice Sutherland, again
speaking for the Court, further strengthened the position of
the President in the independent handling of foreign affairs.
The decision gave force to an executive agreement with Soviet
Russia concerning title to property in the United States which
had formerly been held by a Russian corporation of the czarist
regime but which had been confiscated by the Soviet government. The Court regarded the agreement as to the property as
an integral part of the arrangement whereby the United States
gave recognition to the government of the U.S.S.R. In respect
of what was done here, suggested Sutherland, the Executive
had authority to speak as the sole organ of the government of
the United States. The advice and consent of the Senate was
not required. An international compact need not always be in
the form of a treaty. The validity of the agreement, furthermore, was not impaired by the fact that it ran counter to the
policy of a state in determining the title to property held within its borders.[14]

[12] *Ibid.*, p. 320.   [13] 301 U.S. 324 (1937).
[14] See also *United States* v. *Pink*, 315 U.S. 203 (1942).

If Supreme Court decisions signify with the solemnity of judicial utterance the current course of development of the Constitution as to the control of foreign affairs, activities of Congress and of the President even more sharply delineate moving frontiers. The famous "destroyer deal," made by President Roosevelt with Great Britain before our entrance into the second World War, with the faintest legislative sanction or none at all, later received something in the way of retroactive approval in the Lend-Lease Act. The so-called "Atlantic Charter," the product of President Roosevelt and Prime Minister Churchill, which represents a statement of attitude as to the rights of nations in the world order, is assumed by many to exercise a kind of compulsion upon the development of American foreign policy. Leaders in the Senate, while defending in general language the prerogative of the Senate in the making of treaties, advocated approval of the U.N.R.R.A. compact as an executive agreement supported by Congress. The results of the monetary conference held at Bretton Woods reflect themselves thus far not in a multiparty treaty but in efforts of Congress to enact a measure on the basis of which the Executive will play the part in international monetary affairs which was outlined at the Bretton Woods Conference. Throughout the period after its enactment the Lend-Lease Act gave to the President a tremendous amount of power for the disposal, at his discretion, of government-owned resources for the benefit of our allies. Even though the disposal was supposedly restricted by statute to ends connected with the war, power nevertheless remained to influence the lines of non-military foreign policy through the allotment of lend-lease materials.

In the development of American foreign policy through the making of agreements with foreign nations by the Executive with a minimum of legislative restraint, perhaps even more important are the international conferences attended by the President himself. The conferences held during the recent war were no doubt predominantly military in character. They were concerned with the winning of the war. Yet, in participating in them, the President was not merely Commander-in-Chief of the Army and Navy but also the official spokesman of the United States. It is hardly possible that commitments involving other things than technically military matters, including items on which Congress had not passed, could have been avoided. Although as to a postwar international organization for the preservation of the peace both houses of Congress went on record as favoring our participation, the resolutions passed to that end constituted mere expressions of sentiment and not legislative authorization to making binding commitments. The steps taken by the President prior to Senate ratification of the agreement reached at the San Francisco Conference in the summer of 1945 were taken on his own responsibility. The same is true as to the readjustment of European national boundaries and other subjects which must inevitably have been discussed and tentatively settled. In other words, the power of the President to make agreements with foreign nations largely free of restraint from either or both houses of Congress was at least temporarily enhanced by the necessities of war, and the tradition of executive independence in such matters has steadily become more deeply intrenched.

Although this is not to say that there will be no reaction or that the reaction, if it comes, will be a reflection of great statesmanship on the part of Congress, Congress and the people are at the present time ignorant of much that the President does in the process of international negotiation, and they are even more deeply ignorant of the complex of considerations in terms of which he makes individual decisions. In time of war this condition is perhaps inevitable no matter how lamentable it may be, yet inevitability does not keep it from being dangerous. For the postwar era we must, if democracy is to be preserved, see that the American people, and officials of all branches of the national government, develop a working knowledge of the handling of our foreign affairs. This does not mean setting up in the State Department a propaganda agency for making the people think and feel as the administration in power happens to think and feel. It means rather that the people who fight and pay for world wars and whose economic prosperity depends on conditions throughout the entire world must awaken to the fact that the day-to-day handling of foreign affairs is vital to their own welfare and calls for their informed attention. In matters as important as these, no President is wise enough do to all our thinking for us. As for our professional specialists in foreign affairs, they, like experts in other fields, must be our servants and not our masters. When their paternalistic leadership from behind the scenes runs into catastrophe, they have fine capacity for constructing plausible stories as to how it all happened and for blaming the backwardness of public opinion—see, for example, the State Department publication, *Peace and War: United States Foreign Policy, 1931–1941*, published in 1943—but their custom is to hoard the information upon which sound policy ought to be made rather than to release it freely to the public whose servants they are supposed to be.

To make the point in other language, we can say that either the merging of powers over foreign affairs in the hands of one branch of the government or their division between Congress and the Executive will be accompanied by danger unless the people know and understand the broad outlines of what is being done and why it is being done. Concentration of power remains dangerous for the reasons which led to the provision for the separation of powers in our state and federal constitutions. Division of authority is also dangerous in the absence of public understanding of issues because under those circumstances the checks exercised by one branch of the government upon another are too often made in terms of departmental jealousy or personal pique rather than in terms of attempts at better understanding of the popular will. Both the legislative and the executive branches of the government ought to participate in the process of popular education about foreign affairs, but neither branch is to be trusted with full powers. As a guide to sound public opinion, Congress, like the public which it represents, is only sporadically interested in foreign affairs. It has no tradition in terms of which it must keep itself informed about them. Few individual pronouncements of members of Congress reflect the breadth of knowledge and understanding which would entitle them to speak with authority.

As for the executive branch of the government, employees variously located have broader information about segments of the foreign field than do most individual members of Congress. This information is likely to be highly specialized as to area or subject, however, particularly as far as employees of the State Department are concerned. Their contribution to public understanding of foreign affairs is restricted by the bureaucratic conviction that only experts can be trusted to understand or act upon their specialized information. It is significant of their attitude that, whereas they now make to public opinion the concession of putting on chatty radio programs and in other ways seeking to persuade the people to accept whatever strategy they may have decided upon, their publication of diversified materials on the basis of which thinking people might arrive at sound judgments about foreign affairs continues to run many years behind.

For other reasons than those already specifically mentioned, members of Congress and the people who elect them must be better educated as to the interrelation between foreign and domestic affairs. The control of world trade, than which few problems will be more important in the postwar era, will involve our tariff program and the already tremendously complicated regulations of domestic commerce in terms of which Congress seeks to regulate our internal economy. If in the postwar period we continue to effectuate our international policy by cutting off some or all exports from the United States to particular countries, such a program will so vitally affect the productive and the commercial enterprise of the United States that Congress must be, at least potentially, a participant. If we attempt to lift the world out of a depression by a gigantic spending program, as during the 1930's we attempted to lift the United States, Congress must participate in the decision and share the responsibility. If we assume the desirability for the sake of peace and order in the world in the years to come of freely sharing the vast resources of the United States with less prosperous sections of the world, a decision to that end would so vitally affect the welfare of all the American people that the decision should not be made without their full awareness as to its meaning and without evidence of that awareness being reflected in overt acts of Congress. It is not enough to say that, if we can spend billions in waging war in foreign lands, we can spend other billions in time of peace to promote a world welfare and prevent another war. It is not enough to say that continued foreign spending is essential to the preservation of prosperity at home. On this point, we have seen in past years the building-up in foreign lands of debts to the United States which the debtors would never be able to pay, under the justification or pretended justification of maintaining our domestic prosperity. A growing awareness of the depletion of our natural resources is already leading many people to the conclusion that some more satisfactory way of conducting our domestic exchange must be found than that of dumping large quantities of our resources into the hands of other nations who can give us nothing acceptable in return. Whatever our decision as to these matters of policy, the decision will be costly in terms of wealth and of adjustment in ways of doing things. No man or group of men should be permitted to lead us far in the direction of permanent commitments without a clear mandate from the American people. That mandate can come only after the issues have been made clear. The issues will be made clear only as they become the subject of democratic action in the selection of representatives to make choices in the field of policy. Congress, quite as much as the President, must share in the decisions.

To elaborate on the relation of the conduct of foreign affairs to the conduct of affairs at home, international, industrial, and commercial policies are inextricably entangled with our domestic policy toward business and industrial combinations. That policy might be said to be one of promoting the growth of ever bigger and more powerful corporations and combinations of corporations, while quieting our uneasiness about such concentrations of power in nongovernmental hands by maintaining a limited antitrust program to demonstrate that the government is still "boss." It is obvious that already each of a number of corporations has more wealth at its disposal and exercises control over the lives of people to a greater extent than do the governments of each of a number of the states. It is not unusual, indeed, to hear such comments as that the state of Delaware is but a tool of the Du Ponts or that Montana is an administrative unit of the Anaconda Copper Corporation. While such characterizations are obviously too sweeping for complete accuracy, they nevertheless illustrate an important tendency in the flow of power in the United States. Furthermore, apart from the question of comparative strength, corporations, in the process of conducting their operations in a number of states, render control by any state extremely difficult, leaving the federal government the only potentially effective master.

The position which corporations and corporate groups have come to occupy with respect to the several states is suggestive of the position which at an early date they may come to occupy with respect to international affairs. A number of small nations are already virtually at the level of tools of particular organized economic interests. The interrelations of corporations formed under the laws of different nations are, in some instances, so complex as to be bewildering almost beyond comprehension, and the strength of combinations is such that they are able virtually to defy governmental control. By means of their control of patents and of intercorporate agreements as to their use and by means of their monopoly control of raw materials and the instruments of production, trade policies of national states may be virtually dictated from corporation offices. Through its investigations of the misuse of patents and its search for various types of violations of antitrust laws, the Department of Justice has discovered between American corporations and various European cartels a degree of collaboration which almost puts to shame the results thus far achieved in the collaboration of national states for purposes other than war. Evidence has been collected to show the continuation of intercorporate collaboration even after certain of the nations involved had gone to war one with another, and the appearance created by the record is that, as the collaborators were being forced to suspend action, they did so like men retreating into a storm cellar, with full expectation of coming out and resuming their activities after the storm had passed.[15] Evidence has been discovered that intercorporate agreements which clearly violate the antitrust laws of the United States or other laws of this or other countries are lived up to meticulously by the parties involved as parts of their program of carrying on commerce and developing industry according to their patterns rather than in terms of policy as expressed by law.[16]

All this has gone on and is likely to continue in the future on such a scale as to suggest that national states are faced with problems of control of corporations comparable to those which have faced the states of the American Union. It suggests the necessity of intergovernmental combinations to control corporate offspring which do business away from home. It suggests also that the world state, if and when it comes, may come not merely for the prevention of war but also for the control of state-created organizations which have grown so powerful as to become laws unto themselves. For democratic nations these problems are problems not for behind-the-scenes diplomacy or for settlement merely by executive agreements but for public discussion and debate and for action by all the branches of the government which operate for the promotion of the public welfare. The conduct of foreign affairs, like the conduct of domestic affairs, calls not for exceptional and extra-constitutional action but for the full implementation of government for which the Constitution provides.

[15] See various parts of the *Hearings before the Senate Committee on Patents* (77th Cong., 2d sess.) on S. 2303 and S. 2491.

[16] See Wendell Berge, *Cartels* (1944); Thurman Arnold, *The Bottlenecks of Business* (1940) and *Democracy and Free Enterprise* (1942); and Joseph Borkin and Charles A. Welsh, *Germany's Master Plan* (1943).

IX

NEW HORIZONS FOR THE JUDICIARY

*

THE larger part of a decade has passed since the day in February, 1937, when President Roosevelt submitted to Congress his plan for establishing the constitutionality of the New Deal by packing the Supreme Court. The one-time remark of Attorney-General Cummings, that on every constitutional question the government started with a handicap of four justices against it—that the situation was like a game in which the score was four down and five to go—now seems like ancient history. Seven of the justices then sitting were replaced by Roosevelt appointees, one received the presidential blessing by promotion to the chief justiceship, and one has been replaced by an appointee of President Truman.

After an unprecedented outburst of destructive activity in 1935 and 1936, in which it announced eleven decisions holding acts of Congress unconstitutional, the Supreme Court quietly signed off as to performance in this field. As a result, with the exception of a minor provision, no act of Congress has fallen to the judicial ax[1] since 1936—the longest period of its kind since announcement of the Dred Scott decision in 1857. Instead the Court has come almost to assume the constitutionality of any measure which Congress has enacted, and it has abandoned precedents incased in its own past decisions when they have stood in the way of the execution of new policies sponsored by Congress or the President. As far as judicial appraisal of action by the federal government is concerned, as

---

[1] As of October, 1945.

distinguished from state action, interpretation of statutes has largely taken the place of interpretation of the Constitution, and administrative rules and orders having the force of law have taken the place formerly occupied by statutes. Except in a relatively few critical cases, the question to which the Court gives attention is not whether a statute violates the Constitution but whether an administrator has properly interpreted a statute. Even in the field of statutory interpretation it seems to be the tendency virtually to assume the validity of rulings which administrators have based upon acts of Congress. In the light of these changes in the performance of the judicial function, it is important to re-examine the nature of that function in order more adequately to appraise the significance of the changes.

In large part, the function of a court is to apply law in cases or controversies which are brought before it. It determines rights and obligations and, in terms of established judicial procedure, settles disputes between private parties or between private parties, on the one hand, and the government, on the other. To describe the function of a court in this fashion, however, seems to imply definiteness and distinctiveness on the part of the law in a degree in which they do not necessarily exist prior to the decision of the case in hand. The common law from which the mass of our legal concepts has been derived is itself a product of the process by which courts decide cases. Even if we accept the generalization of conservative legal theory that judges do not make the law, "they do but find it," we cannot escape the fact that laymen can learn what the common law is only by reading what is said in judicial opinions as they are rendered in case after case. The courts are the mouthpieces of the law, and the law comes to be known only as judges declare it.

Of law which exists in the form of written constitutions and statutes, this at first appears not to be true, yet no constitution which itself is a law, and few statutes, are so explicit in all their details as to require no interpretation, no judicial declaration or "discovery" of legal meaning. Certainly the Constitution of the United States and many of the statutes enacted by Congress require a tremendous amount of development through interpretation. How, then, does a judge determine the meaning of the Constitution in areas where the Constitution itself does not clearly define that meaning? How does a judge make or discover constitutional law? In deciding the case of *McCulloch* v. *Maryland* in 1819, Chief Justice Marshall outlined a standard for interpretation of the implied powers of the federal government in the following language: "Let the end be legitimate, let it be within the scope of the Constitution, and all means which are appropriate, which are plainly adapted to that end, which are not prohibited, but consist with the letter and spirit of the Constitution, are constitutional."[2] In order to be helpful, however, Marshall's words themselves require interpretation. The case at hand may turn on the question as to whether or not the end involved is legitimate or within the scope of the Constitution. It may turn on decision as to whether the means involved are appropriate or are plainly adapted to the legitimate end or are prohibited or consist with the letter and spirit of the Constitution.

Obviously, it is necessary to search further in order to understand in any detail the standards which guide judges in interpretative development of the Constitution. In finding the meaning of words in the Constitution and statutes, judges make some use of the layman's crutch—the dictionary. Yet the value of dictionaries is limited by the fact that in English, as in any living language, the meanings of words are in steady process of change. The word "commerce," for example—one of

[2] *McCulloch* v. *Maryland*, 4 Wheaton 316, 421 (1819).

the key words in our Constitution—has been astonishingly fluid.[3] As an authority on meanings, the dictionary is a man-made institution without pretense of guidance by a higher power or by a basic substratum of natural law or even by superior wisdom, to all of which jurists sometimes lay claim. "Why should we follow the dictionary?" Justice Holmes is said once to have remarked to his brethren. "Let the dictionary follow us."

Judges have relied heavily upon the common law to provide the key to the content of constitutional terminology. Only within the common law could they initially find with any precision at all the legal meaning of such terms as "jury," "grand jury," "due process of law," "case," "controversy," etc. Yet the common law also had its limitations. It, too, was in process of change. Members of the Supreme Court have often disagreed as to the particular chronological point at which they should tap the common law in a search for meaning of constitutional words and phrases. The famous Charles River Bridge case, decided by the Supreme Court in 1837, provides an example. The case had to do in part with the question whether the contract in the charter granted to a private corporation by a state should be construed broadly or narrowly. Chief Justice Taney, relying on a relatively recent common-law decision by a court in England, held for the Supreme Court that any ambiguity in the terms of the contract operated against the holders of the charter. It would present a singular spectacle, he declared, if, while the courts in England were restraining the spirit of monopoly and confining corporations to the privileges plainly given to them and their charters, the courts of this country should be found enlarging these privileges by implication.[4]

[3] See Walton H. Hamilton and Douglass Adair, *The Power To Govern* (1937).

[4] See *Charles River Bridge* v. *Warren Bridge*, 11 Peters 420, 544–46 (1837).

Justice Story, on the other hand, wrote a dissenting opinion in which he derived his theory of interpretation of contracts not from relatively current English decisions but from those of the distant past, saying:

> I stand upon the old law; upon law established more than three centuries ago, in cases contested with as much ability and learning, as any in the annals of our jurisprudence, in resisting any such encroachments upon the rights and liberties of the citizens, secured by public grants. I will not consent to shake their title deeds, by any speculative niceties or novelties.[5]

If in support of Taney's argument we have the principle that the cases most recently decided show what the law now is, we have on Story's side the principle that it is the settled interpretation which determines the law. The point here involved is that the common law left the question of major importance to be decided by the Supreme Court in its interpretation of common-law terminology in the Constitution.

To some extent, judges interpret the language of the Constitution in terms of the meaning which that language had or is supposed to have had at the time when the Constitution was adopted. In the Dred Scott case, for example, Chief Justice Taney took the position that Negroes could not be citizens in 1857 within the meaning of constitutional terminology because they had not been regarded as citizens or fit to be citizens at the time of the adoption of the Constitution. Whether because people do not generally understand the variable nature of verbal meanings, however, or because they have but limited respect for words when used to obstruct popular desires, laymen have little patience with the limitation of constitutional meanings to those of the 1780's. Some judges, furthermore, insist that such limitation cannot be justified. For illustration take the following language, already quoted elsewhere,

[5] *Ibid.,* p. 598.

of Justice Holmes as spokesman for the Supreme Court in
Missouri v. *Holland* in 1920:

> When we are dealing with words that also are a constitutent act, like
> the Constitution of the United States, we must realize that they have
> called into life a being the development of which could not have been
> foreseen completely by the most gifted of its begetters. It was enough
> for them to realize or to hope that they had created an organism; it has
> taken a century and has cost their successors much sweat and blood to
> prove that they created a nation. The case before us must be considered
> in the light of our whole experience, and not merely in that of what was
> said a hundred years ago.[6]

In any event, it is no easy task to discover the content which
particular words had in the minds of our forefathers. In reply
to Chief Justice Taney's contention as to Negro citizenship,
other judges and many laymen denied that at the time of the
adoption of the Constitution the Negro "had no rights which
the white man was bound to respect." There was no way to
settle this controversial question of fact to the satisfaction of
all concerned.

Furthermore, the Constitution must operate upon phenom-
ena about which the Founding Fathers could have had no
opinion. How can we discover, for example, whether they intended to include radio broadcasting within the concepts of
commerce, and interstate commerce at that? How can we discover whether by means of the due process clause of the Fifth
Amendment they intended to limit the power of the Interstate
Commerce Commission to fix railroad rates at a point high
enough to yield a fair return—five, six, eight per cent—on the
fair value, with value measured by a variable complex of factors such as original cost, reproduction cost, depreciation, etc.?
Railroads as we know them today, and the Interstate Commerce Commission, to say nothing of radio broadcasting, were
beyond the wildest dreams of the framers of the Constitution.

[6] *Missouri* v. *Holland*, 252 U.S. 416, 433–34 (1920).

It is clear, then, that if we are to solve modern problems in terms of the Constitution someone must read new content into old language. It is equally clear that if anything that meets the desires of an interested party can be read into the Constitution without reference to the basic pattern prescribed in the document, a written Constitution loses most of its meaning. Actually, the constitutional system operates in such a way as to embrace new concepts within the words of the Constitution while at the same time guarding the essential features of the system. By the exercise of power alleged to represent legitimate interpretation of the Constitution, Congress and the Executive create issues some of which litigation brings before the federal courts, and eventually before the Supreme Court, for adjudication. At the same time the states, in the exercise of powers alleged to be reserved to them, give rise to other issues of federal constitutionality, also for eventual adjudication by the Supreme Court. That Court, therefore, becomes the arbiter of constitutionality, the final authority as to the meaning which it is permissible to read into the language of the Constitution. It is, in a sense, as it has at times been characterized, something in the nature of a continuing constitutional convention, yet it is a convention which functions within the pattern and in terms of the principles of a constitution which has already been established.

What, in more detail, is the process by which justices of the Supreme Court perform their functions? By textual study of the Constitution itself, by use of available guides such as those already discussed, and by reference to other decisions of the Supreme Court and to a lesser extent of other courts, they seek to discover the original and basic meanings of the relevant provisions of the Constitution. The meanings of most provisions of the Constitution on which present-day decisions turn have already been projected at considerable length by means of cases already decided. These earlier decisions provide guidance to current judicial action which is only less authoritative than that provided by the Constitution itself. Situations arise, however, in which all guidance seems to fail and in which the task of the judge comes to be starkly that of making the law in terms of which the case before him is to be decided, or at the very least it comes to be that of making law incidentally in the process of deciding the case. The duty of the judge at times extends so far, indeed, as to involve the un-making of law now deemed incorrectly made by other judges engaged in the same process.

In those areas in which legal guides are largely wanting, the common-law jurist takes guidance from conceptions of right and justice—conceptions as to what ought to be in rela-tions between man and man, between man and society, and between man or men and government. His philosophy of life, his attitude toward his fellow-men, his conception of the ideal economic and social order—all become important in shaping the extensions of law for which he will be responsible in deciding cases. Almost every man likely to be chosen for a judicial position is the product of the central stream of our culture, with the result that his lawmaking activities consist of projections of the sentiments of the dominant groups in so-ciety. Judge-made law reflects usually the dominant beliefs of the community as to what ought to be, with an anchor on the side of conservatism in the essence of law itself which implies stability and established connections with the past. If per-chance a judge lives too long, so that his personal sentiments fail to keep up with changes in the dominant sentiments of the community, his decisions may be out of line with the latter. In the long run the matter is likely to be relatively unimportant, however, for the choice of his successor or successors in office will bring the law once again into line even at the expense of the overruling of past decisions.

All this must not be taken to imply, however, that the judge may absolve himself from responsibility by deciding cases in terms of the transient whims of the community. If he is to serve the community properly, he must strive to reflect in his decisions the ideals and standards of settled and rational attitudes, making himself oftentimes the articulate voice of the community on matters on which the community itself is inarticulate. When the question involved is one of federal constitutionality, he has the obligation to rationalize the decision in such a way as to show how it fits into the scheme of principles and ideals which are embodied in the Constitution. For example, no decision which denies a claim to a constitutional right should stop with statement of positive reasons for the action of the court. In addition, it should throw a beam of light upon the bulwark of constitutional safeguards in such a way as to demonstrate that the bulwark is undamaged by the decision. On the other hand, no decision which restrains governmental action in order to protect constitutional rights should stop with statement of positive reasons in justification. It should also restate in some fashion the principle that rights against government are not absolutes and demonstrate that constitutional grants of power to government are not nullified by the action of the court. Similarly, the court should explain each decision in terms of the basic structure and fundamental principles of the Constitution—the principle of federalism, the principle of the separation of powers, etc.—in so far as they are relevant. The purpose of this process of rationalization is not merely to insure the rightness of the decision which the court is to announce, important as that insurance may be. Beyond it is the even more important function of making clear to all the people the process of constitutional unfolding which proceeds under the sponsorship of the judiciary.

The Supreme Court, in particular, has duties almost at the level of a priesthood of the law—duties of supervising constitutional development in terms of the ideals of our constitutional and social system. Performance of those duties, once again, is not limited to striking down federal or state statutes which are found to violate the ideals or principles or the clear language of the Constitution. It involves, rather, the illumination of issues and the development of constitutional law in terms of the whole background of ideals and principles which may happen to be involved. In the language of Justice Cardozo as recorded long before he became a member of the Supreme Court:

> The restraining power of the judiciary does not manifest its chief worth in the few cases in which the legislature has gone beyond the lines that mark the limits of discretion. Rather shall we find its chief worth in making vocal and audible the ideals that might otherwise be silenced, in giving them continuity of life and of expression, in guiding and directing choice within the limits where choice ranges. This function should preserve to the courts the power that now belongs to them, if only the power is exercised with insight into social values, and with suppleness of adaptation to changing social needs.[7]

The difficulty of the judicial task lies as much in the appraisal of social values and changing social needs as in logical development of the language of the Constitution. There is always the danger that the judge will become the legal spokesman, not for the settled and dominant sentiments of the community as a whole, but rather for that of a faction with whose interests he incorrectly tends to identify the interests of the community. Under the cover of constitutional interpretation the judge can become a defender of, or a crusader for, the interests of a particular warring group and mold the development of the Constitution accordingly. Although the tendency of judges in the past has been to drift somewhat in the direction of what was currently regarded as conservatism and particularly to protect

[7] Benjamin N. Cardozo, *The Nature of the Judicial Process* (1920), p. 94.

rights of property as against so-called human rights, a bias on behalf of a minority such as an allegedly oppressed group—whether it be labor or a religious sect or a section of the population—could also make itself effective in the molding of constitutional law. To run ahead of our story, there are critics who would say that this kind of bias, particularly as to the rights of labor, now operates more frequently and more dangerously than that on behalf of the rights of property.

Judges with differing conceptions of social values and changing social needs check one another sharply when biases stand out in judicial decisions. When, for example, in 1936 the majority of the Supreme Court, speaking through Justice Roberts, held unconstitutional the processing tax provisions of the Agricultural Adjustment Act of 1933, it reflected deep antagonism to the control of agricultural production by the federal government. Justice Stone, dissenting, by implication accused his colleagues of resorting to "a tortured construction of the Constitution" and declared tartly that "courts are not the only agency of government that must be assumed to have capacity to govern."[8] He pointed out that, "while unconstitutional exercise of power by the executive and legislative branches of the government is subject to judicial restraint, the only check upon our own exercise of power is our own sense of self-restraint."[9] This suggestion that, in the interpretation of the Constitution, judges needed to exercise self-restraint so disturbed Justice Sutherland, one of the extreme conservatives on the Court, that he tried to answer it in a dissenting opinion a little more than a year later when a shift in alignment left the conservative wing in the minority. He wrote as follows:

The suggestion that the only check upon the exercise of the judicial power, when properly invoked, to declare a constitutional right superior

[8] *United States* v. *Butler*, 297 U.S. 1, 87 (1936).
[9] *Ibid.*, pp. 78–79.

to an unconstitutional statute is the judge's own faculty of self-restraint, is both ill-considered and mischievous. Self-restraint belongs in the domain of will and not of judgment. The check upon the judge is that imposed by his oath of office, by the Constitution, and by his own conscientious and informed convictions; and since he has the duty to make up his own mind and adjudge accordingly, it is hard to see how there could be any other restraint.[10]

According to Sutherland, the oath of office taken by each justice required him to decide cases in terms of his own best judgment. Self-restraint, therefore, had no place among judicial duties. To surrender one's deliberate judgment, indeed, except as it might be modified by the persuasion of those holding different views, would constitute a violation of his oath of office.

Since Justice Stone never formally engaged in counter-rebuttal, we do not know in detail what his reply would have been. We might expect him to say, if he were to speak so frankly, that it requires an act of will to keep alive intellectually and to apply the essential meanings of the Constitution to changing conditions of American civilization and that self-restraint to the extent of resisting intellectual rigidity is part of the duty of every judge who insists upon retaining his judicial position. Few of Sutherland's critics questioned his integrity or his ability to reason cogently from the premises which were deeply intrenched in his mind, but they did question his selection of premises and the scheme of priorities in terms of which he marshaled them for the decision of cases. They did not feel that he must necessarily change the character of his intellectual assumptions because other people thought otherwise or that he must even be aware of the limitations of his own thinking any more than most men are aware of the approach of senility, but they were, nevertheless, firmly convinced that

---

[10] *West Coast Hotel Co.* v. *Parrish*, 300 U.S. 379, 402 (1937).

men whose thinking was outmoded in terms of the welfare of the society to be governed had no rightful part in the making of policy for that government. Their limitations could be corrected only by the appointment of their successors.

As we review the course of American constitutional history, we can say that on few occasions prior to the 1930's did the Supreme Court use its power of judicial review of acts of Congress in such a way as to flout what might be called dominant public sentiment and that on no occasion prior to the date mentioned did the Court hand down a series of decisions in such a way as to block an integrated program of government which had widespread and enthusiastic popular support. It will be recalled that the first case in which an act or part of an act of Congress was held unconstitutional—and in this instance it was a very small part of the act indeed—was *Marbury* v. *Madison*, which was decided in 1803. No similar action was taken until 1857, more than half a century later, when in the Dred Scott case the Supreme Court held unconstitutional part of a statute which, incidentally, had already been supplanted. Restrictive action by the Supreme Court speeded up after the Civil War with the increase in the legislative activity of Congress, so that for the thirty-five years from 1865 to 1900 twenty-four Supreme Court decisions are listed in which acts or parts of acts of Congress were held unconstitutional. From 1900 until 1934 inclusive the Court decided forty cases in which acts or parts of acts of Congress were disapproved.[11] As has already been said, few of these sixty-six decisions ran counter to dominant and settled public sentiment on public

[11] For a list and discussion of these cases see U.S. Library of Congress, Legislative Reference Service, *Provisions of Federal Law Held Unconstitutional by the Supreme Court of the United States* (prepared by Wilfred C. Gilbert, 1936). For a summary and extension of the list see Lawrence B. Evans, *Cases on American Constitutional Law* (5th ed.; edited by Charles G. Fenwick, 1942), pp. 61–63.

issues. For the most part they represented action on legislative provisions about which there had never been any clear public sentiment at all or on which the sentiment had been sharply divided or on which the sentiment which had once existed had largely dissipated. Furthermore, between the Civil War and the 1930's the several decisions were scattered over the years and were not grouped together at any point in such a way as to block an integrated program of the federal government.

The group of New Deal decisions which were handed down by the Supreme Court in 1935 and 1936 provided a striking contrast. During those two years, eleven decisions held acts or parts of acts of Congress unconstitutional. Furthermore, the tenor of these decisions, coupled with that of certain decisions on state statutes, revealed the Supreme Court standing squarely in the way of the integrated program of the New Deal—a program which, Maine and Vermont dissenting, won enthusiastic popular sanction in the presidential election of 1936.

This unprecedented stand of the Supreme Court in a time of crisis against all but relatively unimportant trickles of change doubtless had many explanations. One of them may well be found in the fact that in 1937 the average age of "the nine old men" was more than seventy-two years. While a few men keep intellectually alive and flexible until well beyond that age, most people suffer a decline in capacity such as to justify their retirement well before the average age listed has been reached. Another explanation may lie in the sharp division which had been apparent in the Court since the early 1920's. In terms of that division a liberal minority, consisting of Justices Holmes, Brandeis, and Stone, and of Justice Cardozo as a replacement for Justice Holmes, crowded a conservative majority into a well-rationalized position which may have been more conservative and was certainly better thought out and better phrased than it would have been without the existence of the liberal opposition. In other words, while the liberal justices were educating liberal laymen and liberal lawyers in a rationale for adapting the Constitution to the conditions of mass-production industrialism, they were temporarily defeating the ends of liberalism by giving disciplinary opposition to the standpat members of the Court, particularly those "four horsemen of conservatism"—Justices Van Devanter, Sutherland, McReynolds, and Butler. Another explanation probably lies in the fact that the Supreme Court was not called upon to appraise critical New Deal legislation until after the country had begun its rise from the trough of the depression. Drastic monetary measures upon which other action might well have been disastrous for the country were either upheld or handled in such a way that advantage could not be taken of adverse judicial action. The nullifying action of the Court was taken in terms of a number of statutory provisions which were deemed important by New Deal leaders and their followers but which a growing minority of conservative opponents deemed unnecessary for the further protection of the nation, if, indeed, they had ever been necessary at all. Another explanation lay in the fact that even the liberal minority on the Supreme Court felt itself unable to stomach the disorderly procedure in terms of which legal rights were handled.

At any rate, whatever the weight to be attached to these and other explanations, the Supreme Court took a position directly athwart the program sponsored by a popular President. Although that program had as much positive and conscious support as is ever given to any governmental program except in time of war, the majority of the Court was unable or unwilling so to rationalize the principles of the Constitution as to give its sanction. The development of constitutional law, which ought to be a process of relating the principles of the

Constitution to programs supported by the people which meet the basic needs of the people, failed to make the adaptation and lost its vital contact with the public welfare.

The resulting attempt of the President to pack the Supreme Court with new members with a more flexible outlook is an old and familiar story. In February, 1937, the President sent to Congress a message and a bill in terms of which he proposed various reforms of the federal judiciary, including a plan whereby a new justice was to be appointed to sit alongside each member of the Supreme Court seventy and a half years of age who failed to take advantage of his retirement privileges. The bill would have authorized increase in the membership of the Supreme Court in this fashion up to a total of fifteen. It was privately assumed that no justice who had reached the designated age would endure the insult of having an alternate sit beside him because of his advanced age and that the several elderly justices would therefore retire. If they failed to do so, however, the appointment of new members would so out-number the conservative wing of the Court that measures not objectionable to the existing liberal wing might be expected to be upheld.

Although the members of the Supreme Court maintained an attitude of aloofness toward the controversy started by the President's proposal, they recognized the discredit which would be reflected upon the Court if the bill were passed. In ways of their own, therefore, they became, in effect, partic-ipants in the controversy. A new case had been argued before the Court involving the power of a state to fix minimum wages for women. At a critical moment, by virtue of the shift of Justice Roberts from the group of four with which he had stood a year earlier on the same issue to the group of four which had then registered dissent, the Court upheld the state statute now in controversy and overruled the famous Adkins case, thereby demonstrating that, without any change in membership, it could in important respects adjust constitutional law to current conceptions of justice and of the public welfare.[12] Then in a series of decisions it upheld the power of Congress to enforce collective bargaining upon industry.[13] These decisions, although handed down by a closely divided Court, represented a victory won by the New Deal without the necessity of packing the Supreme Court. Then at a strategic moment Justice Van Devanter, one of the four extreme conservatives on the Court, announced his intention of retiring at the end of the current term, which was only a few weeks ahead. Chief Justice Hughes struck a blow at the pending bill in the form of a letter which had the approval of Justices Van Devanter and Brandeis in which he answered questions of Senator Burton K. Wheeler as to the status of the work of the Court and as to the effect which an increase in membership of the Court would have upon it. His skilfully phrased letter avoided the political conflict as such, but at the same time it marshaled a persuasive argument against any increase in the membership of the Court. All in all, the public was gradually coming to the opinion that the proposal to pack the Supreme Court was both unwise and unnecesary. This crystallization of sentiment, coupled with the opposition of those who had always been opposed to the plan, brought defeat to the plan and nominally to presidential leadership as far as judicial reform was concerned.

The defeat, however, was one in name only. Without actual changes in personnel, the Supreme Court backed away from the intransigent position which it had taken, decided the cases already mentioned in terms of an evolving rather than a static

[12] *West Coast Hotel Co.* v. *Parrish*, 300 U.S. 379 (1937).

[13] See *National Labor Relations Board* v. *Jones & Laughlin Steel Corp.* 301 U.S. 1 (1937) and cases decided therewith.

Constitution, and upheld the Social Security Act and other measures which constituted parts of the program for solving modern economic and social problems. Then, with the retirement of Justice Van Devanter in the summer of 1937, began a series of personnel changes in terms of which eight of the present members of the Supreme Court are Roosevelt and Truman appointees, while the remaining member of the old Court, Harlan F. Stone, who many years ago was Roosevelt's law teacher, holds the chief justiceship. All the new justices were appointed in the knowledge that they had approved or shown open-minded attitudes toward the general program of the federal government which, for want of a better term, continued to be called the New Deal.

This does not mean, however, that President Roosevelt and the Senate simply appointed to the Supreme Court a group of "yes men" whose primary qualification was their willingness to place the stamp of their approval upon anything which the political branches of the government saw fit to do. It means, rather, that the present members were expected to continue and are continuing the retreat begun by their predecessors from untenable positions which the latter had taken. The dike had broken before any new member had been appointed. An apt figure is that of black-robed justices running before the escaping flood waters and hoping to establish new peripheral lines of constitutionality in the foothills as the area of governmental power approaches the limits of popular desire. In other words, because of the fact that over a period of years, the old Court failed to perform properly the function of steady adaptation of constitutional law to the needs of the people, the new Court finds it necessary to make what appears to be a sharp break with the line of constitutional reasoning in the immediate past in order to bring constitutional interpretation into harmony with the public welfare which the Constitution was framed to promote. Having made that necessary break, the next task of the Court will be and, indeed, already is, that of re-establishing lines of continuity with the more distant past in order to guide current constitutional development in terms of the essential principles and ideals of our constitutional system. Intermingled, therefore, with an unprecedented number of frank reversals of past decisions have been efforts on the part of the Court to get "back to the Constitution."

To indicate how vastly the face of our constitutional structure has changed in a few short years, it is necessary to mention briefly some of the particular changes which have taken place, even though most of them have already been discussed more at length in other connections. First of all, ignoring the distinction between direct and indirect effects upon interstate commerce in terms of which the old Supreme Court limited the scope of the federal commerce power in 1935 and in 1936, the new Court seems to have given almost unlimited scope to that power for the control of agricultural production and for the protection of rights of labor. Particularly where labor legislation has been involved, the present Court, unlike its predecessor of some two decades earlier, has not merely recognized the existence of constitutional power of regulation on the basis of the commerce clause but has been inclined to interpret broadly the regulatory power which Congress through various labor statutes has conferred upon administrators. The Court, in other words, shows no tendency either directly or indirectly to use its power of judicial review to sabotage the program to which the country at large, however vociferous the voices of the dissenting minority, now seems to be committed.

Again, in connection with the exercise of both state and federal power, the Supreme Court seems quietly to have devitalized the due process clauses as far as what is known as substantive due process is concerned. That barrier to governmental interference with the rights of property, elusive of definition though it was, had stood squarely in the way of recognition of the changes in the character of private property which the changes in the essential character of our economy were forcing upon us. In the hands of Justice Sutherland and others who had accepted his point of view, it was a potent weapon. His successors, regarding it as an overused weapon for the achievement of undesirable ends, seem to have thrown it into the discard.

These and other constitutional changes which have taken place in recent years do not mean that the Supreme Court has abandoned its duty of appraising governmental action in terms of constitutionality. It means, rather, that the Court is attempting to reconsolidate constitutional interpretation along lines which are tenable in terms of current conceptions of the public welfare. It is attempting now to rationalize current governmental action in terms of the basic principles and ideals of the Constitution. Ultimately, perhaps, when the extension of governmental action reaches the approximate limits of the area to which the dominant sentiments of the people would have it go, the Court may again resume the function of limiting the scope of governmental power by constitutional interpretation. For the time being, however, its task is largely one of reconstruction—of reconstruction which has been made enormously more difficult by virtue of the fact that for a period the membership of a few years earlier failed to rise to the challenge of judicial obligation.

In the light of the dimensions of the task of reconstruction and adaptation and in the light of the realism with which the task must be faced, it is not surprising that to external observation the Court seems divided as seldom ever before. Each of the group of nine men—not so old now, the average age at one

time recently having been less than fifty-seven years—has his
own ideas as to methods and extent of reconstruction and is
not of the caliber or personality likely to yield easily to the
opinions of other men. When they finally came, furthermore,
the long-delayed changes in the membership of the Court
came with such rapidity as to leave the group without a sufficiently large nucleus of justices accustomed to the ways of
the tribunal and without a desirable background of experience
at working together as a group.

It is not surprising, therefore, that, in the interpretation of
federal statutes and in passing upon the constitutionality of
state statutes, the justices divide in large numbers of cases.
While lines of division are not hard and fixed as they were in
earlier years when Justices Van Devanter, McReynolds, Sutherland, and Butler almost always voted together and when
Justices Holmes, Brandeis, and Stone made up a well-defined
liberal clique, tendencies toward habitual alignment are apparent. For a time Justices Black and Douglas seemed to move
together with the rhythm of Siamese twins. They now sometimes act separately, but such occasions are still rare. Justice
Murphy is frequently aligned with them, and Justice Rutledge
only less often. For want of a better word, this group, or the
first three of them, at any rate, might be classified as the "liberal" wing of the present Supreme Court. Chief Justice Stone
and Justices Frankfurter, Reed, and Jackson make up the
"conservative" wing,[14] while the position of Justice Burton is
not yet clearly defined.

Although these groupings represent only tendencies and not

[14] For analyses of judicial alignments see the several articles of C. Herman
Pritchett in American Political Science Review, XXXV (October, 1941), 890–
98; Journal of Politics, IV (November, 1942), 491–506; Southwestern Social
Science Quarterly, XXIV (June, 1943), 12–22; University of Chicago Law
Review, XI (December, 1943), 49–61; and American Political Science Review,
XXXIX (February, 1945), 42–54.

permanent alignments, diversity of opinion has been rife in the changing Court, and individual justices have, at times, been something less than polite in voicing criticisms of positions taken by their brethren. Justice Roberts, prior to his recent retirement, denounced the creation of uncertainty in the law by the overruling of past decisions, on one occasion likening decisions subject to change to a restricted railroad ticket, "good for this day and train only."[15] On another occasion he expressed himself somewhat more at length as follows:

Respect for tribunals must fall when the bar and the public come to understand that nothing that has been said in prior adjudication has force in a current controversy.

Of course the law may grow to meet changing conditions. I do not advocate slavish adherence to authority where new conditions require new rules of conduct. But this is not such a case. The tendency to disregard precedents in the decision of cases like the present has become so strong in this Court of late as, in my view, to shake confidence in the consistency of decision and leave the courts below on an uncharted sea of doubt and difficulty without any confidence that what was said yesterday will hold good tomorrow, unless indeed a modern instance grows into a custom of members of this Court to make public announcement of a change of views and to indicate that they will change their votes on the same question when another case comes before the Court. This might, to some extent, obviate the predicament in which the lower courts, the bar, and the public find themselves.[16]

Statements such as those of Justice Roberts have been given widespread publicity, partly because newspapermen can dress them up in such a way as to capture public attention. In contrast with most of the materials which come from the Court and which are unintelligible to general readers and even to newspaper reporters themselves, the cry of uncertainty in the law has been taken up in terms of comprehensible emotional

[15] *Smith* v. *Allwright*, 321 U.S. 649, 669 (1944).
[16] *Mahnich* v. *Southern Steamship Co.*, 321 U.S. 96, 113 (1944).

symbols by lawyers and others of conservative leanings whose real concern is not so much with stability in the law as with preventing the kinds of changes which are now taking place. As a matter of fact, in spite of a considerable number of decisions which have been overruled, there is much greater stability in certain fields than there was some two decades ago. In the matter of utility rate regulation, for example, the Court then talked in terms of its self-created rule that rates fixed by government, in order to be constitutional, must yield a fair return on a fair value. The determination of fair value was based on an utterly unscientific and indefinite mixing of a variety of considerations which can never be reproduced exactly in two sets of circumstances. The only thing about which anybody could feel perfectly sure was that utility corporations interested in stalling off the enforcement of new rate schedules could keep government orders in litigation for seemingly endless periods. The Court in recent years, on the other hand, has sloughed off most of the accretion to due process of law in terms of which this fog of indefiniteness was created, with the result that regulations which do not grossly invade and discriminate against particular property rights are likely to be held constitutional. As far as acts of Congress are concerned, indeed, the impression is created that we can almost assume the constitutionality of any measure which Congress sees fit to enact within the pattern of the governmental program which has been in process of development since 1933. Such a statement implies a kind of stability or, at any rate, a kind of certainty in law which has long been absent, even though it is not the kind which is sought by most critics who profess concern about the judicial creation of uncertainty.

It can be said, furthermore, that law can never be completely stable in an evolving society and that, in periods of social and economic readjustment, legal changes must be particularly drastic if law is to be kept in harmony with the changing needs of society. The United States today is obviously in such a period of transition. The present members of the Supreme Court, taking up the task of adjustment which should have been begun more adequately by their predecessors, are attempting to rethink the principles and ideals of the Constitution in terms of the measures deemed necessary, in the language of the Preamble, "to form a more perfect Union, establish justice, ensure domestic tranquility, provide for the common defence, promote the general welfare, and secure the blessings of liberty to ourselves and our posterity." If they find the task difficult and if they disagree among themselves as to how it shall be done, we ought to phrase our criticisms in the light of the weight and dimensions of the burdens which rest upon them.

X

THE CONSTITUTIONAL SYSTEM TODAY

*

DURING the course of our constitutional history we have witnessed a running battle between the advocates of increased power in the federal government and those who would restrain the exercise of that power. The two groups alternate in ascendancy. Neither has ever been completely victorious. If, by comparing the flow of governmental power today with that of earlier periods, we gather the impression that restraint is now a thing of the past, we do well to remember that a variety of checks still stand as barriers. The principle of federalism, for example, still reserves great areas of power to the states; the separation of powers both potentially and actually exercises restraint; constitutional prohibitions and procedural restrictions still operate; and conceptions of welfare and of rightness still mold or exercise influence upon the molding of governmental action. We do well to remember also that the increase in governmental power in the United States has not been merely the product of the outcome of a struggle between groups who differ abstractly as to what the province of government should be. In addition, the force of economic circumstance, the change in our mode of living from that of small-scale production and distribution to that of mass-production industrialism, has called for more sweeping operation of governmental controls.

Furthermore, it should be remembered that the increase in the scope of governmental power by no means signifies that government exercises all the power that society generates. The organization of men and machines and the utilization of material wealth have added greatly to the total of power to be exercised somewhere. Tremendous allocations of power loom up in the private corporations by means of which production and distribution are carried on. Indeed, it is this growth of power in the hands of technically nongovernmental agencies which has persuaded many people of the necessity of expanding governmental power to a degree commensurate with the power of the agencies to be controlled. In spite of the legal fiction that a corporation is a "person," there is no comparison between the amount of governmental power needed to enforce the public will upon John Smith, citizen, and upon the Standard Oil Company of New Jersey, the General Motors Corporation, the Aluminum Company of America, the American Telephone and Telegraph Company, or a host of similar institutions. These agencies, which we permit to administer much of our economy, make no pretense of internal exercise of their powers according to principles of democracy. They provide no genuinely popular choice of either governing personnel or policies. They enforce no bills of rights to restrain the activities of their officers. They do not resort in any genuine sense to federalism or to the separation of powers or to the principle of control by laws and not by men in their internal operations. In general, their professions of public service are limited to those which can be made on the assumption that what is good for the corporation, namely, the opportunity to produce and sell goods at a profit, is also good for the public.

If perchance we accept that assumption, we must recognize in doing so its broader sweep than that of the like assumption which we might make about the business of a single individual. Corporations of the dimensions here under discussion, and those of lesser size to a lesser degree, wield tremendous power over the lives of employees, competitors, the employees of competitors, and the general public with which they come in contact. They possess much of the wealth in terms of which production and distribution are carried on. They mold as well as submit to the desires of the public in determining what shall be produced. Except where there is free competition—and there is little free competition where huge corporations are concerned—they influence the quantity and quality of the goods purchased by controlling price. Through their control of raw materials, patents, and productive machinery, they guide and restrain consumption by limiting as well as by speeding the development of new and better products. By means of agreements with other corporations they may, to the extent to which it can be done within or by getting around restrictive laws, regulate the economy of the United States in relation to the economies of foreign countries.

Friction among the several states in the 1780's quickly demonstrated to our forefathers that the states would not live peaceably together without restraint from a central source, even though the states embodied in their individual constitutions the varied safeguards deemed necessary for the protection of the rights of the people. It is even more obvious that corporations, whose "fundamental laws" contain no such safeguards, and which, although creatures of individual states, range so widely in their activities as to make adequate state control impossible, must in some way be subjected to over-all supervision. The federal government has considered but has never resorted to a requirement that all corporations doing business in interstate commerce secure licenses from the federal government and that, as a condition of securing the licenses, they submit to varied types of federal control. Instead, Congress has enacted, on the basis of the commerce and taxing powers, various measures for the regulation of our economy which incidentally control in some degree the activities of the corporations by which the principal blocs of our economy are operated.

Even so, in spite of the rapidity with which the powers of the federal government have been extended, nothing like complete governmental control of our economy has been seriously contemplated. The strategy of the federal government has been merely to regulate in such a way as to prevent serious abuses and to supplement private enterprise where that enterprise fails to meet public needs. It has encouraged competition among producers and distributors in the belief that the regulatory effect of competition provides a healthful substitute for direct governmental control, that it achieves the right kind of order in society with a minimum exercise of governmental power. Such has been the strategy of antitrust legislation and of various statutes which, while regulating particular activities of corporations, are so phrased as to encourage, or at least not to interfere with, competitive operations.

In part also the federal government has used the same strategy in the field of labor legislation. While it directly establishes maximum hours and minimum wages in industries producing for interstate commerce and deals in similar fashion with some other matters, its strategy is largely that of maintaining a balance between capital and labor to the end that the aggregations of power represented in the two may work out an equilibrium beneficial to both and to the general public with a minimum exercise of the coercive power of government. Since the chaos of unrestrained industrial warfare would be intolerable in a society such as ours, this banking of aggregations of private power one against another provides the only acceptable alternative to direct governmental management of the economy. As such an alternative, it has in its behalf one of the arguments used in support of federalism and the separation of powers, namely, that it achieves desired ends without promoting possibilities of tyranny by even greater consolidations of power in the same hands.

Indeed, if we view government in the United States in terms of aggregations of power rather than in terms of concepts of sovereignty, we may say that recent years have brought the development of a new type of federalism. At the top, as always, is the federal government. Below that government, however, we find not only the states but also, and often on lines roughly parallel with the states, the more powerful corporations of the country, with labor unions in some instances not much lower than the same parallel lines. A properly descriptive chart might show a pipeline carrying supplemental power from the federal government to labor unions, to inflate them up to positions of equality with employing corporations so that the process of collective bargaining can be carried on between parties at the same bargaining level.

To understand the implications of this new type of federalism, we need to work out still further the likenesses and differences involved in the comparison between the states, on the one hand, and corporations and labor unions, on the other. One of the functions of the federal Constitution is to restrain discriminatory action by one state against another state and its citizens. The corresponding restraint of intercorporation strife is much less sweeping. We have legislation which is intended to prevent combinations in restraint of trade and unfair trade practices; but if such legislation, when adequately enforced, interferes with the operation of the law of the jungle in the business world, normal business relationships are nevertheless regarded as properly those of combat, veneered with certain civilizing restrictions. While such relationships among individuals and small groups may be healthful and invigorating, their existence among huge aggregations of power implies the development of momentum in the hands of leaders which may be highly destructive. It is sheer preponderance of corporate power as well as the logic of mass-production industrialism which speeds the growth of large corporations at a faster rate then that of small ones and steadily enlarges the percentage of enterprise which is under corporation control. Furthermore, whether the preponderance of power is used to work changes in our economy or to restrict such changes in the interest of the current profits of the corporation involved, the decision as a matter of course is made in terms of the alleged interest of the corporation itself and not of the interest of the public. The corporation has no positive relation to the public welfare which the state, by contrast, is supposed to serve except on the questionable assumption that whatever ends are chosen for the corporation by its nondemocratically chosen leadership are good for society because that leadership has found them good for the corporation which makes up part of society. This generalization applies as fully to labor unions as to corporations, except that many labor unions follow the forms of democracy a bit more closely in selecting leaders and in deciding upon action.

Corporations differ from states in their power to combine one with another as well as in their privilege of engaging in business warfare. The Constitution forbids the states to make compacts with one another without the consent of Congress, and two or more states may not merge into a single state without congressional authorization. Although corporations run afoul of the law if they engage in combinations in restraint of trade, the prohibition is much less sweeping and effective upon them than upon the states. Furthermore, corporations may, as a rule, completely merge their identities without violating the law. The mergers may involve consolidation not merely of genuinely willing units but also of those which have been beaten down by the process of competitive slugging and maneuvering wherein the victory goes to the strong, the shrewd, and the skilful. There is no corresponding situation wherein the state of New York, for example, could compel the New England states to merge with it.

To put the matter in another way, whereas the voluntary or involuntary consolidation of a bloc of states which might wield such power as to threaten the domain of the federal government is virtually impossible, we have no effective guaranty against the amassing of such power by the merging of corporations as seriously to handicap the enforcement of federal law. Just as, during certain periods of our history, railroad and banking corporations proved too powerful for effective control by the states, so the concentration of corporate power might in the future become so great as to defy federal control. Judging by such evidence as the barrenness of our antitrust policy during most of the last half-century, we may conclude that the federal government already has its hands full in dealing with the corporate entities spawned under the corporation laws of the several states.

A contrast of growing importance between states and private corporations as centers of power over the lives of the people lies in the fact that, whereas the states have no important contacts with foreign governments, the activities of many corporations involve both agreements and competition with corporations created under the laws of foreign governments. Whether the relationship be one of competition or collaboration, the use of the power of American corporations in conjunction with that of the corporations of other governments involves the economic enterprise of the countries affected and creates problems with which governments ought to be in position to deal but with which no single government is in position to deal adequately. Although the public generally is not yet aware of these problems, awareness is likely to develop as cartel and intercorporate relationships come increasingly to determine the course of foreign trade and the pace and character of the development of economic enterprise. We may well be driven to a decision whether we shall strengthen government in the form in which we have developed it and sought to civilize it over the centuries, so as to enable it to control the corporate units of the new federalism, or whether we shall permit the energetic but relatively barbaric concentrations of corporate power to become the successful rivals of government. As has been suggested elsewhere, it is conceivable that the approximation of a world state, if and when it comes, will come not so much for the largely negative function of preserving peace as for the positive function of restraining and co-ordinating the activities of corporations which operate across the boundary lines of existing national states.

Certain it is, in any event, that the American constitutional system during the decades ahead must increasingly involve supervision of the sweep of enterprise upon which the well-being of the American people depends. If it is to leave tremendous concentrations of power in the hands of corporations rather than absorb such power for its own use, it must at least be kept strong enough, and it must so use its strength, as to mold the conduct of nonmoral corporation in terms of dominant conceptions of public welfare. It must hold its own with respect to corporations as it has more than held its own with respect to the states.

But the question remains: Should tremendous concentrations of power in the hands of privately owned and managed corporations be permitted at all? For argument either way we must take into account the fact that the operation of an economy such as ours has become calls for the lodgment of power somewhere. The choice of place must be between corporations and government. In behalf of corporations, it can be said that they are specialized instruments for the performance of economic functions, whereas government is, or has been, primarily organized for other purposes, and has its hands more than full already. Although the contention ought to be proved rather than taken on faith, the operators of business enterprise lay claim to an incomparably greater degree of efficiency than that of the operators of government.

The argument against corporations as instruments of great power must rely heavily upon the difference in the motivations which drive government, on the one hand, and private corporations, on the other. The basic motivation of government is, or should be, public service. That of private corporations is profit and power, without obligation to be anything else. The argument must also take into account the basic differences in internal operation. The operation of government is, or should be, democratic. Most private corporations, on the other hand, are dictatorships or oligarchies, and we do not recognize a duty on the part of their owners or managers to make them anything else. They absorb into their dictatorial or oligarchical operations an ever growing percentage of our competent men and women upon whom the nation should be able to rely for the implementation of democratic government. In appraising the health of our democratic institutions, we may well ask ourselves whether lifelong commitment to dictatorship, as employee or as manager, provides satisfactory training for political democracy.

It may be that we shall have to find ways to democratize our corporations in order to preserve democracy in government. Thus far we have done very little about it. Some corporations have persuaded or coerced employees to purchase stock, or have given the stock, to promote loyalty and better service; but such stock ownership has had little to do with control. It remains to be seen whether the influence of democratic government will make corporations democratic or whether the example of the concentration of power in private corporations will mold political government in the image of dictatorship— or whether, anomalous as the suggestion may seem, the two systems can function permanently in integrated relationships.

However that may be, our policy thus far has been to permit the growth of power in the hands of corporations while expanding the supervisory power of government. To the extent to which government makes the conduct of corporations reflect the disciplined desires of the American people without itself taking over the performance of their functions, it will have averted some of the dangers which traditional federalism is intended to avert. As in traditional federalism, decentralization of power, other things being equal, leaves performance to people who better understand its conditions. Corporations, like states, can have a large place in the American constitutional system. The problem in each instance is to know what the place should be, to keep them in it, and to encourage the best possible performance of their functions.

Our techniques of control include, as has been said, the restraint of corporate power by efforts to bank corporations one against another in a competitive system, with the enforcement of certain civilizing rules of the game. As far as the rights of labor are concerned, our techniques involve also the restraint of corporate power by banking labor unions against the incorporated owners and managers of property and giving the unions such governmental support as seems necessary to enable them to bargain effectively with employers. However, by no means all the control which is necessary can be exercised through the careful balancing of technically nongovernmental groups against one another. Direct intervention takes a great variety of forms. By means of police legislation such as the Federal Trade Commission Act, the Truth in Securities

Act, the Public Utility Holding Company Act, the Pure Food and Drug Act, etc., Congress attempts to prevent antisocial conduct on the part of business enterprise—which means, in general, on the part of enterprise concentrated in the hands of corporations. Congress uses the taxing power for regulatory purposes as well as for the raising of revenue. Through its power to spend money which it raises by taxation or by borrowing or through the direct operation of enterprise, Congress either restrains or stimulates the activities of private corporations, provides yardsticks for appraisal of the management of private enterprise, and supplements that enterprise in areas where it cannot profitably operate. By the exercise of its lending power Congress sponsors governmental loans to protect private enterprise against the ravages of general depressions and more localized misfortunes. To a steadily increasing extent the field of prices, which was once largely immune from governmental invasion, is becoming subject to governmental control. Regulation of the value of the currency, and the control of currency and credit which is exercised through the Federal Reserve System and in other ways, represent other steps in the direction of governmental efforts to systematize the operations of our whole economy.

All these and many other regulatory activities stem from powers found in or read into the language of the Constitution as originally adopted. They are carried on by means of machinery which is or which rests upon the original basic structure for which the Constitution provides. In general, however alien the specific measures mentioned are to the thinking of the Founding Fathers, the ultimate conceptions of welfare which they represent differ little from the fundamental assumptions of morality and rightness and of the essential worth of free human beings which guided the thought and action of the Founding Fathers. The external circumstances of life have changed and, along with them, the immediate relations of government to the lives of the governed; but the purposes of government remain those of preserving the conditions of order and opportunity wherein each citizen may confidently strive to realize his highest potentialities.

Basically our constitutional system lends itself well to the achievement of these ends in spite of the necessity for changes in methodology. The changes, it is true, often occur belatedly, so that the possibility of adequate adaptation is chronically in question. Illustrations can be drawn from each of the three branches of the government. Although the work of neither branch can be considered in isolation from the other, the tripartite arrangement of the government provides a convenient outline for analysis.

As for the legislative branch of the government, members of both houses of Congress, employees of the executive branch, and political scientists generally are greatly concerned about the slowness with which that body grows up with the growth of its legislative responsibilities. Congress, it is true, continues to perform reasonably well its service as a forum wherein the gradually evolving sentiments of the people can be brought to focus. In spite of abuses perpetrated by individual members, it performs important services through investigations which show the need of enacting or amending legislation and which disclose results of executive and administrative activity, whether good or bad. With a watchful eye upon the policies and methods of the executive branch, it enacts most of the revenue and spending measures sponsored by that branch. It enacts routine legislative measures which are needed from time to time, and, more spectacular if not more important, it debates all and enacts part of the policy-making measures urged upon it by the President.

Congress is sharply criticized, however, on the ground that

it shows no real capacity for independent leadership. Although it is the repository of the legislative power granted by the Constitution, it has shown little evidence of ability or desire to plan an integrated body of statute law for the exercise of such powers as ought to be exercised by government in relation to our integrated economy. Its legislative action is limited too closely to measures sponsored by articulate and powerful pressure groups or by the executive branch of the government. The minds of most individual legislators are fixed too directly upon the needs and the political reactions of their own constituencies and not enough upon the national responsibilities of a national legislative body. When Congress refuses to follow the President, its refusal is usually in terms of opposition to particular measures, or, less frequently, in terms of the determination to enact particular measures of its own choosing. It does not build a well-rounded legislative program of its own and seek to substitute it for that sponsored by the President. As far as the making of consistent national policy is concerned, therefore, Congress, like the judiciary, stands out more and more clearly as a restrictive agency, while such positive leadership as is exercised comes largely from the President.

This generalization, it is true, is derived from only a few years of our national experience. Only within relatively recent years has anyone, whether his responsibility was legislative or executive, assumed that the responsibility of the federal government for the public welfare extended much beyond enactment of a few restrictive and usually unrelated measures to clear paths for positive drives of private enterprise. Theodore Roosevelt succeeded in stirring up some enthusiasm for a general program of conservation of natural resources. Woodrow Wilson sponsored a series of measures having to do with the tariff, trusts, labor, and banking. It was only with the coming of the first World War that positive and integrated planning for much of our national life came to be regarded as a legitimate responsibility of government and then only for the immediate purpose of winning the war. In this field as in others the postwar slogan was "Back to normalcy!"

The first real attempt at over-all supervision of our peacetime economy came with New Deal efforts to cope with the depression. Although many New Dealers hoped to use the crisis as a means for intrenchment of a broad scheme of government control, presidential justification of emergency measures was offered largely in terms of the necessities of the emergency. The country did not thoughtfully debate the question whether government should intervene broadly in the management of our economy, decide in the affirmative, and direct the President to impose and Congress to accept a plan of regulation. Rather, the course of events may be summarized somewhat as follows: Bewildered and frightened by the growing seriousness of the depression, the people looked eagerly to Washington for leadership in the crisis. Members of Congress, as bewildered and confused as their constituents and lacking any tradition of national leadership, had nothing to offer. Both Congress and the people looked for leadership, therefore, to the incoming President, who had probably been elected not so much on the merits of his own platform or of his demonstrated capacity for leadership as on the ground that his predecessor, Herbert Hoover, should be ousted from office as a penalty for having a world-wide depression during the course of his administration. It so happened—and we should keep in mind the fact that it might well have happened otherwise—that the new President fairly oozed confidence in his own capacity for leadership and in the capacity of the country to recover from the depression, and that he had the magic touch which could convince the people that they had nothing to fear but fear itself. With the support of a "brain trust" to keep him equipped with plans and program and with the support of a loyal group of politicians to help him put plans and program into action, he fairly took into his own hands for the time being the direction of the dominant forces of the nation.

To repeat, however, we might have done otherwise. The President whom we elected in the process of banishing President Hoover might have taken fright at the immensity of his responsibility, as James Buchanan took fright at the beginning of the Civil War, might have failed to win the confidence of the people, and might himself have been banished at the end of a four-year period. In the absence of adequate presidential leadership, Congress in time might have come forward with a group of leaders who would have made themselves the architects of national policy—although this is not to imply that the beginnings of such leadership were already in evidence or that its development would have come without great travail. Substantial groups of men on other occasions, however—as witness the Second Continental Congress—have been able to do great things when situations demanded greatness of them. The working-out of policy determinations and compromises in small groups of representatives is of the essence of the process of representative democracy. We have no reason for believing that Congress could not in time develop within itself capacity for constructive and integrated planning of the field of operations of the federal government.

Perspective on the problem is distorted by the fact that, when in the midst of the depression the people demanded leadership from the federal government, Congress was thrown off balance by the fact that it then had no leadership to offer, whereas President Roosevelt was ready and eager to lead. During succeeding years he kept Congress off balance by his superior skill at maintaining leadership, so that Congress, even if perchance it wanted to do more, was kept frantically busy adjusting itself to the presidential program or chipping away at particular features of that program to which it was opposed. Yet this situation is not necessarily permanent. Whereas it seems probable that the need for strong leadership in the federal government will continue indefinitely, Mr. Roosevelt is no longer President. Some of his successors—whatever the truth as to President Truman—will not have his capacity for leadership or, to the same extent, the confidence of the people. Congress will then have to take more leadership than that involved in operating around the edges of policy developed in the executive branch of the government.

All this is not to suggest that the duties of the presidential office ought to be limited to executing policy evolved in Congress. Both branches must operate in the field of policy. The relationship between them ought not to be one of principal and subordinate but one of equals struggling toward creative compromise. Only in terms of such a relationship can we be assured of the continued evolution of inchoate bodies of public sentiment into clear statements of public policy and into harmonious governmental programs operative in terms of the principles of the Constitution.

Turning more specifically to the constitutional aspects of the problems of the executive branch, we find that branch at present perhaps more alive to the changing tasks of government than either of the other two. Therein are housed the men and agencies which are most dynamically aware of the necessity for expansion of governmental functions from those of the old-fashioned policeman to those of the supervisor. Therein have taken place the principal organizational changes involved in adjusting government to the performance of its new functions. In the light of these facts, it is not surprising that therein also do we find the most evidence of organizational chaos and the least tolerance for the principle of the rule of law and the other checks upon arbitrary government which largely determine the character of our constitutional system. It is not surprising that men charged with responsibility for positive action show intolerance of restraints at every turn which are calculated to keep them in the path of official rectitude. Few men recognize the necessity for such restrictions as far as their own conduct is concerned. Furthermore, when the public welfare seems to call for speedy and drastic action, few men can get completely away from the position that the end justifies the means.

The constitutional problems of the executive branch, therefore, are those of adapting organization and procedures to the performance of new functions along with the maintenance of such safeguards as are necessary to protect the people against the arbitrary and unco-ordinated actions of their governors. It is undoubtedly true that "the day of the positive state is upon us." But the more positive the state, the more important it is that the administrators of the state shall not mérely hold themselves, but shall be held by constitutional restrictions, to performance in harmony with the will of the people. The task before us—almost the equivalent in difficulty of that of the men who drafted the original Constitution—is one of developing an executive and administrative mechanism which can at once stimulate the economic enterprise upon which the welfare of the American people depends and hold a tight rein upon the corporate agencies of such enterprise, doing all this in such a way that governmental administrators are given adequate powers for the performance of their functions without the possibility of transforming themselves into the people's masters.

As for constitutional problems in relation to the judiciary, the task of the judiciary, although rendered more difficult by the sweeping changes in the field of governmental action, remains fundamentally what it has always been. That task is to find and declare the law in the process of applying it in particular cases. Since cases properly brought before a court must be decided, the law must be found, however difficult the search. Evidence as to what the law is may consist of specific language in a constitution, a statute, or a judicial decision. It may consist of the meanings of a variety of apparently competing words in a variety of documents. The determining factor may be something almost as indefinite as the "spirit of the Constitution," an understanding of the broad principles on which the Constitution rests. It is therefore the task of the judiciary to maintain the symmetry of the law as far as the character of changing legislation will permit, whatever the conditions of change in the world to which the law is being applied. In a word, it is the task of the judiciary to interpret and develop law in terms of the abiding conceptions of right and justice which give meaning to the community life of the American people. With adequate attention to the selection of personnel and with adequate devotion on the part of that personnel to the task to be performed, no insuperable barrier stands in the way of achievement of the ends of justice which the Constitution contemplates.

In summary, in the adjustment of government in the United States to current needs we must take into account the changes in the content and organization of economic life which require an amount of over-all supervision of our ways of living together which was undreamed of when the Constitution was adopted. We must adjust government to the performance of its new functions without losing sight of the basic ideals of our society and without impairing beyond the range of absolute necessity the safeguards which are embodied in our constitutional system. Necessary piecemeal adjustments in Congress are under consideration and may lead to adoption of basic reforms or to the abandonment of provincial attitudes which interfere with proper performance of congressional functions. The reorganization and disciplining of the executive branch will inevitably receive much attention during the years immediately ahead. The judiciary, against the background of battle of 1937, is already working hard at the task not merely of current adaptation of law to constitutional principles but of gradually smoothing out the aberrations for which an unimaginative judiciary of a few years ago was responsible. A sense of constitutional responsibility in government officials alone, however, is not enough. The ultimate safeguard of the constitutional system is watchfulness, understanding, and participation on the part of the American people. With the people properly on guard and properly active, the growth of constitutional power in the United States should be a matter of pride and not at all of anxious concern.

INDEX

☼

Adair v. *United States,* 112–13
Adams, John, 52–53
Adams, John Quincy, 80
Adamson Act, 113
Adkins v. *Children's Hospital,* 114–15, 225–26
Administrative justice, 128 ff.
Administrative tribunals, 146 ff.
Agricultural Adjustment Act, 93, 95, 220
Alien and Sedition Acts, 54
American Bar Association, 33, 145–46, 150–51
Anti-Federalists, 13
Articles of Confederation, 4, 13, 18, 20–21, 90
Atlantic Charter, 193, 202
Attorney-General's Committee on Administrative Procedure, 147

Bail, excessive, 7
Bailey v. *Drexel Furniture Co.,* 35, 92
Bank of the United States, 57
Bankruptcy, 15–16
Barkley, Alben, 71
Beard, Charles A., 77
Bills of attainder, 6
Bills of credit, 29
Bills of rights, 7 ff.; *see also* Civil liberties
Bituminous Coal Conservation Act, 84–85, 142–43
Black, Hugo L.: in *McCarroll* v. *Dixie Greyhound Lines, Inc.,* 41–42; in *Driscoll* v. *Edison Light & Power* Co., 122; in *Federal Power Commission* v. *Natural Gas Pipeline Co.,* 123; in *Magnolia Petroleum Co.* v. *Hunt,* 123–24; in *Milk Wagon Drivers Union* v. *Meadowmoor Dairies,* 161; in *Bridges* v. *California,* 163–64, 169, 171–72; in *Korematsu* v. *United States,* 164, 177–78; in *Thomas* v. *Collins,* 181; classification as a liberal, 230
Block v. *Hirsh,* 113
Board of Trade v. *Olsen,* 93
Bowles v. *Willingham,* 152–53
Bradley, Joseph P., 109
Brandeis, Louis D.: in the Southwestern Bell case, 117; in the Oklahoma Ice case, 119–20; in *Crowell* v. *Benson,* 139; in *St. Joseph Stock Yards Co.* v. *United States,* 140; classification as a liberal, 223, 230; opposition to court-packing plan, 226
Bretton Woods Conference, 202
Bridges v. *California,* 163–64, 169, 171–73
Buchalter v. *New York,* 16
Buchanan, James, 248
Burke, Edmund, 2
Burr, Aaron, 56
Burr conspiracy, 30
Burton, Harold H., alignment on the Supreme Court, 230
Businesses affected with a public interest, 110 ff., 118 ff.
Butler, Pierce, classification as a conservative, 224, 230
Butler, William M., 105

Calhoun, John C., 57
Cardozo, Benjamin N.: in *Helvering* v. *Davis,* 95–96; in *Panama Refining Co.* v. *Ryan,* 141–42; in *Schechter* v. *United States,* 142; on expansion of legal principles, 178; on the nature of the judicial process, 219; classification as a liberal, 223
Carpetbag government, 30
Carter v. *Carter Coal Co.,* 84–85, 142–43